CLAYOQUOT

CLAYOQUOT

The Sound of My Heart

Betty Shiver Krawczyk

ORCA BOOK PUBLISHERS

Canadian Cataloguing in Publication Data
  Krawczyk, Betty Shiver, 1928 –
  Clayoquot

  ISBN 1-55143-076-2
1. Krawczyk, Betty Shiver, 1928 –   2. Clayoquot Sound Region (B.C.)
– Biography. I. Title.
FC3845.C53Z49 1996   971.1'204'092   C95–911171–9
F1089.V3K72 1996

The publisher would like to acknowledge the ongoing financial support
of the Canada Council, the Department of Canadian Heritage, and the
British Columbia Ministry of Small Business, Tourism and Culture.

The names of some of the people described in this book have been
changed to protect their privacy.

Cover design by Christine Toller
Cover photograph by Adrian Dorst

Printed and bound in Canada

Orca Book Publishers   Orca Book Publishers
PO Box 5626, Station B   PO Box 468
Victoria, BC Canada   Custer, WA USA
V8R 6S4   98240-0468

10 9 8 7 6 5 4 3 2 1

*This book is dedicated
to my wonderful mother
Martha Winifred Rhodes Shiver
and to the memory of my beloved daughter
Barbara Ellen Camp*

ONE

It is the month of July, 1988. I must go to the stream now, while the tide is out, and fill up the drinking water jugs. But I'm not eager. I'm afraid of cougars. In my mind's eye, I can see them, one or two perhaps, a mother in her prime teaching her half-grown offspring to hunt as soon as a likely victim presents itself. They will be hanging around in the treetops down by the stream, waiting for me. Still, I must go.

If I don't, Mike will think me a coward. Mike is my son. At least, I think he is my son. He was the only baby born in the hospital the night I gave birth to my second child, so he must be mine. But he has this peculiar split-brain condition that disapproves of most of his sixty-year-old mother's perceived eccentricities, while growing more wildly eccentric himself by the day. And although I occasionally wonder how some or all of my eight children might perceive any given project that I am involved in, Mike, inherent enemy of the established order that he is, is not the first to come to my mind. Furthermore, I will always be older and wiser and more experienced than he is, at least in some things. And God knows, I've paid my dues in the brave, yeah, even foolhardy department. In fact, it was to save this particular son's wilderness-oriented ass from the American military that eventually landed us in Clayoquot Sound on the west coast of Vancouver Island.

Not that I bring this up to Mike very often. He has a son of his own now, the same age as Mike was when we all emigrated. I am not sorry for the emigration, I am glad. Yet, sometimes I am quite annoyed by Mike's insensitivity to my experiences. It's as though he thinks himself the older, the wiser.

At bottom, Mike doesn't really think I should be out here by myself. He has to go into the village to work, and Tofino is ten miles away by water, too far for him to make it back and forth to our homestead every day. However, there isn't much he can do about my insistence on being a permanent homesteader. Mike built the A-frame, but I own half the property it sits on. So he comes out once or twice a week to see if his contrary old Ma is still alive. He usually chops wood and brings in the water while he's at it. Only last evening when he was here the tide was unusually high and backed up into the streambed. When that happens the steam's banks turn to marsh and mud, and the fresh and salt water merge their differences. The water then is, of course, undrinkable. Mike told me before he left that I would have to get the water myself today. Before noon. While the tide is out.

Well, now. It has always been sort of interesting to me how necessity can dictate events. In spite of the fact that Mike considers me incompetent because I can't row the dinghy properly, or lift heavy things, or start an outboard motor, I have suddenly been promoted nevertheless. Now I'm supposed to just march right out to the stream and become cougar breakfast.

Still I know if I don't face this thing down, I will never be able to live out here with any freedom of movement. I have to go. I touch the whistle hung on a string around my neck to make sure it's secure, and check the hunting knife strapped around my right leg. I feel like I'm heading off on an African safari, but these little accoutrements provide some sense of security, however false. Whatever may happen, I, at least, have done my part. I walk to the sliding glass back patio door and step outside on the deck.

Dammit, why doesn't it rain, I ask aloud as I scan the sky. This is supposed to be a rainforest, isn't it? A curious marten looks up crossly from the woodpile and then scurries away. Mean-tempered little creatures, martens. Visitors unaccustomed to their ways think them cute, and I suppose they are. And so is Julian, my three-year old grandson, but both can create a frenzied chaotic ruin of one's kitchen supplies in three seconds flat. Still, I bear no malice toward this particular marten. At least this one is busy earning his own living. If it would just rain, I think, I could catch rain water to drink and forgo running the cougar gauntlet. But it is July, and sometimes the summers in Clayoquot Sound can be bone dry. However, it did rain some last summer, I remember, because last July was the month of the squiggly black things in the rain water.

I'm not sure what they were. Maybe mosquito larvae. But when I was confronted with this wretched, incomprehensible form of life, I fairly swooned. So disgusting, these diminutive whirling dervish microcosms churning up the water in my water barrels with their constant, feverish back flips. Any woman who has raised eight kids has stared down many a mess, and I'll put my stomach and nerves up against anyone's, but there was something about these things that was profoundly disturbing. However, then as now, our waterline to the stream had been chewed up by bears. Bears seem to love the taste of plastic piping. Or maybe they see the water lines as visible proof of disrespect for their space. I suspect it's easier and safer for an enraged bear to bite a hunk out of the line than to directly confront the human who put it there. In any event, the bears vote on the presence of alien objects in their territory with their teeth whenever possible, and a bear-chewed waterline bears no water.

But that first summer I didn't realize I could have just scrubbed the floors with fresh seawater, I thought I had to deal with these barrels of infected rain water because first, they were there, and secondly, because I needed scrubbing water. So I put a big pot on the stove to boil. After fifteen minutes of a rolling boil I checked the water. The repulsive little black beasts had inexplicably disappeared! I regarded the pot with a mixture of awe and relief. Some men are like that, I had thought. A little pressure, and off they go into the wild blue yonder, vanished without a trace. Well, at least I was forewarned now. Life in the jungle was raw. Only the fittest survived. Which is why I am presently eyeing the treeline down by the steam with more than a little hesitation. It's still morning and cougars are only supposed to hunt in the evenings. However, I have heard enough cougar stories from the oldtimers to realize that cougars will come out and tend to their hunting any time they take a notion.

My obsession with cougars is not just the result of an intemperate imagination. There have been several attacks in the area, one fatal. A child. Overwhelmingly, the victims are children, although one cougar got confused in Hot Springs Cove and attacked a man who was gathering wood from his wood pile. Evidently, the man was bending over when the cougar sprang onto his back from a nearby tree. Cougars, if they become hollow-bellied-hungry enough to attack an adult at all, seem to prefer to attack humans who are bent over.

Cougars are normally very shy creatures and in the past their reputation has certainly been that they will go out of their way to avoid humans. But something pitiful has happened to them of late. Some of the old homesteaders say it is the clear-cutting on the island that is making the cougars crazy.

Clear-cutting is the logging method used by the giant multinational logging companies like MacMillan Bloedel and Interfor. In this method every living tree is cut down in a given area. The unwanted trees and brush left behind are often burned, leaving great open spaces that are foreign to the hunting habits of the cougar. Pack hunting wolves, however, thrive in this new, unexpected windfall of open spaces.

The wolf and the cougar both feed on the small black-tailed deer that used to abound on Vancouver Island. The wolf thinks clear-cutting is great, because s/he catches prey by chasing deer into the open and simply running them down. The cougar, however, is a cat, and like all cats, hides and stalks and pounces. As there is nowhere to hide in a clear-cut, no tall trees from which to leap and pounce, the cougar, like The North American Free Trade agreement, is looking for new, mostly non-existent markets. And so it is the odd cougar, the young ones who are newly on their own and not-yet-great hunters, or very old ones who know how to do it but haven't the physical strength to carry through, who turn their attention in the direction of isolated homesteads and villages. They prefer small pets that can be taken with a minimum of fuss.

I have no pets and the only time I actually bend all the way over, at least under a dense tree canopy, is when I have to fill the water jugs from the stream. Like I will have to do shortly. I pick up the water jugs and with one last glance at the safety of the A-frame, start off down the pathway to the stream.

I love the A-frame. It's a home-made house. Mike built it all by himself, except for the actual erecting of the frames which required a sort of barn-raising beer party. The A-frame is perched on a rocky bluff and when the tide is in I get the wonderful sensation of living in a houseboat, surrounded by water. I used to dream of living in a houseboat. In a free-floating houseboat one is totally out of reach of one's creditors in the immediate sense. At least they can't drop by or call you on the telephone. And if one doesn't like the neighborhood one can jolly well mosey on around to another cove. Houseboat living precludes being arbitrarily summoned by one's children or grandchildren for this or that little emergency. The dear ones must survive on their own until grandma wants to emerge. Still, I have most of those advantages now, perched as I am above my rocky bluff. And when the tide is out I have the additional sensation of being suspended in space. The structure is just one huge room with sleeping lofts upstairs but there are lots of windows and skylights, and wherever I stand or sit inside the house I can see through to the outdoors. Which makes me very happy.

I don't know what it is with this wilderness gene. If I had known from the beginning what kind of life makes me happy, I could have saved myself a lot of misery. I was raised in the country, in East Baton Rouge Parish, in the state of Louisiana. I loved the country, but the aim seemed to be, on everybody's part, both black and white, to get out of it as fast as possible. It's hard to hang on to something that is so down-graded by everybody else. In fact, my brother and I couldn't beat the country dust off our shoes fast enough. Downtown. Just show us the way. The funny thing is, both my brother and I have since spent a lot of years trying to get back to the heart of nature.

But one really can't go home again. My brother has retired halfway up a mountainside north of Phoenix, Arizona, which is a different face of nature, one a long way from the swamps of Louisiana. And while the Clayoquot Sound evokes some childhood memories for me — the heavy rainfall is sweetly familiar, as is the fresh, sea-borne air — still most is strange. It's like meeting a new man, the strongest attraction is centered on the one with the most challenging blend of the strange and the familiar. Only my fascination with the Sound hasn't worn off. At least not yet. I have lived in some impressive places in my life, as well as some that were only a step or two above the hovel category, but none have filled me with such joy as this place. If only I didn't have to go get the damned water.

Before I became intimate with Cypress Bay, which our little cove claims to be part of, I knew little of pebble beaches. A beach was supposed to have white sand and at least be good for wading, if not swimming. Our little beach cares for none of these affectations. This beach is sort of a marine Calcutta, swarming with life, each organism trying to survive, often under great odds. There seems to be an abundance of squabbling and death-dealing altercation between the different species, but there are also some manifestations of tolerance, if not downright cooperation. I put down the water jugs and pick up an oyster shell.

The shell has several rows of barnacle townhouses, all occupied. A single oyster shell can carry dozens of barnacle townhouses, large and small, over its surface. As these particular tenants sense that their entire planet is in danger, they decide it's time to hunker down and play dead. What curious creatures they are. Do they imagine their planet, their world of the oyster shell, to be flat? It is, rather. It certainly isn't round. Perhaps, like the barnacles, we believe our world to be flat, but unlike the barnacles, are convinced that it is round, or not quite round, by our scientific elite. The barnacles presumably have no scientific elite to confuse their perception of their own particular universe. Then again, perhaps our universe, scientists and all, is really no bigger than the back of the monstrous sea turtle that the ancient Chinese sages imagined the world rested upon. Maybe the ancient Chinese were right in principal, they just didn't think in universal terms. After all, does anyone know for sure what lies outside the universe of our universes?

I carefully place the shell back in its original position. Is that a small collective sigh of relief I hear? The seaweeds are full of tiny hitch-hikers and the stationary rocks are smothered with scallops and oysters and mussels. I am always on the lookout for interesting shells because I make little craft things in the evenings. At least I try to make little craft things. I don't have the particular gene that makes one good at that sort of thing, but I don't believe in letting a lack of innate ability get in the way of expressing myself creatively. However, it seems almost impossible to find a large shell that isn't housing a bunch of squatters of one sort or another and this is definitely hindering my craft-making.

As I pick up the water jugs to resume my journey I glance across the cove. The bears have come out to play. More precisely the bears have come out to eat. Small black bears, two of them. Teenagers, I think. I've seen them at least a half a dozen times in the last few weeks, but always through binoculars from the safety of my front deck. I think their mother has kicked them out. They are not so close to me as to be threatening in any way. I stand motionless, watching.

I must be downwind of the bears, because they give no indication that they are aware of an audience. They are totally focused on the task at hand which is to try to turn over the largest of the rocks under the bluff by the stream. This is the largest of the streams and I can hear the sound of its waterfall from my front deck if the birds aren't making too much racket.

The bear mother has taught her children, before she decided these big kids were old enough to fend for themselves, that the outgoing tide left little presents underneath the rocks. Tiny crabs and other dainties. But the bears must wrestle the rocks for their treats. When one particularly large rock won't yield to the strivings of one, the twin comes over and offers assistance. The rock is stubborn. The bears have each taken a turn and turnabout, before the rock finally gives up and rolls over. The bears pounce on the tiny, luckless crabs now pitiably exposed, and after a couple of moments of intense feeding, amble down to another cluster of rocks. But the wind has shifted. The hateful stench of humans has evidently reached one of the twins. S/he rears up on hind legs and looks in my direction.

I doubt if the bear can see me with its poor eyesight. But this one is definitely spooked. S/he suddenly turns and bolts for the rocky bluff that fronts the towering cedar trees. The other follows, lickety-split. They aren't taking any chances.

The sea birds don't give a damn. They are fishing too and I almost have to kick them out of my way, they are so intent at table. They remind me of my kids, when they were all at home and mostly made of mouths and stomachs. But I like them, raucous bunch that they are. Even those greedy guts, the seagulls.

But the loon is my favorite. I love its romantic, mysterious cry. The diving ducks are in some rare category of marine maladaptation. Just from watching, it seems to me ducks, like the loon and the canvasback, need an inordinate length of runway in order to get airborne. If they are startled while in the water and try to make a quick exit, they splash and flounder and half-drown themselves. The mallards and pintails don't dive for their food, they just tip upside down in the water and show their cute little behinds. But they're much better designed for emergency take-offs. The haughty blue herons look great in the air, sweeping low on their wide, wonderful wings, but, when they land and go beachcombing, they walk with the peculiar hesitant gait of the stork. There are two families of blue herons living somewhere around our cove and they bring their youngsters here for fishing lessons. They all have better luck catching fish than I do.

The bald eagle likes our neighborhood, too. Everybody likes to watch the eagle. Monarch of the mountain. The power and grace of the eagle's flight and strike is awesome. However, the bird has a whimpy cry. A kind of whistling sound, more suitable for a smaller bird. One of nature's little trade-offs, I guess. A kind of reigning in of the high flyers. Mother Nature fixed it so the eagle wouldn't get a swelled head in both the looks and voice department, otherwise the bird might think itself the favorite of the skies, like the human male thinks he's the favorite of the earth. I mustn't tarry any longer. Duty is calling. But first I decide to take a little side trip to Mike's shop to see how the catamaran and "The Raven Lady" are coming along.

Mike built his shop halfway between the house and the first stream, but it skirts the edge of the bush, back away from the beach. So I sing. Loudly. My voice is awful, but it warns the other land animals that I am out and about and please let's not have any mutually startling and embarrassing encounters. I come from a family of singers and musicians on my mother's side, but I found out early when nobody would sing with me, that instead of the soft, fine voice of my mother's clan, I had inherited the hog-calling voice of my father. Daddy was a country preacher and when he called on heaven to hear his voice, heaven heard. And hell, too, for that matter. But here, in the wild, my voice is an asset. It frightens the wild animals. I step into Mike's shop and inspect the half-finished sailing catamaran.

A catamaran is a double-hulled boat with flat bottoms that can supposedly be brought up onto shallow beaches without fear of grounding or capsizing. I am very interested in this boat. One of my main interests in it is that it will have no motor. I hate motors. Which gets me into a lot of heated arguments with men. Don't I understand, they ask, that the world runs on motors? Yes, I answer, but I don't like the way the world is running, at which point they wander away, young and old, kin and strangers alike, shaking their heads at my simplistic, superficial grasp on life. Certainly the world needs some working on, but to put most of the blame on motors!

But that's one of the big reasons why, at my advanced age, I'm trying to homestead here in the wilderness. I desperately want to get away from motors. Primarily automobile motors. Cars are the biggest polluters in the world and the biggest budget-busters devised by man and fobbed off on women. When I was owned by a car, every time I thought my pitiful little savings might actually amount to something, my car would promptly take care of that bit of optimism. The motor would begin to cough, whine, ping, hemorrhage vital fluids and threaten to expire. Emergency time.

But boats, I thought when I first came to Cypress Bay, will be better and cheaper. It stands to reason. Boats have fewer moving parts. A respectable citizen is less likely to get decapitated by drunk or maniacal drivers. Boats are simpler, safer, and less expensive to keep than cars. Besides, they're fun.

This, of course, was before I had to actually depend on a boat to take me over ten miles of totally unpredictable waters to the nearest village. My fascination with boats was one romance that hit the skids almost as soon as it left the dock.

Mike owns two boats. Both are skiffs. One he built himself out of wood; the other is a large aluminum herring skiff. Both have outboard motors. I can't start either one. I can pull on the start cords until my arms threaten to fly off into the cove, but no go. The wooden skiff is beautiful, but the sides sit too high up out of the water to suit me. It gives me the sensation that we're going to topple any minute. The aluminum boat is better; it is massive enough to dispel any notion of toppling, but when the waters are rough it pounds like a jackhammer.

When I discovered the jaunty little green and white speedboat for sale in the village of Ucluelet, I thought my personal water transportation problem was solved. This little gem started with a key. And there was a regular steering wheel. Vinyl bucket seats. Definitely civilized. Uptown. The owner took me out for a spin. It seemed like something I could manage. Only when I got the little darling out to Cypress Bay and started fiddling around with it, did I realize I had made a big mistake.

This boat, I discovered, was an addict. A speed freak. If it couldn't go fifty miles an hour, it didn't want to go at all. I, personally, do not want to go fifty miles an hour. Especially in these waters, where there are crab traps everywhere, and partially submerged logs that have escaped their booms, and great, concentrated patches of seaweed that harbor your worst nightmares. Anything over fifteen miles an hour exceeds my comfort zone. But at that speed my perky, obviously spoiled, little boat wallowed sullenly in the water, giving off vibes of sheer disgust. Only when Mike took over did the boat come to life and shoot across the waves like a greased pig in a cornfield.

But I don't care how efficient it is, as Mike insists, that little speedboat is simply too sassy for its own good. It will get its come-uppance some day and I don't want to be there when it happens. In fact, if I could just learn how to row our dinghy around the cove properly, I'd feel I was making progress.

Rowing a dinghy sounds simple enough. The water in our cove is only about three hundred yards across at high tide, and the surface generally as smooth as a baby's bottom. But the apparent placidity of the cove is deceptive. There can be strong under currents. Besides, something is definitely amiss with this particular dinghy. It has a mind of its own and it doesn't play with a full deck. It backs up when I'm trying to urge it forward, turns right when I want to go left. And occasionally, quite inexplicably, it will start pulling in circles. There are times when I suspect that, apart from the peculiarity of the dinghy, there is something lurking on the bottom of the cove—a strange, mysterious, dangerous something. After all, I've read Stephen King. Old Indian burial grounds down there, or some sort of spirit life that has an evil affect on the dinghy, causing a compelling suction action that threatens to swallow it and me, down into a swirling, suffocating, terrifying whirlpool of unfathomable depth, never to be seen or heard from again.

Of course, I don't mention this suspicion to Mike. He is the second oldest of my eight children, bossy as all get out, and if pressed, will use any little thing to try to further his arguments that I shouldn't be out here alone. No sense in just handing him ammunition to use against me.

I leave the catamaran and move on to "The Raven Lady." "The Raven Lady" is Mike's latest sculpture-in-progress. Bossy or not, I have to admit that the boy is talented. She isn't even half-done yet. When finished "The Raven Lady" will stand about ten feet high. She's made of stainless steel and will have a strong, generously proportioned nude body with long, flowing hair and a raven perched on one outstretched arm. She will be beautiful. Mike is very creative. He builds boats and houses and sculptures and knives and paintings and stories and poems, and somehow it is all the same to him, all one.

I leave the shop and resume my song as I make my way to the stream. The sky is clear, but there are wafting mists hugging the mountains. The birds are still feeding and the dewy breeze is so salty-sweet that I feel giddy. What have I ever done in my life to deserve to live with so much beauty? The song I'm singing is an old gospel tune from my childhood called "Buela Land."

The chorus goes:

> *I'm living on a mountain*
> *underneath a cloudless sky*
> *I'm drinking from a fountain*
> *that never will run dry*
> *I'm eating of the manna*
> *from a bountiful supply*
> *For I am dwelling in Buela Land.*

Buela Land is heaven, of course. I'm a long way from the Louisiana Southern Baptist churches and their notions of heaven, both physical and philosophical, but my brain track was thoroughly saturated with these songs when I was a defenseless child. Besides, I like this one. It's a happy song. I think I am already in Beula Land, at least for the moment, and I'm not even dead yet. But as the mists that have been hiding the denuded mountains around the cove begin to lift, I feel a creeping disquiet wash over my happy song.

I'm sure there are no clear-cuts in heaven. There couldn't be, they're too damned ugly. The mountains look like they've been napalmed. But maybe I just don't understand this clear-cutting practice. The man representing the logging company that sold us our ten acres said the mountains had been replanted and would soon be sprouting a new forest. Well, I knew then that there must be a difference between an old growth forest and a tree farm, but at the time I didn't understand to what degree. And as I gaze upon these stripped mountains daily, I am beginning to wonder if the logging companies, after all, know what in tarnation they are doing.

At the steam I blow several ear-splitting blasts from the whistle around my neck. It's one of those high-powered whistles, guaranteed to intimidate man and beast alike. The birds rise in one body like a shot, at least, the ones that are designed to do so. The others flail across the water like so many faulty little motorized scooters, and I can hear the sudden scurrying sounds of the small panic-stricken land animals trying to vacate the area. Quickly, while every living thing about is still stunned, I stoop down and begin to fill the jugs with the clear, gurgling water.

On my second trip to the stream I notice that the wild rose bushes on the opposite bank are weighted down with hundreds, no, thousands of small, heavenly-scented blossoms. As there are obviously no cougars out today, I make a third trip for roses and asparagus.

Sea asparagus is a long-stemmed, cranky-looking plant that resembles chicken feet but is tender and tasty when lightly stir-fried. It grows wild in thick clumps at the high tide line. As I head home laden with flower and sea plants, an eagle swoops low, makes a complete circuit of the cove and heads away over the mountains. What do the eagles think of the clear-cuts, I wonder? The clear-cuts must seem very strange to them, to all of the animals, in fact. After all, a good hunk of their world has disappeared.

But I have wild roses and sea asparagus and pure, sweet water and I won't let those poor scalped mountains intrude upon my enjoyment of an incomparable summer day in July in the Clayoquot Sound.

At the time, of course, I have no inkling that those same wounded, bleeding mountains, on another incomparable summer day in July several years later, will throw me into a conflict so passionate, unrelenting and uncompromising that I, a perfectly respectable if somewhat eccentric grandmother, will wind up behind prison bars, condemned as an enemy of the state.

TWO

 I certainly wasn't raised to be a protester. I was raised a poor, country, southern white woman. But who can tell, once one is an adult, what actually went on with one's parents and siblings and the neighbourhood in general? Memory is so selective, so subjective. At a sibling confab several years ago we were tickled and somewhat amazed to learn that we each, my brother and sister and I, had felt the others to be favored in the family. I know I felt the other two to have been favored. Actually, I still do. My brother was the older, and the only boy, so he got most of the attention. What was left went to my sister because she was the baby and delicate to boot. I was a big, healthy girl who could amuse herself, so nobody took any special notice of me. Which was just fine as far as I was concerned.

You really didn't want my father to notice you. If he did, you were in trouble. Not that he beat any of us ever, but the threat was always there. We were to be seen and not heard, and seen as little as possible. My mother was different. She was warm and loving. Although I always knew she favored my brother and sister, she was so full of love some of it slopped over on me, too. After I grew up I once confronted my mother with my secret knowledge, and she was hurt and astonished and insisted that if she paid more attention to the other two it was because they needed her more than I did, that I was always more emotionally independent. I remembered that line, and I've used it myself to fend off similar accusations from my own children. Kids are crazy. How can a parent ever hope to please them?

Sixty years ago southern Louisiana was mostly one big swamp. Today it has been drained, sprayed, paved, air-conditioned, and citified until it bears no resemblance whatever to any childhood memories of mine. When I visit, it is a matter of taking very short steps from an air-conditioned house to the air-conditioned car to drive to the air-conditioned store or movie or library. When I visit in the summer (and summers in southern Louisiana are eight months long), I have to get up before the sun to take a walk. If I'm a bit late, when I open the door and step outside the thick, wet, suffocating heat in all its glory will wrap around me like a broiling blanket, and I know in my gut where it's coming from — it was sent to us straight from hell. But, as children, we hardly ever noticed the heat.

As kids we each had a small, electric fan to sleep under at night and a mosquito net. Sometimes in the midst of summer Mama would call us in to cool down in the middle of the day. But by evening a little breeze would soothe our flushed cheeks, caressing our faces and arms and legs, while the scent of the wisteria blossoms from the gigantic vine smothering the front porch mingled with the heady smell of Mama's narcissus growing in a neat little row by the back and the wild seven sisters roses that climbed and leapt and danced along the half-rotten fence that enclosed the weather-beaten old house. And there was always corn and strawberries and melons from the garden cooling their heels on the back porch, while Mama fried up some chicken for supper, two or three plump, tender fryers, while the survivors scratched around blissfully in the chicken yard. And sometimes I thought we must have been God's chosen people because we had so much food and so many flowers.

But when I asked Mama about it she laughed. No, she said, we aren't rich, in fact, we are poor. This bit of information shocked me. If we were poor, why was she always laughing and singing and playing on the old piano? Besides, Daddy had his business, didn't he? He brought home money all the time that people gave him for his goods.

On our early school records, before Daddy got converted and became a preacher, our father was listed as a salesman. One could say he was that, but, as he sold blankets, sheets, and bedspreads from his car, he was more of a peddler. He bought these goods wholesale and then resold them to country people who had no credit to speak of, a dollar down, fifty cents a week until an item was paid for. He was good at what he did and even during the most terrible economic times, we fared better than a lot of our neighbors. I don't remember exactly when it was that Daddy also became a medicine man.

He didn't prescribe medicines, he just sold them. There were two to be exact. One medicine was an external liniment that Mama and Daddy cooked up in washtubs over the stove and was supposed to be good for whatever ailed you on the outside of your body. Daddy bought this recipe from another country entrepreneur who was, I think, on his way to jail unless he came up with some money quick. Be that as it may, after the liniment was cooked and bottled, my brother and I had the job of sticking the labels on the bottles. We refused to go into the kitchen until this powerful stuff, which was capable of cleaning out head colds and infected sinuses with one application along with its other magical properties, was safely enclosed and capped in the individual bottles.

The other medication Daddy sold was an internal tonic called Liberty Tonic. Daddy bought this tonic already bottled from a distributor. Liberty Tonic was supposed to be good for whatever ailed you inside. This concoction was so vile tasting that, when confronted with a spoonful, you weren't sure you hadn't rather just die. The first time I read Tom Sawyer and got to the scene where Tom gives Aunt Polly's medicine to the cat and the cat jumps out the window, I laughed so hard the teacher asked me to leave the room until I could compose myself. I think the main ingredients of Liberty Tonic were iron and castor oil and Mississippi River mud. After Liberty Tonic came into our lives, feigning illness to stay home from school became a thing of the past. Even when we did get sick, we would deny it in order to try to ward off being purged with the dreaded tonic.

When I was very young, I was given to wild nightmares and nervous imaginings in the dark, which usually brought my mother running with soothing, cool, damp cloths for my forehead, and maybe even a cold cup of milk flavored with vanilla and sweetened with cane syrup. But when a generous dose of Liberty Tonic came to replace the cool cloths and milk, I started sweating out my nightmares and nocturnal fears, instead of calling for help. In this sense Liberty Tonic could definitely be credited with improving the health of the children in our family, and I suspect, a lot of other families, both back and white, in East Baton Rouge Parish. But we were hardly ever really sick, anyway, as we had plenty of fresh air and exercise and ate only organic food.

Mama had a Cajun touch. The trout and catfish that Daddy caught got fried crisp in cornmeal batter, and the shrimp and crabs and oysters went the same route or else slipped into their good night in great pots of rice laced with okra and onions and hot red peppers. Mama was no slouch with soul food, either. Of course, we didn't know back then that the collard, mustard, and turnip greens cooked with velvety pieces of fatback, and the bowls of black-eyed peas and lima beans, and the pans of hot biscuits and corn bread, so sweetly textured that it would make you swallow your tongue, as my father was fond of saying at the table, that these foods, such standard fare for all southern country people, would someday be elevated to the realm of the exotic, and served in eastern restaurants as ethnic food. But this has been a relatively recent development. When I first left the south, I was aghast at what other people ate. What, no red peppers? No gumbos? No fried okra? No cornbread? No grits? Lord, have mercy on us. But even stranger than the food, I found on my first venture outside the south, were the people.

Louisiana people are just louder, funnier, more talkative, and full of laughter than other folks. This willingness to laugh at just about anything has been a hard one for me to shake and has caused a right smart of trouble in my life. I think Louisiana people hold on to this trait because it is their only defense against their politicians. Also, there is this urge to argue about anything and everything under the sun whether one knows anything about the issue at hand or not. When I was a youngster, the rural schools for blacks were few and far between, and even the schools for whites were sorry specimens, so nobody's personality was over-burdened with the ego-crushing effects of education.

If you don't realize how much you don't know, then your opinion is as good as anyone else's. In fact, back in those days the entire state of Louisiana was so backward and ignorant I am ashamed to have come from such a place. And yet the people, both black and white, were so distinctive and colorful in their mannerisms and expressions that when I left the state most other people I met seemed oddly restrained in their phraseology and mode of speech, cold even, with rigid body language, they seemed to have unfinished personalities and undeveloped senses of humor. Years later, when I developed an ear for subtlety, I realized this wasn't necessarily so. And of course, a lot of the jeu d'esprit of the black people's humor was developed to cover the pain and humiliation of apartheid, and the whites' funny bone was whittled at the expense of blacks, women, and Jews. If any of the more sensitive southerners found a contradiction in this, well, many things in life are contradictory and we'll understand it all by and by, when God chooses to reveal His plan to us.

I didn't like the way things were turning out, myself. True to the Biblical vision that women should go forth and multiply, I married early. In fact, I married the first grown-up man who came to court who could actually prove he was financially solvent. And he had already been in the service, slightly wounded, and honorably discharged. I was sixteen. By this time Daddy had got religion and was studying to be a preacher, and I just wanted out. Mama objected, but Daddy didn't think school was doing me any good anyway, and at least this prospect had a small business of his own. It wasn't Daddy's religious fervor that made me so anxious to quit the homestead, it was Daddy himself. And the entire southern mentality about women. I had absolutely no freedom living at home. I couldn't go out with a boyfriend on a casual date, or be anywhere after dark but home. It was the virginity thing that was so damned important. Sometimes I wished I could just take my intact hymen and given it to my parents and say, here, this really doesn't have a lot to do with me and it keeps you in a constant state of anxiety. The threat of the loss of it keeps me a semi-prisoner, it prevents me from moving freely in the world, this thing is my enemy, I hate it, do with it what you will, just let me go. But no. The hymen is strategically located and it is to be given in marriage or not at all. So I gave this gift without price, this irrecoverable tyrant that had sucked up all my natural girlhood freedoms in keeping it intact, to my husband.

He didn't much appreciate it. It certainly wasn't all that special to him. It was just another in his collection. In fact, he was a bit of a compulsive collector of intact hymens. He couldn't seem to stop after we got married. He finally collected one too many. By then I had three little boys, the youngest just a baby. I tried to get a divorce, but Louisiana law in those days frowned on any woman who wanted to leave her husband for any reason. The man supported me and my kids, didn't he? The judge ordered me back into the domestic domicile, at which point I packed up my sons and moved to Phoenix, Arizona.

I didn't go alone. My parents and my sister came with me. They had all moved to Baton Rouge from the country and didn't like living in the city, and the preaching was never much of a money-making thing anyway. Daddy's church affiliation had used him more as a country evangelist, and he didn't have a regular church of his own. Maybe he would be able to get one in Phoenix. His sister lived there along with numerous nephews and nieces, and maybe they would also be able to help us find a place to live.

They did. We had hardly any money, but living was cheap in Phoenix. At least on the south side. We settled in with the other poor whites, Hispanics, blacks, and a smattering of Orientals. Daddy got his peddling business established. My sister found a job in the cafeteria of the hospital on the south side and I went to work as a waitress in a downtown restaurant specializing in seafood. Mama, as usual, took the hardest, lowest paying job ... housework and taking care of my children while I worked. We got by, and in truth, after a period of readjustment, had more disposable income than we had enjoyed in Louisiana. We bought a house, still on the south side, but rather nice with a big yard. However, I felt poorer, less secure than down south. Louisiana soil is so rich that all you have to do is throw the seeds down on the ground and jump back out of the way. Phoenix is desert and didn't seem to grow anything except cactus without extensive and expensive irrigation.

There were very few vegetable and flower gardens on the south side. Deprived of the comforting sensation of a multitude of good things to eat and smell and look at growing all about me, I felt measurably poorer. Back home, we'd had enough chickens and pigs to feed a small army. I don't think there was a single live pig in all of the south side, and damned few chickens. Of course, this was the city.

Most of our new friends and neighbours worked in the affluent north side as cooks, gardeners and housekeepers, or else staffed the kitchens and dining rooms and bars of the big hotels and restaurants that catered to the winter tourists who came to soak up the glorious, unending Arizona sunshine.

Now I knew what Mama meant about being poor. In spite of Daddy's modest entrepreneurism we had become part of a class of people that in the south was occupied only by blacks. We had become the servant class.

There was no point in trying to discuss this startling revelation with Mama. She always countered that it was the poor who would gain heaven, not the rich, and the harder the row to hoe down here, the greater the glory up there. My sister wasn't any help, either. She was just trying to survive her job in the cafeteria, which seemed to involve a lot of lifting of heavy pots and pans. This girl had been petted all her life and lifting heavy pots and pans wasn't what she had trained for. Daddy was in a phase of blaming the Bolsheviks for every ill known to mankind. I didn't even know who the Bolsheviks were, and I don't think Daddy did, either. All he knew was that they were atheists. Whatever, the Bolsheviks were in Russia and I couldn't see they had anything to do with the fact that this enormous city of Phoenix could be divided into almost two equal parts ... one part who used servants and the other part who were servants. I even tried to discuss this with Jose, one of the waiters at work. We had our supper breaks at the same time.

"Don't talk stupid," Jose replied when I told him of my observations. "This is America, the land of opportunity. And I own my own house."

"You mean you've paid for it? Or does the bank actually own it?"

"Sure, what does it matter? Nobody can take it away from me."

"Not as long as you make the mortgage payments. Just miss some of those and see how much you own."

"I don't plan to miss any. I've been working for Sam for almost thirteen years. I make enough money my kids will get an education. They won't have to be waiters. And we got a good boss. Sam is the best boss in Phoenix."

Jose was right about Sam. Sam was a warm, personable, caring employer, but that wasn't the point. I decided to start going to some union meetings. I was still working for Sam five years later when our union went out on strike.

Sam's restaurant no longer exists. The building itself has been torn down, but, if it hadn't been for the strike, I would probably have been there when the last brick was shovelled out. Sam's restaurant was a rock of stability for me in a business that was fraught with instability. And I was alone now, except for the kids. My brother, who had married and was working for an air research company was in Phoenix, but he lived and worked on the outskirts of town and I didn't see him often. My sister, tiring of the heavy cafeteria pots and pans had become a nurse, where the pans at least weighed less, married, and convinced her husband that they should go back to Louisiana with my parents. They were all horrendously homesick, including my brother-in-law who wasn't even a southerner, but who had heard so much about the south that he thought he was. They all tried to convince me to return, too, but I declined. I was doing very well. The children were all in school now and I had some savings. My car was paid for, I had lots of insurance, I owed no one. Until the strike.

The strike pay was twenty dollars a week. My savings evaporated as the weeks turned into months. And yet I was solidly behind the union. We were striking primarily for more pay for the secondary kitchen workers, the prep cooks, dishwashers and bus boys. Sam paid more than most, but we were asked by the union to consider the entire hotel and restaurant work force. And this was a pitiful thing for some of the other workers. We all knew of unconscionable exploitation by some employers. The numerous abuses other than just low wages and backbreaking work, the difficulties of split shifts, inadequate or no lunch breaks or breaks of any kind for eight hour shifts, the under-compensated overtime ... the list was endless. The proposed union contract was actually very modest and as Sam was already doing what the union asked for, I thought he would sign the contract. But he didn't. On general principles, he said.

I walked the picket line for almost two months, and then savings depleted, went to California. Some of the waitresses I knew in Phoenix had found jobs. I found a job, too. The wages and tips were better because the restaurant where I worked was unionized. But I couldn't get settled there. I was living in an enormous house with my friends, but I was the only one with children in the house. My roommates didn't mind my kids as my boys were quiet and well-behaved, but I minded their boyfriends. Their boys were not quiet and well-behaved.

I didn't want to go back to Louisiana. In the society that I knew there I would have absolutely no freedom to do anything, especially now that I was divorced. I would be considered an easy mark by every man who chanced across my path unless I stayed right under my parents' noses. Of course, things had changed in the ten years or so since World War Two had ended, at least according to my sister. Women were doing all kinds of things, she said. Yeah, maybe. I just didn't believe the attitudes about what constitutes a virtuous woman could change all that quickly. At least among the people that I knew. A virtuous woman was one who lived in the house of a male protector, either a legal husband or a legal father. There was just no way a woman could head her own household without being suspected of whoring. If not for money, then at least for fun. Not until she was eighty years old, anyway.

The west had its advantages. Nobody gave a damn where you lived or with whom you lived or what your background was. The downside was, nobody gave a damn about you, either. I tried to make some sense of all of this.

I began to think about politics. It was the Republicans who fought against our strike and eventually had it declared illegal. I remember that Senator Goldwater was especially opposed to our union. When our strike was broken, a right-to-work law was established or reinforced, I can't remember which, that meant there could be no more closed union shops. That is, people could no longer be compelled to join a union, even if in their workplace the majority were union members. Now, on the face of it, this sounds reasonable. But it doesn't pan out for the benefit of the workers. A lot of the workers didn't understand the necessity of having a union, that a union would raise their pay and benefits in the long run, all they knew was that the union would take a bit of their hard-earned money for union dues and they resented this. So the workers were pitted against each other, and everybody lost. Except those who, like Senator Goldwater, were already rich.

My self-confidence was seriously eroded by the strike. With good reason. I no longer had a home, my savings were all gone and we were living hand to mouth. I think if I hadn't felt so defeated, I wouldn't have married the second time. I was looking for some sort of emotional and financial security.

I might as well have looked in a sink hole. The marriage lasted only a little over a year, barely long enough to produce a baby girl. A beautiful baby girl. I named her Susan. She would fit in nicely with my three outstandingly intelligent and handsome sons, Joey, Mike and Andy. It has always been a source of astonishment to me how my rotten choices in men produced such wonderful children. But there were four of them now, and not a father lurking around anywhere. And no child support.

I started thinking about those lush gardens in Louisiana, and the pigs rooting around in the pen, and the soothing proximity of the moss-hung woods. When my parents wrote urging me to come home, I accepted the invitation. I needed help. My aunt was keeping Baby Sue for me while I worked, but I was barely making expenses and I was flat worn out. By the time I got back to Louisiana I wasn't even worried about social restrictions. I didn't have time for socializing. Besides, I truly didn't care if I never had a man again. I was only twenty-eight, but I was finished with Mother Nature's jokes. All she wanted was for people to have babies, and she didn't care beans about how wildly unsuitable the matches were. And if she sent any more dark-eyed, dark-haired men with flashing white teeth my way again, I would spit in their faces. But it was John Camp who showed up, a tall, muscular young man with sandy hair, intelligent green eyes and an unquenchable thirst for knowledge.

John was so different I didn't know what to make of him. I had never talked to an intellectual before. In fact, I had never met one before. I was so stunned by the discovery that a man could find so many things to think about that I married him. And for once, I made a good choice.

But that was long ago. It is the month of July again, 1989. I have come to terms with living with the cougars. I still take precautions, but go more freely into the bush. This year I have a garden. The garden consists of half a dozen four-by-four boxes set at precarious angles in the highly uneven terrain around the A-frame. A proper garden is impossible without a greenhouse. Maybe next year. In the meantime I have planted Winged Beans in the planter boxes.

The Winged Beans represent a victory of sorts. A victory of perseverance over computers. I first heard of these elusive beans on TV. Not that I have a TV out here. Out here is to get away from TV. But I was visiting a friend in Victoria who had her set turned on when I stopped by to call. A Catholic priest was speaking from somewhere in Africa, somewhere where the pygmies live. It seems the pygmies were in ill health because of the destruction of their environment, and they weren't reproducing at a rate to sustain their population. The priest decided to try this Winged Bean, planted it in large numbers and now, after several seasons of eating Winged Beans, this particular pygmy population is back in good reproductive health.

The priest appealed to all Third World countries to consider planting this bean because not only is the bean itself very nourishing, but also the leaves, the stalk, and the root. It sounded like a winner to me. I went to a seed supply store in Victoria.

Never heard of the bean. Neither had any other of the suppliers. Next stop, the library. I have the utmost respect for libraries and librarians. Librarians will not only give you books to read, they will look up all sorts of information for you, the more obscure the better. They'll give you addresses for just about anywhere in the whole world, they'll dig out the names of companies gone broke twenty years before, spell difficult words you can't think of, give you whatever statistics you need, tell you the time, and furnish you with all the major magazines and newspapers in a dozen different languages.

Ah, yes. I love the library. The only time I ever got even middling angry with my grandson Jason was about a library book. He was fifteen at the time and into Kung Fu. There was a spectacular photo of Bruce Lee that he wanted to part from the book. I lectured him for a good fifteen minutes and then requested that he repeat what I'd said.

"Yes, Grandma. Libraries are probably the only truly democratic institution in our entire society. Just about anybody can get a library card. You don't have to pass any kind of a test to get a card, or have lots of money. Nobody will fault you for your reading tastes. You can get information in libraries not taught in schools or approved by churches. If learning is one of the highest goals of human life, then it is the library that should be recognized by society as the greatest teacher, for instead of stuffing selective material inside kids' obstinate heads just long enough to pass exams, as the school system does, the library gathers arts and information indiscriminately and spreads it before all who will partake of its bounty. May I be excused now, Grandma? I promise I'll never again even think about tearing a page out of a library book, even if it has the best photo of Bruce Lee in the whole world."

I let him go, tolerably satisfied that he understood the enormity of his proposed act.

But after such a long and fruitful association with libraries, when it came to locating the Winged Bean the Victoria Library struck out. The computer could find nothing, absolutely nothing, on the Winged Bean. A couple of weeks later I was in London, Ontario, and I went to the main library there in search of the elusive bean.

Again, nothing, in spite of the librarian's undivided attention at the computer and telephone for at least twenty minutes. When I returned to Victoria I went back to the main library there. I refused to believe that a competent library like this one wouldn't have something somewhere, on the Winged Bean. This time I bypassed the computer minders and went straight upstairs to the second floor where the gardening books live.

I had decided to just work my way through the whole damned section if I had to, but after a bit, the gardening librarian came over and inquired if she could help. I explained the dilemma. Her face lit up. I could tell this one enjoyed a real challenge. Maybe she didn't get too many in gardening.

"Perhaps your Winged Bean has another name," she suggested.

"Perhaps." I agreed.

"Was this an American or Canadian program you saw about the bean?"

"I don't know. I was visiting and when my hostess came down, she turned off the TV. I only saw part of the program."

She nodded like a doctor getting the symptoms in order and turned to the first shelf. "Well, let's start with this little book and see if we can find your Winged Bean under another name." She deftly slid a slender little volume entitled Unusual Vegetables from between two thick gardening books and flipped to the index.

"Ah, here we are," she said almost immediately. "Asparagus Pea, also known as the Winged Bean."

My jaw dropped. "Really?" I blurted.

She smiled as she handed the book to me. "Really. That wasn't such a big problem after all, was it?"

If librarians have a common fault, it's a tendency toward smugness. After copying the information, I took my quest to the nearest gardening shop. The clerk in attendance had, like the others, never heard of the bean. She doubted I would find it in Canada, but gave me the name and address of a large seed catalogue house in the States. I wrote and voila. The Winged Bean seeds, alias Asparagus Pea seeds, came by return mail.

And they're coming up nicely. But I'm worried about the slugs. They grow as big as boa constrictors around here. They must have plenty to eat in the wild, or they wouldn't grow to such monstrous sizes, yet let me put down one strange plant and they attack as if they haven't had a square meal in a year. In fact, it doesn't even have to be a strange plant.

I transplanted several wild onion plants into one of the boxes, the same wild onions, mind you, that the vast hordes of overgrown slugs had been detouring around every day to get to my planter boxes. But after I replanted the onions, these hopelessly corpulent critters, left behind somehow when most prehistoric things either disappeared or evolved into something more reasonable, almost broke their fat little necks trying to get at the same onions they had ignored when they were outside my boxes. Like children, they figure if it's something I'm trying to keep away from them, it's bound to be good. They don't want what's on their plate, they want what's on mine, and they stomp through my planter boxes with impunity.

But I can't bring myself to kill them. They're kind of sweet once you get over the feeling of revulsion about their plump, slimy bodies. It's the expression on their cute little faces. So innocent. And their little antennas are charming. So I carry them away from the scenes of their crimes on pieces of bark, scolding all the way. And then I heard about the seaweed.

Slugs hate salt, you see. For good reason. It melts their gelatinous bodies. So the solution to the slug problem is to spread liberal amounts of seaweed around the planter boxes. I have liberal amounts of seaweed and have spent the entire morning spreading it high against the boxes. If this works then I have solved at least one problem in my environment. But I am getting increasingly worried about the clear-cuts on the mountains that ring the cove.

The mountains seem almost as bare as ever. And there are great deep fissures in the mountainsides that seem to be widening and deepening. I go south every year either just before or right after Christmas. My father died twenty-five years ago. Mama lives with her sister and is still quite well, but she's approaching ninety, so I spend some months with her in the winter. Mike said that after I left last year for my trip there were landslides around the cove. That's worrisome.

Sometimes I think the sole purpose in life must be to solve problems or why would there be so many problems to solve? Why would nature and circumstances hit us with so many, so often? And then there is that mother mystery of them all, what are we doing down here in the first place? Could this have been an honest mistake on Mother Nature's part, one that she regrets? But most of her other creatures are so beautiful, so perfect. The slug in his or her slugness is all that a slug should be; how did humans get so faulty?

Sometimes I wish that John didn't live so far away. After all, we have a history of communication. At least about some things. Like the meaning, or lack thereof, of the universe. And soon after we married, John and I were immediately plunged into the heart of those two great bugaboos, race and religion.

THREE

 John was a couple of years younger than I, but he seemed much older. I was working in a restaurant right across from the university and John came in practically every day. He would appear during the lull of the afternoon when we had time to talk, and I learned during the course of our conversations that he had been in the Marines and that he had served in Korea for three years. He was working on a Master's degree in physics and wanted awfully to take me out to dinner.

I told him I didn't have time, because I had a house full of kids, and besides, if I went out with him it would cause a whole peck of trouble at home with my parents, which I didn't need. Fine, he countered. In that case he would just come get acquainted with my parents. I said no, I'd rather he didn't, my life was already terribly complicated and I certainly didn't need an affair, that would only make me more tired, and he said he wasn't thinking affair, he was thinking marriage. I looked at him. You don't know what you're talking about, I said. Maybe not, he answered, but how complicated can it be? Pretty damned, I said. I keep getting kids. I love them, but I can't afford anymore. Fine, he said, I don't particularly need any of my own seeing as how you have so many, anyway, I'll be making the living. Are you right sure of that, I asked, remembering that I had heard that song before. Positive, he answered, and when I looked into those searching green eyes, my heart didn't pound with excitement, but my gut warmed a bit with the notion that whatever else this man might be, he at least meant well. Then you can come for coffee and cake on Sunday, I said.

John sat in my mother's kitchen and ate huge helpings of blackberry cobbler and drank unending cups of hot, black, chicory coffee. This pleased my mother, but my father was puzzled. What was this physics thing that John had majored in? And more importantly, would it support a ready-made family?

John tried to explain that physics is the study of matter and energy. Not that I knew any more about it than Daddy did. But I was enormously interested in the answer to Daddy's second question. Oh, yes, John answered without hesitation. Although he was still going to school he already had a job at a chemical plant in Baton Rouge, and yes, it was enough to support a family. Modestly.

Some of my friends and relatives seemed surprised that a young man like John just starting out in his career was willing to take on such a heavy burden. There were even a few suggestions that, in spite of his education, he might be a tad unhinged. But several weeks into our courtship I came to realize that a man like John wouldn't let a bunch of kids stop him from marrying any woman he set his mind on. And I liked that. It showed strength of character. I liked to think that was the way I would have felt, had I been a man. John didn't care a lick for material possessions. It was brain things that were important to him. He lived on the ideas that came out of books and inside his own head. There was a downside to this, as I discovered after we'd been married for several months.

John hated money. On payday he would hand his check over to me and I would give him back an allowance. This wasn't necessarily a bad arrangement, as I now had more time for budget managing than he did. However, the man was definitely not to be trusted with any extra money. He was a compulsive book buyer. If I gave him extra money to pick up some needed item for the household, what I frequently got back was a book about some new theory on quantum mechanics, or the unified field theory. Once I gave him money to buy birth control and he brought home a book on thermodynamics. Naturally, this caused some stress in the household.

But on the whole, my new husband was wonderfully easy in many ways. Because he was always thinking, he just flat didn't care what he ate, wore, drove, or how he appeared to anyone else. And he got on with the kids. He thought his new stepsons were good boys and in truth they were. They weren't babies anymore. Joey was twelve, Mike eleven, and Andy a very tall eight-year-old. It didn't happen often, but occasionally the two oldest would have a disagreement that ended in a flailing-fist melee that I couldn't break up and in these instances, I would haul out the belt, which would settle the matter. John firmly disapproved of this time-honoured method of riot control, and I said oh, yeah, then how would you do it? I don't know exactly how he did it, just his tone of voice, I suppose, but the belt was retired for good. John never tried to pal around with the boys, but they liked him well enough. It was Baby Sue who hated John on sight.

She knew right off that John would be an usurper of her authority, a bitterly resented interloper. If John sat down beside me, Sue would immediately drop whatever activity she was engaged in, rush and thrust her plump little body between us, trying to push John away. John was highly amused by this. Baby Sue wasn't amused. But she gradually came to the conclusion that this huge, hateful person had come to stay, and by the end of the year had included him in her routine. But there was one thing about my new husband, besides his book buying compulsion, that did disturb me somewhat. He was an atheist.

In our neck of the woods atheists were as scarce as intellectuals who were as scarce as hen's teeth. I downplayed John's atheism to my family, as they already thought him strange. He wasn't terribly sociable, like most southerners, and he read and studied too much. But he was providing financially for me and the kids and that kept the criticism at bay somewhat. I took this atheism business with a grain of salt myself. I mean, how can anybody really be an atheist in a place where Bible thumping is everybody's favorite pastime. This was something to argue about with John privately, but I didn't worry my head with it much. I went to church as usual and took the kids with me. And I was pregnant again.

The economy was expanding and even though there would be another mouth to feed, the future looked bright. The country community where we were living at the time was mostly populated by Catholic Cajun people. They traditionally had large families, so we were not in any way unusual by having more children. And even after we bought a new house in the suburbs of Baton Rouge and took up residence among more sophisticated people, we parents of the generation that came to be called the Baby Boomers were prolific regardless of race or creed.

We used the G.I. Bill to buy our new house, which meant we only had to pay one dollar down and a bit of closing costs. It was a three-bedroom located in a new subdivision with the grandiose name of Kingcrest Parkway. We would have preferred a four- or five-bedroom, but we couldn't afford that yet. I reasoned that as John got promotions we could add on later. I loved the neighbourhood with its neat rows of upscale houses with the generous enough lawns and attached garages. And I loved rolling the two words of our new address off my tongue ... Kingcrest Parkway. Oh yes, mam, we live on Kingcrest Parkway. No more swamps for us. Why, our house is brand spanking new. We moved into our new place two months before our new baby was born.

But before we moved, I did something that I had never done before in my whole life. I wrote a story. It was sort of an accident.

When Baby Sue was born in Arizona, I had used a maverick doctor who believed in and practised natural childbirth. It had gone very well and I wanted to repeat that experience but couldn't find a doctor in Baton Rouge who would go along with the no drug concept. Which was maddening. In those days traditional doctors were still keeping women handcuffed and leg-shackled down for their own convenience during delivery. My sister, who was now working as a nurse in Baton Rouge and aware of my desire for a more natural birthing process, brought over a magazine one evening on her way to work. In the magazine was an article about how to convince your doctor that you know more about having a baby than he does. In those days almost all doctors were men. The name of the magazine was *True Story*, a magazine for and about women.

John was working the night shift and after he had left for work and the kids were finally in bed I sat down to read this article. It was interesting and informative. But as I flipped through the rest of the magazine I noticed that there were no other articles, the rest of the magazine space was taken up by anonymous stories told by women about their own lives. Or presented as such, anyway. Some of the illustrations and even some of the titles struck me as tacky and brazen, but, as I read through the magazine, I found the stories themselves, while written in a melodramatic fashion, mildly interesting. The stories dealt with the everyday lives of working class women ... unfaithful husbands, ungrateful kids, unpardonable in-laws. The deep down gut stuff. Yes, I could relate. And the magazine was having a contest. Write your story, they said. We want to hear it.

The contest people preferred typewritten scripts, but would read hand-written material if it was neat. I put the magazine aside, pilfered a pack of unused notebook paper from the boys' supplies and started to write. I wrote through the entire night. I was still writing when John came home at six in the morning. I put the story aside then. There was breakfast to be conjured up, kids to be gotten off to school. Baby Sue and I napped together that afternoon and I finished the story that night after John left. I attached a note to my script advising the editors that if my story won anything to please make it enough to buy a typewriter as I had a right smart case of writer's cramp. And then I went to bed, exhausted.

After my bemused husband mailed the script the following day, I put it out of my mind. There was all the pandemonium of moving into our new place and my advanced stage of pregnancy didn't help any. I wasn't feeling well. I kept having false labour pains. I didn't want to go into the hospital too soon, because the sooner one went, the sooner one lost control of the process. But by the time I actually got to the hospital, I knew this delivery would be more difficult than the others. There was no fluid, it would be a dry birth. To add insult to injury, the doctor induced labour. I forgot all about my breathing exercises and my determination to have a drug-free birth. Yes, sir, I certainly would like something to ease the pain, something strong, please, forget what I said about anaesthesia, I'll have some after all, just tote that tank of gas over here, please....

When it was all over I felt like I'd been hit by a truck, and my new daughter's little nose was mashed. But after several hours of sleep we both felt better. My baby's perfect little nose straightened up, and when she opened her eyes and looked at me, my heart was in danger of bursting. She had large, slightly slanted blue eyes and blonde, silky hair. How my black-eyed Baby Susan would love her! We named the new one Margaret Elizabeth. Two weeks after we brought Margaret home from the hospital I went out to the mailbox and found a long envelope from *True Story* magazine. They were buying my story for four hundred dollars!

Lord have mercy on us poor sinners! What a shower of blessings this was. Four hundred dollars in those days was equivalent to four thousand now. Well, not quite, but it seemed so then. John was working days. I rushed inside to the telephone. I never called him at work except in a state of dire emergency, but I just couldn't wait until he got home.

John came to the phone, his voice all screwed tight and anxious sounding when he said hello. I blurted out the astonishing news. He was too dumbfounded to say much of anything except "Well, I'll be. What do you know about that?"

I hung up and called my mother and then my sister. I would have called my brother and sister-in-law in Phoenix, but they wouldn't be home at this hour, and by the time the boys came in from school I had simmered down a bit. After dinner that evening we all sat around making lists of things to buy when my money arrived. Besides a second hand typewriter for me, the boys needed new shoes and new jeans and I needed a tooth filled. John would get a new book of his choosing and the babies something pretty. I would have liked a few new pieces of furniture, as our old stuff looked poor-white-trash-shabby in our house, but that was out of the question. This time. But not for long. I had found my vocation. I would just knock out two or three of these little stories a month and pretty soon we'd all be rich.

I was dreaming. While I was right in thinking that most of the stories were written by professional writers, making something out of nothing is a hard row to hoe. My first story sold so quickly because it was mostly true, except for the ending. I'd written in a happy ending just for the hell of it. Why depress people with sad endings? But I couldn't seem to stop writing.

I couldn't understand it. It was as though selling that one story had made me into some sort of addict. When I was cooking or sweeping or folding clothes, my fevered brain would be busy plotting stories, and at night, after the little ones were in bed, I'd write. Often I would set the alarm for three or four or some other ungodly hour in the morning so I could get in a couple more hours of writing before the baby activated. But it didn't seem to matter how desperately I wanted to succeed at this, my stories came back from editors as fast as I sent them in. Occasionally, I'd get a personal note from an editor and that was enough to keep me going. A year and a half went by without another sale ... but there was a bull's-eye in another department. We were going to have another baby.

It wasn't that we were trying to have more children. We used birth control. But the pill hadn't come out yet and the diaphragm just didn't seem to work. I also used spermicides, John used condoms, and we tried to calibrate all this with the rhythm method. And to add to the mystery of this latest news of impending procreation, for the past several months John and I had hardly had sex. We were too tired. John was taking more graduate courses, besides working full time and trying to do his father things. I kept the household running, and the boys out of reform school, the babies pacified and all of us fed, clothed, washed and ironed, and continued to pursue my writing career when I should have been sleeping. Neither John nor I could understand what had happened. We finally came to the conclusion that we had sex in our sleep, only we were both so worn out neither of us could fully awaken to take precautions — even to remember what had taken place. But none of us had any complaints about the first baby John had sired, so we all just accepted another pregnancy as the natural order of things and went about our respective businesses. But there was trouble abrewing in the woodpile that was to have a profound effect on our relationship with our entire southern environment. School integration was on the way.

As a poor, southern, white woman struggling to gain a firm foothold in the middle class for myself and the family, I was conditioned to believe that black people were inferior, and if given a chance, down right menacing. But I didn't get my conditioning right, and this was my parents' fault.

I received mixed messages from them when I was growing up, which propelled me into the anxiety-ridden position of having to decide the integration issue for myself. The conclusion I came to was that segregation was wrong because it hurt people, people who had never hurt me, people who had only helped me in my life. Particularly people like the Best family.

Eda, the wife and mother of the family, helped Mama around the house. She didn't seem inferior or menacing in any way. In fact, we were plumb fond of her and her husband Willy, who helped Daddy around the farm. The Best kids, like their parents, grew up to be ambitious, hard-working people. Eda often sat at the table with us during the day when I was growing up, and I would no more have thought of sassing her or Willy than I would have of sassing my parents. So when the United States Supreme Court ruled that the doctrine of "separate but equal" which upheld segregation in the south was unconstitutional, and that the public school systems in the south must integrate, part of me sat up and clapped. The other half of me cringed, dreading the confrontations that I knew were going to try and stare me down.

It's always hell to go against the grain of the society in which one lives, to adopt a way of seeing that isn't shared by the majority of one's peers. In the beginning I tried to weasel out. After all, I was a very busy woman. I didn't have time to engage in the polemics of integration. But when it came around to our very own elementary school, which our very own children attended, John and I, at least, got down to some heavy discussions. Some of the public schools in New Orleans were closing, or thinking of closing. White parents evidently preferred to boycott rather than integrate, and our schools could be next.

John could very well have been a redneck on the issue as his own family was quite prejudiced and sometimes education can't make a dent in the ideas sucked in with mother's milk. But John, true to form, winged out into some esoteric never land of abstract thought.

John thought all races essentially the same. I could see that. But he also thought there wasn't enough difference between humans and chimpanzees to spit over, or humans and elephants for that matter. He wasn't even sure there was any compelling difference between animate beings and inanimate objects. In fact, he admitted to the possibility that the entire universe and everything in it was made out of the same building blocks, and that the earth itself was a closed system where matter could neither be created nor destroyed. And that the blood and flesh and bones in my hand could be the same atoms from millions of years ago that were in the bodies of dinosaurs. And that nothing was even really very solid, including the table my hand was resting on; that the wood was really a mass of whirling, shifting particles that only seemed solid in relation to other bodies of particles. And that there actually was no such thing as black or white, merely differences in the intensity of light. And that black people, far from being born in some inherently inferior state were the first humans, the originals from which all other races descended.

I liked it. It had a ring of truth. And yet, while he was on my side, he had explained the entire question out of existence. But this was no help to me. The issue was closing in. Ours was a young neighbourhood. Most of the children went to the same school and many of the families went to the same church as the kids and I. And Sunday School and Bible class and Wednesday night prayer meeting was definitely heating up.

I was about the only one I knew in my church who thought that maybe the schools ought to go ahead and integrate. I kept arguing the Christian dogma of love thy neighbour. And if black people, who lived cheek by jowl with the whites in the countryside weren't our neighbours, who the hell were they? The bitterest arguments I had were with Tom Synder, who was an usher in the church, and like me, on the executive committee.

Tom and his family lived three doors down from us. Our kids played together. Tom and I were also constantly thrown together through all the church activities and we locked horns almost daily over the issue of school integration. But one evening our argument took an ugly turn.

Tom came over just before dinner to collect his small son. As I was outside with the kids, I bade Tom good evening. He spoke pleasantly enough, but then asked me if I had come to my senses about integration.

"If you mean I should join the forces opposed to integration, then no." I answered. "Why should I? I claim to be a Christian. And doesn't loving your neighbour as the Good Book commands mean that we should love the colored people, too?"

"Yes, mam, we should love everybody as God commands, but nowhere in my Bible does He say to send my children to school with colored kids."

"But doesn't loving mean to treat equally?"

"No, mam. It doesn't. Because the coloreds are different from white folks."

"Tell, me, besides having dark skins how are they different?"

"They're not as smart," he answered. "You know that. Coloreds just can't do things like white people."

"I know lots of smart colored people. They're just not allowed to show how smart they can be. And I also know lots of dumb white people."

"Betty, you just don't want to face up to what's behind the school integration move. Don't you see that the colored people just want to put the white race down? You let colored kids go to school with white kids and the next thing they'll want to intermarry. You want your little blonde-haired baby daughter to grow up to marry one of those black coons?"

I looked at him through the gathering dusk. His broad, florid face had flushed a deep crimson. The kids, bored with the same old argument, had wandered off. I was trying to keep from having a fit. I didn't want to just lash out at him, and call him stupid names.

"Why do you use only my blonde-haired baby daughter as an example?" I asked. "I also have a black-haired baby daughter. She's half Italian. Are you saying that it would be okay for this daughter to marry a colored?"

"Of course not."

"Then tell me ... do you think there is some sort of inherent superiority in being born blonde?"

"I told you. You know what I mean."

"Yes, I do know what you mean, and I think your meaning is disgusting. There's lots of white men in this town who think it's just fine for colored women to give birth to a white man's child. Just look at all the high yellows, the mulattos, and quadroons in the colored population. Some of them are whiter than I am. So lots of white men certainly don't mind sharing a black woman's bed and making high yellow babies, they just don't admit to it. And what some of these same white men are so sugar-tit-scared of is that a black man might make a high yellow baby on a white woman. I just don't see the difference. If white men making mixed babies on black woman haven't pulled the white race down, I don't see how white women having babies by black men could."

There was a long silence. I could barely make out his expression in the twilight, but I could smell the heat of his anger.

"You're the one who is disgusting," he spat and then whirled around on his heel and disappeared into the evening.

"God don't love ugly!" I yelled after him. A childish saying. But that was the last of our conversations, or arguments. The Synder children no longer came over to play and Tom avoided me at church. Which suited me just fine. But I was suffering, nevertheless.

More than any specific church dogma, my positive feelings about religion were based on the good will of most of the church people I had known. Even when I was a little girl, I loved going to church. In Sunday School the teacher told us fantastic stories about Jesus walking on the water and Jonah being swallowed by a whale. These stories were right up there with Jack and the Beanstalk and Alladin's lamp. I also liked the grown-up services with the upbeat music and clapping of hands, and the preacher's thumping of the pulpit as he warmed to his sermon, his body threatening to explode all over the platform as he stomped up and down, gesturing wildly as he preached hell fire on Judgement Day. But in spite of the threats, in the end he would plead with us to be sorry for our sins, to come to Christ, to rededicate ourselves to the Lord and He would forgive all. I always liked the ending of church the best at evening services.

I felt firmly planted in the church as a child. And to go along with the wonderful music there was often good things to eat at the church and grown-up women of all ages who called me "honey" and "sugar baby." I wanted to give my own children these same experiences of warmth and safety, but I was definitely running into a snag over this integration business. Tom and his wife weren't the only ones who cut me, or iced me to death in church. It was bewildering. At prayer meeting one night I challenged the minister for some clear leadership, some sense of direction in all the racial turmoil. He declined the challenge. He waffled up one side and down the other, and when he finished nobody knew what he had said, including me. What I did hear was that this man wasn't sticking his precious neck out. I bridled up at him and then left the church, flabbergasted.

I just couldn't believe that the churches in our area and even in the entire state were being so cowardly on the issue. There was one exception I remember. I heard a white woman speak on the radio from New Orleans. She and her husband were Unitarians; her husband a Unitarian minister. They were the only white people sending their children to school every day along with the three little black girls who were integrating a public school in New Orleans. These children were escorted in and out of school grounds by the National Guard. I thought this white woman and her husband outstanding. But aside from them, all I heard from the churches I knew about was "no-comment."

How was this possible? This was a moral issue, right? An extremely far-reaching moral issue that affected every living human being in the south and the churches had no comment? The churches were declining to follow in the footsteps of Jesus, our Savior, who was so solidly on the side of the poor and downtrodden? If the church chose not to help influence events, not to help us collectively grow in grace, to search for the good, then what was the church itself good for? To build buildings and be a social club?

And it wasn't just my belief in the goodness of the church itself that was being shaken. If my concept of religion was embedded in the goodwill of the people of the congregation, which under fire was proving so disappointing, what was left? Church dogma itself?

Now I was wading knee-deep in swampy waters. I had always had trouble with the image of God the Father. It wasn't that I didn't believe it, exactly, it was just that I couldn't fathom it with any clarity. I mean, there was this all-powerful God up there in the sky somewhere who was everything and who had made everything in some mysterious way. He was a jealous god, and vengeful, but at the same time compassionate and loving, and if your prayers found favor with Him, He might personally intervene in your life. On the other hand, He also might personally intervene in your life if he didn't like what you were doing. As a child I rather made the decision to treat this concept of an all powerful father god in the same way I reacted to my own father ... unless he was in an extremely jovial mood, just try to stay out of his way. That worked. Imperfect being that I was, it wasn't in my best interests to draw fatherly attention to myself. But I couldn't help but wonder from time to time ... how had God procreated without a wife? And who begot God? But the genealogy of the gods was beyond me. It had always been the image of Jesus that struck a chord with me and was the foundation of my personal religious feelings.

But while I could be cavalier about trying to postulate who was the father, and mother, of God the Father, no one messed around with my concept of Jesus. Humble carpenter Savior. Bearer of my sins, the One who stood between me and His retaliatory Father, between me and the Father's hellfire, the compassionate son, who was also God. Just the same, now I began to brood over what it was exactly that Jesus was supposed to be saving me from.

Lying? Cheating? Stealing? Gluttony? Malice? Let's be reasonable. It's impossible to live in our society and not be troubled by some of these indulgences once in awhile. But are we to be sent to hell for these pitiful feelings and doings? Then there are the devil walkers, like child molesters and mass murderers. Yes, in a way, I could say these people were deserving of hell. But according to the psychiatrists these people are already in hell. They are already there because they are alienated from their victims, from society, from the milk of human kindness, from life itself. They are the walking dead. And I think they live in hell from the beginning, when nobody cared enough to rescue them from their separate hells, which they then spread around to other people. But even with the most happy and contented among us there are usually some little areas of pus and pain in the individual psyche and a lot of it has to do with sex.

As we all know, sex is a big ticket item in the Christian religion. Jesus said that if one even thinks about sex one has sinned. And yet sex is the one thing that people think about often, unless they are too young or too old, or too hungry, or too sick. If any religion wanted to guarantee its survival, it couldn't have hit upon a more cunning stratagem than to pick out one human activity that was constant, declare that activity a sin and offer the services of the religion as the only antidote for that sin. Talk about a closed shop! And as the sin factor renders people then unable to think about sex with any degree of good conscience, hardly anybody can make an objective critical analysis of their own sex lives.

There is a basic contradiction here about sex and humans and Christianity. In the beginning there was no marriage, so how did sex get such a bad name? If sex was inherently sinful and only purified by marriage, and marriage was good and necessary for the propagation of the species, wouldn't nature have fixed it so that the woman's egg would only fall down into the fallopian tube when a golden wedding ring was placed on her third finger by a male dressed in a suit and accompanied by a minister? But it is, after all, not horse sense that the church thrives on, but belief.

As long as people believe in the Trinity, they're home free. They can commit any manner of mayhem, and get forgiveness for any night of debauchery and treachery and be back in the club as a member in good standing by the following morning. While nonbelievers can lead blameless lives and eat hellfire for their pains. But I came to the conclusion that above all, even more than sex and disbelief, the church hated change. Because of this, the church wouldn't let much new information in, so black people had to stand up screaming and yelling to get the church to notice that we weren't still back in Biblical days when slaves were told to obey their masters. This was now, and this was America, and slavery was supposed to have been abolished.

Ah, yes, the church. I left it reluctantly and with sorrow, for I left behind not only the religion of my childhood, but a world view, a vehicle by which I tried to make sense of the world, a system that told me what I was doing here, what my duties were, and where I would go when I died. I left behind some of the best foot-stomping music ever written, comforting prayers, and the good fellowship and social events that marked my days. And the children. Now what on earth was I going to tell my children about religion?

Looking back over a time span of thirty years or more, had I known then that the question of what I would tell my children about my new found agnosticism would be one of the lesser of my tricky questions, I might have fainted dead away and refused to go on with the show.

People who consult seers and fortune tellers strike me as mad. The evils of each day are sufficient thereto. Praise the Lord for that one. Only now I say praise Mother Earth, it is in Her that I live and move and have my being. Whatever, it seems that one's plate is rarely clean of tricky questions. Even here, in the wilderness, where I thought I might ease off the stage, retire from the ring, and gain some peace from tricky questions in my old age, I am besieged with questions of morality.

I killed four slugs this morning. Lately they have been ig-noring the seaweed I placed so carefully around the planter boxes. Just as they have ignored or found some way to circumvent every other repellent I have tried. The wood ash that was supposed to turn the slugs away, merely intrigued them. A sandbox. Goody. Total slug experience. But I've hardened my heart.

I'm not seduced by their cute little faces anymore. I don't care how long their ancestors have inhabited this particular cove. My Winged Beans are in shreds and the slugs mowed down two thirds of my turnip plants. The loss of the turnips was a cruel blow. I am a Canadian citizen now, but my stomach still holds citizenship in Loui-siana, and dammit, Louisianians love their turnip greens. Canadians, bless us all, don't as a rule, eat turnip greens. Turnips, yes, some-times but the tops are inexplicably thrown away. The tops are more prized by southerners than the bottoms, but like grits, it is almost impossible to buy turnip greens in the grocery stores. If one wants turnip greens, one must grow them. I'll do well now to get a couple of messes of greens out of what's left after the grand slug onslaught. And the slugs especially appreciated the sunflowers. They want me to plant some more. But they have crossed over a line with the turnips and now it's my greens or them. I'm also harboring some hard feelings toward two trees that are working against my ever having a garden to speak of around this cove.

One is a cedar and the other a hemlock. Both are very old. They grow along the bank of the cove in front of the A-frame and their shadows fall on the house and the garden boxes, winter and summer. In a rainforest one needs all the sun one can get in the winter. In the spring and summer the house needs direct sunshine to thoroughly dry out and the garden soil, of course, needs direct hits, too. So periodically I go down to talk to these two ancient ones and explain to them why it is time for them to go. After all, they have lived very long lives, and good ones, I surmise, dwelling majestically supreme over the cove. Surely they have seen just about all of cove life worth seeing. But they withhold their permission to be so disposed of, they say they want to go when they are ready, and not before.

Twice I have told Mike that I think the trees should be cut down, and then changed my mind before he could actually commit the murderous deed. For the moment, at least, the trees have won. But I have warned them that the reprieve is only temporary, that when I get around to serious gardening next year, we will have to reopen negotiations. Maybe only one would have to go. They might draw straws or maybe one would volunteer. And then the very idea of cutting these straggly but still magnificent old wonders down to make way for turnip greens sickens me as I catch myself thinking in the way of the destroyers, the technology driven multinationals, the machine organizations that monkey around with nature in a wanton, careless way, plundering and rearranging natural things at will in order to achieve one particular purpose. And is this not what the capitalists do, which is making a cesspool of the world — and which is what drove me to this relatively inaccessible little cove in the first place? From the beach I look up to the mountains and I feel this apprehension that things up there are decidedly not right.

The mountains are simply too steep to have been logged at all, much less clear-cut. The rains are washing all the top soil away before anything can start to grow back. What was the logging company thinking of? And where were the government foresters? Weren't they supposed to be watching out for this sort of thing before it happened?

I have heard of an organization based in Tofino called "The Friends of the Clayoquot Sound." This group is opposing any more clear-cutting in the Clayoquot. One of the spokespersons for this group is a young woman named Valerie Langer and I know her slightly. I will stop in and see what the group is doing, but I don't personally want to get involved. Let the young people do this one. I have had enough fighting. I have fought in almost all of the areas known to woman in a patriarchal society and am tired and long for peace. I deserve peace. Besides, I'm not much good in battle anymore. The Vietnam War broke my heart and wore me out before I even got to women's rights. And it left me an incurable cynic about the established order of things.

But even the Vietnam War didn't send me to jail. The poor old mountains around our cove that are picked as clean as a Sunday chicken finally did that. They will eventually send me forth as a witness to their degradation, to their pain. The mountains, in their raped and ruined state, become feminine to me and in some mystical, metaphysical connection that is easy to hook into in the wilderness, I become one with them, I feel their breath upon my face, my soul entwines with theirs, their fate becomes my fate. But not yet. The time for battle is not yet. I must wait a little while.

FOUR

 My bacon was fried for good with the church people when I joined a very select group of other white citizens who, for one reason or another, hadn't been properly programmed as children into the correct amount of hostility and patronization that whites were supposed to deal out to blacks as the natural order of things. We got together and went down and picketed the elementary school one Saturday morning. We carried signs that urged the schools to integrate peacefully and act civilized. Some white bystanders and passersby yelled obscenities. An old man walking past spit in my direction but his aim was off. The press came and took some pictures. When I got home that afternoon I gathered the boys up, the little girls as yet too young to understand, and tried to explain what was happening, with the schools and with the churches, at least as far as I understood the situation.

The boys seemed to readily grasp my interpretation of events. Looking back, there might be a question of how much they actually understood, and how much they just wanted, as my sixth pregnancy was already manifesting itself in the usual swollen ankles, killing indigestion and non-stop vomiting, not to get me more riled up than I already was. Still, my sons had lived among and played with and gone to school with so many different races in Phoenix that all the commotion about integration must have seemed downright spooky to them at times.

At any rate, our schools in Baton Rouge didn't close, and as a family we survived the neighborhood snubbing. John was too busy chasing the secrets of the universe to care about the neighbors, and the boys and I had a few select friends to whom we could turn for companionship. But the thing still didn't set right with me. It was like the aftermath of the union strike I'd been involved in; I couldn't digest all that I knew about what had happened. Why did people so frequently act in such inglorious and unfeeling ways?

But then in January our new daughter was born, another blue-eyed blonde, healthy and beautiful. No thanks to the medical profession. I was expecting the torture rack complete with handcuffs and leg irons with my lower body elevated, and, in spite of my protests, I was not disappointed. Common sense does not rule the labor rooms, delivery rooms, and nurseries of hospitals. I am convinced that this is because men are in charge of something they can never know personally, which is why the entire birth process, at least back in those days, was unsatisfactory and even downright dangerous.

I just wanted to take my dumpling of a baby home as soon as possible. She looked a lot like Margaret Elizabeth except that her eyes were a deeper blue and her dimples were on her chin instead of at the sides of her mouth. Rose Mary was barely a month old when John received an answer from an application he had sent NASA in Norfolk, Virginia. They would like to hire him as a junior grade physicist.

John was happier than a June bug. His work at the chemical plant was not all that challenging. At NASA he would be doing some interesting work in physics. I was happy, too, that John would finally be doing the work he liked. But I hated to leave my family who still lived in the country across the river, my parents and my sister and her husband and little boys. My own sons, too, had mixed feelings about the move. They were of an age now that they had formed important friendships. But the move would be several steps up the ladder of financial and social mobility, and as I was still chasing my own American dream, and in spite of deepening suspicions that this mobility had a dark underbelly, it seemed a wise move. So we put the first new house any of us had ever lived in up for sale and prepared for the trip to Virginia.

The first people who came out to look at our house bought it. The deal took two months to go through and the new owners gave us another six weeks to actually vacate the premises. By that time Rose Mary was old enough to be semi-weaned and accustomed to the bottle which was a good thing as we planned to move ourselves to Virginia. We got a moving allowance, but would be able to save a lot of the allowance if John drove the moving truck and I followed behind in the station wagon. The boys were to take turns riding in the enormous moving truck with John. That would always leave me with two big boys to help with Susan, now five, the two babies, Margaret Elizabeth and Rose Mary, and Chip, the boys' terrier, while I drove. In retrospect, I can't believe we did such a stupid thing.

The night before we left on this epic voyage I stayed up until midnight frying chickens. Bearing in mind that an army always travels on its stomach, I fried half a dozen chickens to make sure we had a good meal on our first stop on the road. But in the confusion of leaving, I left the chickens behind in the oven, and we were at least a hundred miles outside Baton Rouge when I remembered. Everybody was mad at me, including Chips, who always got the livers and gizzards. But that was only the beginning.

Going through Gulfport, Mississippi the following day I almost lost John. I was in the right lane in downtown traffic when I looked over and saw John making a left turn. I don't know how he had switched to the left-hand lane without my noticing, but as my job was not only to drive and keep John's truck in sight, monitor Joey's handling of the baby in the front seat, and yell orders and admonition when the passengers in the rear seats, including the dog, threatened to lose control, it wasn't too surprising that I might have missed John's switching lanes. But I simply couldn't lose him. So I lay on the horn, yelled out the open window to the startled drivers and passengers in the cars to the left of me that I intended a left turn from the right lane. Appraising what must have looked like a rolling time bomb, they graciously gave way.

Looking back, I don't know what we were thinking of to take

such heroic measures to move five rooms of mostly crummy furniture halfway across the continent. And a dog. Okay, maybe a case could be made for taking the dog, but not the crummy furniture. I guess the ratty furniture was just all we had left and we weren't sure when we would get any more. It was somewhere in western Alabama that I lost sight of John's truck altogether.

We were on an interstate highway that abruptly branched off into a T. In the seat beside me Joey was trying his best to soothe a cranky baby with little success, so, when we stopped for a red light, I leaned over and checked Rose Mary's diaper. This was a single lane highway and several cars had gotten between our station wagon and John's truck so when I looked up and saw what appeared to be the truck we were attached to make a left at the light, I made a left, too. We were a good thirty-five miles from the turn off when Joey voiced his first doubts.

"Mother, I don't think that's Dad's truck," he said worriedly as he leaned over the now sleeping baby, trying to see more clearly through the windshield.

"What do you mean, you don't think that's Dad's truck?" I wailed. "Of course that's Dad's truck. It's a U-Haul, isn't it? Same size and everything?"

"Something about it looks different. And it's going too fast. Dad wouldn't go that fast."

In truth, the truck ahead didn't seem to be worried about anything behind it, in fact, it was so far ahead of us now I could barely see it. But perhaps John is absent-mindedly thinking about his new job, I thought. And drove on. Twenty miles later the truck ahead had left us behind entirely. If John was actually driving that truck, and by now I was convinced that he was not, he had lost his mind and there was no use in following him anyway. My favorite motto in life has always been: He who fights and runs away, lives to fight another day ... so I pulled into the first truck stop on our way back from whence we had come and we all piled out of the car. Leaving the dog sulking at the doorway to the restaurant, we humans went in and found a table large enough to accommodate us. It was at this point that I discovered that I only had three dollars and seventy-eight cents in my purse. When a waitress appeared at our table I decided to be up front about the whole thing.

"This is all the money I have," I explained. "We need five glasses of milk and some whole wheat toast. Is this possible?"

The woman didn't bat an eye. It must be true what they say about waitresses in truck stops being some of the world's sweetest people. About my age but with a no nonsense air, she sat two quarts of milk from the cooler on the table, brought glasses, jam, butter, and a platter of toast. Last, she sat a cup of steaming hot coffee before me.

"My God, that's purentee wonderful," I breathed gratefully. She smiled and went about her business. I glanced at Joey. Teenaged, reserved and sensitive, I knew that the rest of us sometimes embarrassed him. But if he was embarrassed by the situation he didn't let on. For which I was momentarily grateful. Andy, who was yet to hit the teens, was still mostly stomach. The little ones ate hungrily, too. There had been fruit and boiled eggs for breakfast, but this traveling whetted everybody's appetite. However, there was still a bag of apples in the car, and some crackers. So we had enough to eat at the moment, but how to find John? After we had finished eating and everyone had made a trip to the restroom we went back outside. Andy took the dog for a run. While we waited around the station wagon, Joey questioned my plan of action.

"I don't have one, honey, except to go back to the intersection where we lost Dad. Surely by now he's discovered we're not behind him and has gone back to the intersection himself. He's probably there waiting."

Only after Andy got back with the dog, and I changed the baby, and Joey resettled the little ones back into the station wagon, and we were all ready to go, and I turned on the ignition did I notice that the gas tank was riding on empty. Or almost.

But how could that be? We had filled up early that morning. Either the needle was off or there was a leak in the gas tank. Joey and I got out and examined the tank. There was no leakage or smell of gas. What to do? Go back into the truck stop and call a policeman? But what would I tell him? That I had lost my husband? Wouldn't he take a good look at us all after three days on the road and think that John had deliberately lost us? Would we be taken to some sort of family crisis center? Or perhaps the children would be separated from me and taken to foster homes? And my son Mike who was riding in the truck with John, would any of us ever see him again? Forever separated from his mother and brothers and sisters, would he finish his growing up as an only child, a stepfather his only parent? Would he become a troubled adult, repeating endlessly his tragic story of how his mother and five siblings disappeared somewhere along a lonely Alabama highway, never to be heard from again...?

"Get in the car," I told Joey with forced heartiness. "I'm sure the gas gauge needle is just stuck."

"I hope you're right, Mother," he answered doubtfully. "I personally think we should just stay here and let Dad find us."

He was right, of course. But it was early July and the sun was bearing down like a loco mule bound for the barn, and we couldn't all just tromp back into the restaurant just because it was cool in there. And there were no trees around to park under.

"At least we'll go until we find some trees for shade," I said firmly. That sounded reasonable enough to Joey and he gave over. I eased back out onto the highway but I was seriously worried. Joey kept a nervous eye on the gas gauge. We had only gone a few miles when Andy spotted the highway patrolman.

"Mother, there's a police car behind us," he announced excitedly. "And he's signaling for you to pull over."

Startled, I glanced into the rearview mirror. Sure enough, a highway patrolman was flashing the red light on top of his vehicle and gesturing to me. I slowed down and eased over to the side of the road. Why was he stopping us? I wasn't speeding. Did he perceive my driving as reckless simply because of all the kids and the dog, a case of overload? I stopped the car and waited. The officer walked over to the car and peered inside, taking in all the attendant horrors, Joey and the baby opposite me, with bags of diapers and bottles and books, the rear seat with Andy and the little girls and the dog and a bag of apples and three bags of toys and coloring books and a box of crackers and changes of clothing and more books all scrambled up together ... and then he looked at me closely, a tall, lanky man around forty with sharp, suspicious eyes.

"May I see your driver's license, please, mam?" he asked after a moment. His tone was polite but I wasn't crazy about the way he was observing everything about us. He reminded me of the line about Cassius in Julius Caesar that I remembered from school, "Yond Cassius has a lean and hungry look; He thinks too much: such men are dangerous."

But the kids and the dog were fascinated. They all stared back at the patrolman while I rummaged around in the front seat for my purse. My purse wasn't there between the seats, where it usually rode. Flustered, I ran my hand under the seats, the edges, the sides, under the diaper bags and bottles, under Joey's books. No luck. Where could the damned thing be? Frantic now, I turned to the back seat.

"Kids, my purse. Do you see it anywhere? Look around, please."

There was a sudden general upheaval in the rear as everyone including the dog, started searching under the stacks of books, coloring books and crayons, dolls, drinking cups, sweaters, shoes, knapsacks of clothing, thermos jugs, and pillows for the lost purse. The bag holding the apples couldn't stand the pressure and self-destructed, rolling its contents hither and yon. Skip, unnerved by the sudden, intense activity in general and the rolling of the apples in particular, gave up the search. He sat back on his haunches and howled. Which woke the baby who up to that point had been sleeping. She immediately screeched her protest at the top of her little lungs. And then I remembered I hadn't picked my purse up from the table at the restaurant.

"Officer, I've done a stupid thing," I began.

He raised an eyebrow. "Oh?"

"Yes, you see, we had breakfast at the truckstop back there and ... I left my purse there. A good thing you stopped me, isn't it?" I asked, trying to brazen the thing out. "Why, I could have driven a million miles before I had discovered that I'd left my purse. That is, if you hadn't stopped me."

"You realize that driving without a license in your possession is against the law?"

"Yes, sir, I do. I surely do. I'm always careful about that. And I'll go right back to the truckstop and see if my purse is still there."

The officer seemed not to hear. Now he was directing his stern, searching gaze to the outside of the station wagon.

"I realize the old buggy looks a tad tattered on the outside," I blathered nervously. "All that rust and all. Probably why you stopped me in the first place. But everything is in good working order," I went on mindlessly, unable to stop chattering. "Really, my husband had the dear ole thing safety checked before we left home, and while I admit it wouldn't take any beauty contests, because it's been through a lot, you know, with all the kids, it's kind of like me, a smidgen rough on the outside, but the motor still purrs like a kitten."

The officer was not amused. If anything, his hateful eyes grew steelier. Momentarily cowed, I closed my mouth and waited. Everything had suddenly gone quiet, the dog stricken with a case of chicken heart induced by the man's air of authority, while Rose Mary had found temporary solace in sucking her chubby little fingers. Joey sat stiff and protective beside me. Andy and the little ones in the back were still as mice. What was this Nazi going to do, I wondered, arrest all of us and take us to jail?

"May I see your car registration?" the Nazi suddenly demanded. His words cracked through our universe like pistol shots. We all gave a collective jump and stared at him some more.

"Your vehicle registration, please, mam," he repeated. And then we all sprang to life again. Joey was already opening the glove compartment door.

"That's right, son, it should be right there on top," I said encouragingly. "The first thing you see. That's it."

Joey handed over the card triumphantly as if to say, "well, officer, we may be poor white trashy looking at the moment but we are not completely undocumented. But, as we had been down some dusty turn-offs on our trip, the card was covered with a good inch of dust. As I turned toward the waiting patrolman with the card I did an impulsive thing ... I blew at the dust on the top of the card.

I only meant to make the card presentable for the officer's inspection but of course the dust was blown smack into his face. He stood there for a moment, shocked. And he looked so funny! With only his deep-socketed, rapidly blinking eyes visible through the film of dust he was completely stripped of his awful, threatening aura of authority. A bubble of laughter welled up in the pit of my stomach. I tried mighty hard to push it back. I bit my lips and dug my nails into the palms of my hands. I threatened myself with hell fire, the way I used to do in church when I was threatened with a fit of giggles. But it was no use. A loud, semi-hysterical peal of laughter broke loose from my throat and then Joey joined in and our hilarity jumped a barrier and spread to the back seat, and while we were all busy laughing, except the Nazi, of course, none of us heard or noticed John's truck drive up. We were aware of his presence only when his face appeared next to the patrolman's in the car window.

"What's going on?" he demanded, peering in at us much as the Nazi had done. The unexpected sound and sight of this second inquiry struck us as being so hilarious that we all started another round of raucous laughter.

The patrolman took a large handkerchief out of his pocket and wiped at his face with a slow, deliberate motion.

"For some reason they seem to think that blowing dust in my face is just the funniest thing they've ever seen," he complained to John. That set us all off again. We were weak from the explosive, hysterical laughter by now, and if we could have found a floor to roll on we would have been rolling. John suddenly leaned into the car and grabbed my left wrist.

"Stop it!" he commanded. "Stop it right now!"

I was teary-eyed and couldn't see clearly, but I recognized the anxiety in his voice. The humor of the situation began to vanish. In a few moments I managed to straighten up and order was restored.

"Is everyone all right now?" he inquired, rather patronizingly I thought.

"Of course not," I snapped, wiping my eyes. "You lost us, we had no money to speak of, something's wrong with the gas gauge, I've lost my purse, we have no idea how to find you again and then this ... officer pulls us over for God only knows what ..."

"Because I asked him to," John broke in.

"You asked him to?

Yes. When I realized you weren't behind me, I stopped and called the Highway Patrol."

"You mean this man is actually our friend?" I asked astonished.

"Yes and no, mam," the officer replied. "I have to ticket you for driving without a license." His face was clean again, except for one smudge of dust on the very tip of his nose. "But I'll call and see if I can locate your purse. If it isn't at the truckstop, or your license isn't in the purse, you'll have to get a replacement before I can let you drive that car any further. Describe your purse for me, please."

I described the big, multi-colored leather purse. The officer went back to his car. He returned in a few minutes to say that the waitress had found my purse and that he would take John with him to fetch it.

I think your wife should stay with the family," the officer said, addressing John. A look passed between them. John nodded. I saw that look. I'd seen it before, passing so silently between men. That look said that women and children are incompetent and a bit of a nuisance, but they seem to be necessary and we men must do the best we can. Nevertheless, when the officer returned with the purse, I thanked him profusely, in spite of the look and the ticket in my hand.

"I have to have some time out," I told John.

"I think we all do," he agreed. We drove to the next little town and found a park where the kids and I rested in cool shade while John found a grocery store and a garage. By the time the gas gauge was fixed, and the kids and I had been restored to reasonable sanity by a nap and refreshments, it was time to hit the road. I hated to get behind the wheel of the station wagon again. But I had to. Joey wasn't old enough for a license yet and we had to get this caravan to Hampton, Virginia. But I made a vow that once there, I was through with driving. I hated it. It was nerve-wracking and dangerous and something was always ailing automobiles. They were deadly, expensive, hunks of junk. And when we finally rolled into Hampton two and a half days later, I was even more determined to give up driving.

We immediately found a rental house in a small community on the outskirts of Hampton. That night, after the kids were in bed and it was my turn for a long, leisurely bath, I promised myself that I would never drive again. At first John thought I was just exhausted from the trip, but in the days that followed he saw that I was serious about not driving anymore and stopped bothering me about it.

The community had begun as a fishing village but was getting overrun with foreigners like us. Still, the neighbors welcomed us with open arms. An older couple named Lenshaw lived in the house to the left of us. Mr. Lenshaw was retired but his wife still worked as chief cook at the school cafeteria. The evening following our move-in Mrs. Lenshaw came over bearing one of the largest non-ceremonial cakes I've ever seen. As we were so busy getting settled in, our dinner had been scanty and we were immediately riveted by the cake. As soon as Mrs. Lenshaw left we fell to with a passion.

This was a poppy seed cake and it was utterly delicious. Now, a poppy seed cake sounds harmless enough, right? Rather wholesome and nourishing in fact. But this poppy seed cake fell into a different category altogether. It was as velvety and succulent as the richest of pound cakes, made with real butter and rich cream and dozens of free ranging chicken eggs and nestling between the eight different layers of cake, mind you, that's eight layers, one for each of us, including the baby, and I counted them before we attacked the thing, was various jams, strawberry, peach and apricot, and something else, something wonderful that I couldn't quite place, something I think, mildly alcoholic. An incredible creation. The woman was a genius. Highly appreciative of this unexpected gift from the moving gods, we licked up every crumb. Unfortunately our constitutions weren't geared for such rich fare and this cake was so rich it could have bought out the entire city of Hampton and surrounding environs.

My style of cooking was to fill up a huge pot with vegetables, throw in a bit of meat and call it dinner. Side dishes were beans and rice. And cornbread. If a dish called for more than two pots I declined. Dessert was banana pudding or sweet potato pie. This complicated poppy seed cake hit our innocent, unsophisticated semi-empty stomachs like guerrillas on a jungle ambush. We clung to each other for support as we staggered around trying to suppress the rising collective indigestion, while we also tried to sort out the bedding for the night. Our beds still weren't up and some of us, now too weary and burdened with poppy seed cake to care, simply dropped in our tracks.

Around mid-morning the following day we were plied with goodies from another source ... a young woman with her little boy who lived to the right of us. It turned out that, while she had been born and raised in the village, her husband also worked for NASA as a research engineer. But where her husband worked wasn't what impressed me about Ann. It was the offering she brought. Peanut butter cookies. Store bought.

Most southern women are plumb batty about food, spending enormous amounts of time growing it, buying it, preparing it, thinking about it, talking about it, eating it, cleaning up after it until sometimes I hated food. This was a woman after my own heart. Any southern woman who would buy a bag of cookies, put them on a plate, and then offer them to another southern woman had a hellava lot of nerve. I was sure we would become friends.

And we did, after a fashion. My other neighbor with whom I came to spend a few gossipy hours a week was an elderly woman who lived directly behind us, Mrs. Thompson. But I must digress from remembrances of that first neighborhood in Virginia. Mike has just returned to Cypress Bay from Tofino and has brought supplies and a bit of news. There is to be an environmental wilderness meet on Vargas Island over the weekend. There will be discussions of the logging practices in the area. Would I like to go? Yes. Oh, yes.

FIVE

Vargas Island is a small island that lives between Cypress Bay and the village of Tofino. The native people claim part of it, some say all of it, but these claims are not as yet settled and non-Indians also live on the island. Mike and I start out early Friday morning in the speedboat. We pick up a passenger in Tofino, a young woman named Hope. She is a different breed of young woman, physically competent and adventurous, who scorns make-up among a million other goodies that society has to offer. Hope works on a fish farm near us, lives on a houseboat, and some-day plans to have her own fish boat. She also has relatives who live on Vargas Island.

The relatives have offered us the use of their small guest cabin for the weekend. The cabin only has one room so Mike will have to pitch a tent on the beach like most of the other people who will be at the meet. Mike doesn't mind. He and Hope are only friends, so I am not intruding on a relationship. But just as we are getting

Hope's gear into the boat, Chris, a reporter for the local weekly, hails us from the dock.

"I can't make it over to Vargas," she yells down at us, her blonde hair blowing in the wind as she waves a camera in my direction. "Betty, please?"

"I'm not a reporter," I protest.

"You don't have to be. Just some pictures and some names, okay?"

Mike catches the camera and suddenly I'm a reporter. I'm not exactly keen on this, but my spirits are too high to fizzle under this unexpected responsibility. The day is gorgeous. Sunny and bright with a sweet, cool breeze, we are wafted over to Vargas Island by the smoothest of waters. Already a hundred tents are spread out along the sandy shoreline like giant, colorful mushrooms.

We skirt the open beach where the festivities will be held and putter around to the inlet on the opposite side of the island where we find the little doll-sized cabin perched saucily on a rocky outcropping overlooking the inlet. Mike helps us up to the cabin with our gear and then heads back to the main action. He has been asked to read one of his environmental poems later in the evening and must find out the particulars from the organizers. Hope and I put away our supplies, have a bite to eat, secure the cabin, and then start off on the two-mile hike back across the island.

I am surprised by the wildness of the trail. It is more an animal trail than anything deliberately created by humans as there is no rhyme or reason to the zigzags and switchbacks. My legs are short and I struggle, grunting, over huge fallen trees. Nursery logs, they are called, because though dead themselves, their felled flesh is bursting with new life, both plant and animal. The smell is powerfully of the earth. The only sounds are natural ones ... bird calls, humming insects, small animals rustling in the undergrowth. I slide down steep embankments and hop through and over small waterways running under the plant debris piled on the forest floor. When it was young the whole world must have looked like this, I think. There has never been any clear-cutting in this particular spot, nor logging of any kind, and I am spooked by the primordial look, feel, and smell of everything. Yes, way, way, back, before the Indian cultures, even, back when humans were lurking in caves or swinging in the trees themselves, this was the way things were. Or I could almost be on a different planet entirely, one similar to earth, but different, with different animals, perhaps, and at any moment some slimy monster might blunder through the underbrush. I shudder. And I have lost sight of Hope.

I call, but there is no answer. Trying not to panic I unwrap a clinging vine from around my ankle as I slither over yet another nursery log. Where could she be? Cougars? Are there cougars on this island? Probably. Cougars are reported to be on most islands of any size in the area. Sweet Jesus. But no, think. I remember now, a citizen of the island told me there were no longer any cougars here. I yell again, at the top of my hog-calling voice. Still no answer. Quicksand? Could Hope have blundered into a patch of quicksand? No, surely Hope would be yelling blue murder if she had stepped or fallen into quicksand. Anyway, I'd never heard of quicksand around here. Warped time zone? Had I somehow truly slipped into a fractured time warp of a million years ago and the reason everything seems so primeval is because it actually is? I am thrown back at least a million years into the past ...

"Betty!"

I jump a foot. It is Hope, calling me from up ahead. I wait a moment for my heart to calm down and then hurry around a thickly grown-over bend in the trail.

"Why didn't you answer me?" I complain.

"Because I was in the middle of negotiating this stream. Which is what you have to do, too. But it's okay. I came back to help you over. Give me your hand."

I look down, down at the stream. There is a steep drop-off and the only way across is over an enormous downed log that spans the rushing water below. I take Hope's outstretched hand and start inching across the log. The drop is extremely steep. About four feet from the bank I begin to lose my nerve.

"Don't look down," Hope warns, sensing my ambivalence about this dubious undertaking. I clutch her hand tighter. I try not to look down, try just to concentrate on monitoring my footing with brief, sideways glances. I think of mountain climbers and trapeze artists and skydivers and the film I saw about the Africans who scale unbelievably steep cliffs to collect some prized bird's eggs, and wonder how on earth these people, who must have constitutions similar to mine, as we are all human, ever manage such things? Incredible.

"You're looking down," Hope says accusingly.

"If I don't look, I can't see where I'm putting my feet," I explain.

"But you say heights make you dizzy. I don't want you to get dizzy," she answers firmly.

That did it. Now I am paralyzed. If I don't look, I will stumble on the knots and protrusions on the log and risk falling into the stream, but if I do look I may very well get dizzy and fall into the stream anyway. I don't mind getting wet, but that stream is a long way down.

"Are you going to stay on this stupid log all day?" Hope asks impatiently.

There are times when the young annoy me dreadfully.

"I might."

"Then I'm going to leave you here all by yourself."

She is bluffing. I know for a fact she is bluffing. And she knows that I know she is bluffing.

"You'll miss Mike's poem," she says after a moment, obviously deciding on a different approach. "You know how you're looking forward to hearing Mike read his poem in front of all those people. Think how proud you'll be. Do you want to miss all that?"

She has definitely hit on the soft underbelly of my maternal pride.

"No. I don't want to miss that."

"Then let's go. We're already halfway across. You can do it."

I do it. And as if to reward me for being so brave the trail begins to smooth out and before long we have reached the beach and landed smack in the middle of the activities.

The day promises to be a lively one and I am ambushed by a warm, happy feeling. The clear skies and gentle breezes seem firmly in place. Mike's poetry reading has been rescheduled for the following evening. He and Hope go off to one of the workshops, and I, mindful of my reporter's duties, decide to take a stroll and interview people.

People are coming and going from the workshop tents and others are just lazing around in front of their own private tents, others, mostly children, are dipping their toes in the gentle, but frigid, surf. The seawater in Clayoquot Sound never really warms up. Well, maybe a shallow cove here and there, like the one at Cypress Bay, will decide to de-chill enough to accommodate a few hardy swimmers, but most swimmers haunt the fresh water lakes in the area. But this beach is quite beautiful.

Smooth, hard packed white sand, interesting shells. But I am a reporter and must record this event. Perhaps I should first just get an idea where all these people are from. I eye the beach strollers, wondering how I should approach them. "Hi, I'm your basic roving reporter?" No, that won't do. "Hi, my name is Betty Krawczyk; I'm a reporter for the local weekly. Do you mind if I ask you a few questions?" What if somebody asks to see my credentials? I don't have any credentials. Well, maybe I won't interview anybody just yet. I'll count the tents as I walk along the beach, that should be an important statistic. The paper will want to know how many tents were pitched. While I count, I watch the people out of the corner of my eye.

There are so many young people. But after all, this is probably a young people's thing ... camping on the beach, braving the elements. It is difficult to categorize most of these young people. Back in the sixties I knew a hippie when I saw one. I listen to accents and snatches of conversation as I drift past, and I come to the conclusion that many of them seem more yuppie than hippie, especially the foreign ones. After the tent count I take a deep breath and stop the very next people coming my way, two males and a female, all tall and blonde and somewhere in their early twenties. They are from Holland. On holiday, they are pleased to be recorded and have their picture taken. Self confidence bolstered, I am now an experienced reporter and think nothing of stopping and detaining people and inquiring into their lives. What a sense of power I have suddenly acquired! I am quite dizzy with my importance. I talk to people from England, Ireland, Germany, Mexico, the U.S. and from all across Canada ... Newfoundland, Quebec, the prairies and interior B.C. It's wonderful. There are some older people, but they are not quite so talkative, and I think at least one couple I try to interview may be on a clandestine rendezvous, they are so touchy, or perhaps they feel environmentalism to be some dangerously exotic activity that borders on the subversive and therefore mustn't be found out. I do not try to interview the natives at all.

These are local Indians, not tourists. And they make me feel shy and awkward. The questions I ask of the non-natives will sound stupid if posed to First Nation peoples. Questions like, "when did you first become aware of environmental issues?" Long before the rest of us, I'd guess. They've been living in this rainforest since forever; they know it the way a child knows its mother. They live environmental issues, for God's sake. Like the rest of us, only deeper. So I don't interview the Indians.

But the native people here, like the blacks of Louisiana, press heavy on my consciousness. Although I am not personally responsible for their historic oppression, as it is my own race who have confiscated most of the original riches of people of color the world over, I feel some of the weight of that responsibility. The natives around me are fisher people or involved in some other self-employed activity, and I know that some of them are a lot better off financially than I am. But it is not for them that I mourn and feel such guilt, it is for their ancestors and an entire lost way of life. Still, I cannot interview them. I am too emotionally involved. Anyway, the afternoon is drawing on and I spot Mike and Hope standing by the information tent.

The workshops are interesting but by six we are all getting restless. We were promised dinner at six. We can smell the dinner. We can even see it being prepared under the kitchen tent. The native women who have contracted to cook are busy barbecuing generous hunks of salmon and tossing about huge mounds of cole slaw and adding continually to the growing mountain of bannock, the wonderful Indian bread that is cooked on top of the stove. In the face of the tantalizing smells it is impossible to think of anything except food. But in answer to all inquiries the cooks say no, things are not ready yet. They are obviously on west coast time and we must all adapt. However, the crowd is definitely getting surly. The organizers wisely decide that some sort of distraction is in order. A young woman in jeans and masses of dark, curly hair appears on the speaker's platform and introduces another young woman in a flowing skirt who asks us all to form a hand-holding circle. Which is no small feat. At least a hundred and fifty people have to be engineered into place. But when the dogs and children quieten and the shuffling around lessens, the enormous circle is impressive. Beautiful, all these people holding hands against the backdrop of the sea. A marvellous photo opportunity. I try to slip out of the circle unobtrusively to take a few pictures but am chastened on both sides by my circle mates and urged to put the camera away. I am solemnly told that this is a magic circle, to photograph it will be insensitive and profane. Chagrined and apologetic, I slip back into the circle, the unused camera dangling from my neck. The young woman on the platform is speaking in a warm, well modulated voice that carries well over the microphone and everyone is listening intently, food, for the moment, is forgotten.

She is praising us all for being here, she is giving thanks for the sky, the earth and the waters, and I am with her on this — for in my weakened, half-starved state she seems some sort of priestess in the way she holds up her graceful arms to the heavens in a gesture of supplication, all the while urging that we put ourselves in touch with the wholeness of the universe. In order to facilitate this touching she first directs us to become aware of our feet inside our shoes as we stand on the grassy earth, and then instructs us to imagine that we are following her further down into the earth, past the grassy crust, down into the many layered strata of gravel and sand, way down to the underground springs, past the water downward to the hot, dense inner workings of the earth where the rocks become molten ...

Once my imagination is on a roll it goes for broke. This young priestess has no intention, I am sure, of leading me into the very confines of hell itself, but that is where I wind up, deep within the fiery, churning, blasting, red furnaces of the hell of my childhood. And my reaction as an adult is the same as that of the terrified imagination of the child ... my heart is pounding, my scalp crawling with anxiety and apprehension, my upper lip is wet with perspiration, as are my underarms, and the palms of my hands are so damp they are slipping from the grasps of my circle mates and I think I might faint.

"Are you all right?" whispers the tall, thin woman in the gauzy, gaudy skirt on my left. She is peering down at me with some measure of concern.

"I don't feel well," I admit somewhat shakily. "I think I have to lie down."

"Do you have a blanket?" the woman asks kindly.

I shake my head, ashamed to have come so ill-prepared. Almost everyone has brought blankets to spread on the ground.

"The red and green one by the side of the cook tent is mine. Use it."

I thank her and slip out of the circle. My stomach feels queasy and for a moment I think I really am going to be sick. But the moment passes and I stretch out on the blanket and try to relax. I want to get away from the woman's voice on the platform, but the electrical hook-up is perfect and there is no way to escape her voice as she begins to lead her people on the journey back up through the bowels of the earth. I cannot extricate myself from the journey as I, too, am one of her people. I must throw in my lot with the others as we leave the molten inner core of hell, back up through the miles of substratum through the burning, oil-soaked sands up, up through the mineral-encrusted outer earth. And then we are at one with the long, entangled roots of the enormous trees of the rainforest, and we are bouncing off the animal burrows and passing through the sweet, worm-infested topsoil until we arrive safely back on the surface of the earth. I can once again smell the rainforest and the sea all mixed up with the cooking salmon and bannock, and feel the breeze tangy with iodine and salt. My heart beat starts to slow and just as I am feeling happy and relaxed again the damnable priestess on the platform prepares us for another journey. She is going to lead the magic circle away from the earth altogether now and shoot off up into the sky.

"You are leaving the earth," she intones hypnotically over the microphone. Fighting back a surge of panic, I press my face into the red blanket. It's no use. Her voice is too strong for me. "You are gliding through the air, greeting the birds as you pass them on your journey to the clouds, we are headed for the stars ..."

Almost swooning, I press my face deeper into the blanket. I am more terrified of outer space because of my fear of heights than I am of boiling, blistering inner spaces. In desperation I plug my ears with my fingers, trying frantically to drown out the mad woman's voice. This works. I can still hear the drone of her voice but not the actual words she is saying. With my eyes closed and my fingers firmly planted in my ears I find, much to my relief, that this woman's voice no longer has the power to tamper with my nervous system. After a time I am aware that a large body has moved into my territory. I open my eyes and look into the bemused face of my son. He is kneeling beside me.

"What are you doing?" he asks curiously.

"Just resting."

"You didn't like the circle."

I get up and brush off my circle mate's blanket. "I didn't say that," I answer defensively. "In fact, I was rather enjoying it."

He evidently decides not to pursue the matter in the face of more important things. "We'd better get in line for grub. They've finally started serving."

Half an hour later Mike and Hope and I are sitting on the grass eating from sinfully heaped plates. The fish and cole slaw and bannock are tongue-swallowing, foot-stomping delicious. Later there is music and speeches, all with environmental themes, primarily the preservation of the forests. As afternoon turns into evening, an intensity of purpose begins to build among the crowd, manifesting itself in the speeches and music, an intensity fed on the desire to save the natural world from technological destruction, now, while there yet may be time.

The passion here reminds me of revival meetings back in Louisiana. In fact the whole scene seems familiar ... the words — and certainly the accents — a little different, but the motivation, the longing for salvation, the yearning for meaning and substance, the desire to get down to the inner core of what the hell it is that life is all about. That holy spirit that searches for love and cooperation and oneness with the universe is alive and well and walking among us. I hear it in the voices and music and taste it in the food.

Food, after all, is one of the main vehicles for getting in touch with salvation. My Louisiana country people knew that when they dragged out the long rough tables for a singing on the grounds after Sunday morning services, and smoothed out the snowy white tablecloths and piled the platters high with fried chicken and cold meats and salads and egg custard and sweet potato pies. Oh my God, yes. You can't get saved on an empty stomach. And then after clean-up we'd all sit under the shade trees and sing. Everybody sang. And picked a little. Whoever had a guitar or banjo or fiddle brought it out. Hardly anybody could even read music but nobody was shy. Most people didn't even bother going home after the singing was over, because it would be almost time for evening services to start and people were just good and warmed up. But finally, the evening services over, sung and saved out, the singers would go gladly to their homes, warmed and mellowed by the good fellowship. And here on Vargas Island the evening is also waning to a mellow, good fellowship close. The finale is to be the sweat lodges.

It is announced that there will be a mixed sweat, males and females together, except for women on their moon. Women on their moon are asked to wait until the following day when there will be an additional sweat for women only. I know nothing of sweats and sweat lodges, so I turn to Hope for enlightenment.

"What do people wear in the sweat lodges?" I ask, curious.

Hope shrugs. Nothing usually."

I am profoundly shocked. "My heavens."

"You're missing the spirit of the thing," Hope answers grinning.

"So?"

"It's a cleansing ritual."

"So?"

"So people do it naked, that's all."

"Very enlightening. Are you going?"

"No, we have to leave pretty soon. As it is, we'll do well to get to the other side of the island before dark."

Indeed, the big boats that have been hired to take people who aren't spending the night on the island back to Tofino are already waiting offshore. Mike heads back to the village, and Hope and I board a small craft that takes us to the large fishboat that will ferry us around the island. I have never been on a large fishboat before and the ride is pure delight. The moon is up and throws a fluorescent phenomenon into the sea, an incredible light show, green and yellow beams that strike the sides of the boat and follow in its wake. I am mesmerized. The ride is not nearly long enough. Too soon we are let off at the small dock of Hope's relatives , and the magical fishboat slides back across the sea. Hope and I head up the trail toward the house.

Half way there, Hope discovers that we have a problem. We have lost the flashlight somewhere. While the moon is bright enough that we have no problem with the trail that leads to Hope's cousins house, I am sure we must have a flashlight before plunging into the half-mile of deep woods and dense undergrowth that leads to our little guest cabin.

"We're going to stop by your cousin's house and ask him for the loan of a flashlight, aren't we?" I ask.

"He isn't my cousin. Only by marriage. And Janice isn't home."

"Does that matter in terms of borrowing a flashlight?" I ask.

"Yes. I don't get on with Jerry. And Janice told me not to bother him because he is getting up very early to go fishing in the morning. His lights are already out. The cabin's not far and I know the trail. And I've got matches in my pocket. Come on, we'll be there in a jiffy."

"But it's dark in the trees," I protest. Hope is already moving away from the house toward the woods. One of the things I like about her is that she is so independent, but now she is carrying things a little far.

"Hope, one of us could break a leg," I yell at her as I reluctantly follow her retreating figure. She pauses and waits for me to catch up. "I don't like this," I continue. "I'm too old for this sort of thing, blundering around in the dark ... "

Hope laughs. She is not sadistic, just genuinely amused.

"Then why don't you live in the village and knit socks for your grandchildren and weave and stuff? That's what my mother does."

"Do we have to go into that sort of thing right now?"

"No. Just hang on to my shirttail here."

She stuffs the end of her long plaid shirt into my hands and resumes her march into the woods. I am subdued. She seems so sure of herself. We are moving slowly but we are definitely on the trail. I put my feet down carefully, trying to avoid holes and roots. But as the overhanging canopy of tree branches close in above us, blocking out the moonlight, the ancient, primordial terrors of the wild dark skitter along my backbone.

"Are there cougars on this island?" I ask, striving for a neutral and panic free tone of voice as I try to remember exactly who it was who told me there weren't any and if they were indeed reliable.

"I don't know. A few, maybe." Her own voice is preoccupied. I stop abruptly, reining her up short by her shirttail.

"What are you doing?" she demands irritably.

"Hope, I do not like this. Let's go back and wake up your cousin and ask for a flashlight. For Christ's sake, are you afraid of him?"

There is a long pause. I have struck a nerve, I think.

"Afraid of him? Not exactly," she answers finally. "But he's kind of a perfectionist. And if I have to wake him up because I lost the flashlight somewhere, I'll appear so bloody incompetent, don't you see?"

I did and didn't. Nobody likes to appear incompetent especially someone as proud as Hope who has left most of her relatives behind on the east coast years ago to paddle her own canoe with no one to criticize the paddling except these cousins who communicated in detail to the others back east, but this extreme of pride is truly curious.

"And I've been fishing with him," she adds, as if this explains everything. She turns and mushes forward. I follow blindly, clutching at the lifeline shirttail. I'm wearing rubber boots which were fine in the low-lying mushy spots, but we are travelling uphill now and the boots are clumsy, trying to catch every stump and root.

And the cougars are here. I know they're here. If there weren't any before, I'm sure there are now. Cougars follow me around.

They are primarily night prowlers and we have nothing to fend them off with. Hope is short, too, like me, and very slender, why, we both could be taken for children by an exceptionally hungry, not too bright cougar. Just then a large bird of some sort brushes by the back of my head. I scream, simultaneously trying to ward off a heart attack. At least this gets Hope's attention. She quickly lights a match.

"What is it?" she asks anxiously. Her face is a ghostly apparition in the sudden glare of match light.

"I don't know. Something big with wings. Maybe an owl ..."

"I doubt it. You probably just brushed a tree branch."

I am not convinced. Hope lights another match and searches to the right and left of the trail. She seems concerned, not about whatever it was that had startled me but about the nature of the trail itself, a concern she tries not to show, at least for the moment. She lights more matches. There is a divided fork in the trail. After some hesitation, Hope veers to the right. I follow, filled with dread.

"Hope, are you sure this is the way?" I inquire, longing for reassurance.

"Positive. Just pay attention to where you're stepping. We're doing fine."

We are not doing fine. I know, deep in my bones, that I personally will not live to see the morning. In total desperation, I consider deserting. I glance searchingly over my shoulder, striving for a glimpse, even a sliver, of moonlight. If I see one moonbeam of light, I think, I will make a mad dash for freedom and abandon Hope entirely to her nocturnal madness. But the fates are against me. There isn't the faintest glimmer of moonlight, all is blackness. The only link to any possible salvation now is the red plaid tail of Hope's shirt that I am clutching so tightly. Suddenly Hope stops, half turning. What now? I wait, heart in mouth. She lights another match.

"Shit, I don't know where we are," she admits angrily. "The trail should be going off this way by now." She moves several paces to the right. I inch forward, still clinging to her shirt. She moves as though to search for another match and then, inexplicably, she isn't there at all, she is pitching forward and downward into the darkness. My reflexes fail me. I can't untangle my fists from the back of her shirt fast enough and I, too, with a terrified cry, am pulled down into a pitch-black void.

It is the end, I am sure. Groping frantically for something to break my fall, I am clawing empty air. We are descending into a dark bottomless abyss. It is a wilderness revenge pit of some sort left by the Indians of long ago, or perhaps created by the forest spirits themselves, constructed to bring death to the white man, raper and plunderer of all that's good and holy, destroyer of light and reason.

But all may not be lost. The bottomless pit evidently has a bottom after all. A rather shallow bottom as a matter-of-fact. I am all tangled up with dry leaves and branches and bits of stuff that feel like earth and rock and Hope's hiking boots. I untangle myself and stand up. Apparently no bones are broken.

"Are you all right?" I ask the stubborn, hard-headed girl struggling to her feet. At least I hope it is Hope, and not some other unsuspecting victim before us.

"Yes. You okay?"

"Yes, no thanks to you. Where are we?"

I can see her now, vaguely. To our back is the forest, but ahead there is a large clearing and the moon light is again spilling across my vision.

"Shit!" Hope says, her tone one of sheer disgust. "We've been going around in a stupid circle. That's my cousin's house. We're back where we started."

Before I can answer a light suddenly blazes forth from the upstairs window. We are treated to the spectacle of a naked man throwing on his trousers and then rushing over and throwing up the window.

"Who the hell is that out there?" he yells. His voice is distinctly authoritarian. I can tell the man is used to being obeyed.

"It's me, Hope. I'm with my friend, Betty."

"Leave me out of this," I mutter.

"We were just on our way to the cabin," Hope continues, ignoring me.

"Don't you have a flashlight?" he asks, as any sensible person would.

"We forgot it at the meet."

"You were trying to get to the cabin without a flashlight?" His voice is incredulous. "Why didn't you knock on my door?"

"I didn't want to disturb you."

"Come to the house," Cousin Jerry orders, and bangs the window shut.

"Shit," Hope mutters.

"Watch your language," I say happily. Our journey back to the house is effortless, as Jerry has turned on all the outside lights. Once inside the pretty little cottage Cousin Jerry seems not bad at all, a big, bluff middle-aged man making an effort to be pleasant. Soon the three of us are sitting down at the breakfast nook with steaming cups of fragrant tea. Even Hope seems to be relaxing somewhat. Jerry asks about the wilderness meet and then expresses some concern over Indian land claims.

"Nothing specific like that was discussed," Hope answers stiffly.

"You mean no rousing speeches about running the white people off Vargas?"

"No, nothing like that."

Hope's voice is tense and I am wondering about Jerry's concern for his property.

"So, you must own your own land here," I offer by way of conversation.

"Yes, we do."

"My son and I own a few acres at Cypress Bay. How much acreage do you have here? Five? Ten?"

"Over a hundred."

"Really?" I say, surprised. "That's a good chunk of the island."

"It's a relatively big island."

"Yes. Well." I am suddenly uncomfortable with the idea that the native peoples may be claiming the very land that we are resting on at the moment. Jerry senses my discomfort. He moves in.

"So how would you like it if the Indians claimed the land on Cypress Bay that you think is yours?" he asks, his voice and smile both thin and brittle.

"I would probably be disturbed," I am forced to admit.

"See?" he asks nobody in particular and then drains his mug with an air of triumph.

I did see. And yet wasn't sure. Would the native peoples ever try to claim my little piece of the Clayoquot Sound? And if they did, what would my attitude be? The man has certainly given me something to think about. Hope and I decline his offer for another round of tea, and after more apologies for waking him we are given a flashlight and allowed to take a reasonably pleasant, even dignified leave.

This time there is no problem in finding the cabin. As it has been some hours since the salmon feast, we haul out the cheese and crackers and pickles and pineapple juice. After, I am too exhausted for much of a night toilette. I can't find my toothbrush or cleansing cream so after throwing a bit of water in the general direction of my face, I roll into the bottom bunk. Hope climbs up to the top bunk and turns off the flashlight. The darkness seems wonderful, warm and friendly, full of the soothing sounds of the surf. I pop off immediately. Only to be immediately awakened again.

There is something alien in the room. Something that has not been invited and is enthusiastically munching on the leftover cheese and crackers. I sit up and peer into the darkness. I can't see anything. Softly, I call Hope's name. She doesn't stir. The munching sound grows more aggressive.

"Hope!" I yell. She jumps up, cracking her head on the low ceiling.

"What ... what ... "

"Something's eating the cheese and crackers," I explain.

"So?"

"It could be a rat. A big rat."

"No, Betty, it's okay."

Her voice is fuzzing off with sleep.

"No, it's not okay," I insist loudly, mentally cursing the young's indifference to just about anything that threatens to interrupt their sleep when they have their minds set on sleeping. She moans and it sounds like she's turning over.

"Listen, Betty, please be reasonable. Whatever it is will just eat the cheese and crackers and then go away. Go back to sleep. Or, if you insist on playing policeman, then you get up and see what it is."

I digest this for a moment. I'm so tired I can't think straight, but I am fully cognizant of one thing ... I will not get up and confront some enormous rat from the twilight zone.

"Hope, this is ridiculous," I say evenly, striving for a sweet, reasonable tone. "I appeal to your sense of fair play in this matter. First, I am a guest in your house."

"This isn't my house. It's a crummy cabin that just happens to belong to my cousins. You are I are both guests here equally."

"There is blood between you and your cousins," I point out patiently. "Besides, you invited me."

"Well, I didn't realize you were so afraid of small animals."

The crunching from the direction of the table grows louder.

"Small animals, no," I answer, noting the chills racing up and down my spine at the voracity of the chewing. "This is no small animal. Can't you hear him, for Christ's sake?"

"Probably a mouse. Please let me sleep. Just make a shooing noise and it'll go away."

The girl is clearly mad. The monster supping at our table couldn't possibly hear a shooing noise over the racket it is making with the crackers. I search for my get tough-voice, the one I use with all obstinate children.

"Hope, I am your senior by many years. I deserve some respect. I am older than your mother."

"My mother would not be at a wilderness meeting, and she definitely would not be sleeping in this cabin."

"Be that as it may, you must get up and chase out that monster. I insist."

"All right, all right."

Her voice is filled with disgust, but she is getting up. As she turns the flashlight beam on to the table I see that I am right, it is quite a large animal, a martin, I think, or maybe a mink. It runs across the table, leaps to the floor and then scurries beneath some loosened boards near the wall and is gone. Hope picks up the last of the scraps of the cheese and crackers, yanks the door open and throws the scraps after the fleeing animal.

"And take this with you, you inconsiderate creep," she shouts into the night. "Can't you let people sleep? Do you even have a home, you silly little bastard?"

I wanted the animal out, but I am quite taken aback by the vehemence of the eviction. Hope climbs back into her bunk and turns off the flashlight. I fall asleep again immediately, but the next morning I tease Hope about yelling at the animal as it fled for its life.

"You were so fierce," I recall.

"I can get that way when I am awakened unexpectedly in the night."

"That's not exactly good news for your future husband."

"It depends on what I'm wakened unexpectedly for," she answers, leering, obviously in a recovered mood, having slept the sleep that knitted up the ravelled sleeve of care.

It is a beautiful morning. The sun is bright, the sky cloudless, the salt air so fresh it could be the first morning of creation. And we get an early start on the trail. The same trail that seemed so otherworldly and dangerous the day before has become familiar. I slither over downed trees like a snake and trod lightly through the low-lying water holes with the grace of a gazelle. However, on the latter part of the trail, as we are nearing the beach, we run into a new phenomenon. We are meeting small groups of young people who are out exploring on their own. They are friendly and smile and speak as we pass on the trail, but the men and women alike have abandoned their tops.

"The mixed sweats must have broken down some barriers," Hope remarks dryly.

"I don't like it," I say. "I don't think the native women in these parts ever went barebreasted, even when they all lived wild. Did they?"

"You might ask them," Hope answers. "You haven't asked them anything else."

"I have my reasons," I answer defensively.

When we actually reach the beach, I see that things are worse than I had first imagined. Some people, not content with exposing breasts, were now also exposing bums. Young men are playing kick ball in the buff on the beach, and the even more foolhardy ones are frolicking barenaked in the surf. It is not a pretty sight. Several couples pass in their birthday suits, oblivious to my shocked appraisal. Mike finds us, inquires of our night's comfort in the cabin. The native people who are standing around are mostly talking quietly to each other, their own clothes firmly in place on their bodies, while they ignore, or pretend to, the white people's nudity. Which takes a bit of doing as three musicians, two naked woman and a man, stroll right in front of them as they play guitars and sing a lament of lost Indian lands.

Mike turns to me with a wide grin. "Well, Ma, what do you think?"

"I think native people must think white people are nuts. First, the white people come over here to this continent, kill off most of the native people, steal their land, and tell them their religion is no damned good, and they have to trade it in for the white man's religion. Then, generations later, when the white people have stolen and destroyed everything they could that belonged to the native people, including life itself, they come back to the ones that are left and say, wait a minute, brothers and sisters, you were right in the first place, your mind set is better than ours after all, your religion is better, let us apologize, and while we're doing it, we'll feel better if we take off our clothes, you don't mind, do you?

What else could the natives possibly think except that white people are silly and dangerous."

"Well, I can't speak for the native women, but maybe the native men like looking at naked female flesh as much as any white man," Mike answers, refusing to turn a serious face on the thing. "Lighten up, Ma. Go with the flow."

"What does that mean?" I ask suspiciously. "Does that mean you're going to take off your clothes?"

"No. And you'd better not take yours off, either. Hope, you can take yours off if you want to."

Hope takes a mock swing at him, but she isn't fast enough. Mike ducks underneath her fist, laughing, and then runs away. "See you two later," he calls over his shoulder. "There are some people I must see."

"Male chauvinist pig!" we yell after him. But we are not really angry, we have our own agendas.

By late afternoon a chilling fog has rolled in, piercing naked flesh and the nudies don pants and sweaters and jackets, and we all sit around on blankets that are moistened and sweetened by early dew. There is music, several speeches, and then Mike is called upon to read his poem. He is nervous, but his poem is an instant hit. He departs the stage, flushed and triumphant midst enthusiastic applause and whistles.

And in spite of the several shocks to my old-fashioned sense of decorum, when Mike returns me to Cypress Bay the following morning, I am still basking in the glow of good fellowship.

But I am happy, nevertheless, to be back in my own little part of the Clayoquot Sound. How wonderful the home-made A-frame seems to me, how dear the trees and rocks and gently curving sweep of the cove that is busy with the duck families feeding their young, my funny slug-infested garden boxes, the chipmunk in the old cedar tree right off the front deck, and the rising early morning mist that nourishes the rainforest and all of its creatures. I have become anchored here, I feel a connection to the land that I have not felt since I was a tow-headed kid in Louisiana. It's a joy, the sweet, simmering joy of a child held safely on the mother's breast, the joy of lying in a lover's arms.

Clayoquot Sound, you have become my mother and my lover,

more faithful than the latter and more beautiful than either. Ah, had I but discovered you years ago when I was young, we could have grown old together. But I don't like what they have done to you with this clear-cutting business and now I know from what I have learned at the meet — in spite of the distractions of nakedness — that there was no plan for the logging except greed, and that the land itself and the streams and the animals were never considered seriously.

I have to think about this. Action must be taken, but I'm not sure what. I have been through actions before, it isn't than I'm afraid. But I have learned enough from action to approach it cautiously, sideways even, like a crab. The Vietnam War taught me that. But in the beginning, when we first arrived in Virginia for John's new job at NASA, we were stepping on a definite, important rung in the ladder of American upward mobility.

SIX

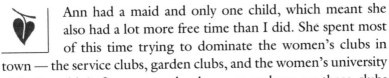 Ann had a maid and only one child, which meant she also had a lot more free time than I did. She spent most of this time trying to dominate the women's clubs in town — the service clubs, garden clubs, and the women's university club. I couldn't figure out why Ann was so keen on these clubs because she considered most of the club women stuffy and provincial. Ann was definitely neither stuffy nor provincial. She was beautiful and smart and well-read. She spoiled Tommy, her little four-year-old, something pitiful, but I put this down to his being the only child. Ann was in the habit of dropping over almost every day for a coffee and a quick chat. One afternoon she came over while I was at the typewriter. I stopped work and put on the coffee pot.

"I hate this town," she said as I pushed back the typewriter on the dining table to serve the coffee. "Yes. I'd like to move to Hampton but R.L. won't hear of it."

"Why not?" I asked. She shook her bright, blonde hair.

"Who the hell knows? Oh, he says it's because the country and the sea air is good for us all, especially Tommy, but I think it's because he just hates change. Does John make all the important decisions in your family?"

"Well, sort of," I admitted. "We came out here because this is where he got a job. I suppose if I made a fuss he would agree to move into the city, but I hate cities. But as the men are the ones who make the money and have to deal with getting a job done that pays the bills, shouldn't they have a little more leeway in deciding where the family lives?"

Ann lit a cigarette and inhaled deeply.

"I knew you were going to say that. You're a smart woman but sometimes you sound like you don't have a lick of sense."

"Well, I haven't been to university like you."

"University has nothing to do with it. I don't think. I'm not sure. Maybe it does. I've just finished reading this book by a woman named Betty Friedan. It's called *The Feminine Mystique*. Have you heard of it?"

"No, what does it say?" I ask, listening for the baby's first little mewing sounds of awakening from her afternoon nap to turn into something more demanding. I found *The Feminine Mystique* a curious title. I was most involved with titles these days, confession titles, something catchy and outlandish, even shocking.

"It's about women married to men who have interesting and demanding jobs, men who like their jobs, and women who are lost in the kitchen and nursery as unpaid labourers. It's about women needing paying jobs, too, to fill out their lives. And more education. But I can't even get R.L. to agree that I should go back and finish my university. He thinks Tommy should come first with me. And he does ... but a child just isn't enough for me and I refuse to go into mass production the way you have. You know what R.L. really thinks? He thinks I should stay busy with church like his mother did. While he, himself, of course, wouldn't be caught dead in a church. But he thinks that's different, because he's a scientist."

"Well, it's certainly true that if you're not a churchgoer, you'll find yourself being a non-churchgoer all by yourself in this town. Or almost. In fact, you're the only other one I know. But I accept the fact that the women here will not be particularly interested in me because of my ... uh, unbelief."

"But it's different for you, Betty. You have so many kids you can barely draw a free breath and when you do, you head for the typewriter. What do you write about, anyway?"

"Oh ... stuff I know. Working-class women's lives. Unfaithful husbands, problems with kids at school, not enough money, in-laws troubles, young girls trying to catch husbands ..."

"They're not such marvellous prizes, you know," Ann broke in, as she jabbed out her cigarette in a saucer. "And that's the trouble. All of us women are taught to think men are such damned bloody prizes. If women spent some of that energy developing their own lives and skills they wouldn't have to spend so much time pussy-footing around men."

I am caught off guard by Ann's flash of bitter anger. But then she smiles.

"Sorry. I guess I natter at you too much, but it's because I feel safe with you. You don't even know most of the women I complain about in this town, and your John is an awful lot like R.L. Do you write under your own name?"

"Oh, no. These stories are all anonymous. They're supposed to be true, you know. Confessions, get it? Professional writers write the majority. That's what I'm trying to be, but I've only sold one story in over two years."

Her dark-ringed violet eyes widened in disbelief as she looked over at the stack of papers by my typewriter.

"Good God! You mean you do all this work for nothing?"

"At the moment, anyway. I'm just learning."

"May I read one of your stories?"

"Of course," I answer quickly. I was always eager to have other people read my stories and offer advice. Besides my own family. The boys offered peculiar plotting suggestions as they were science fiction buffs, and John was simply bewildered by the entire concept of confession writing. I got up and found the envelope that held yesterday's rejection.

"This just came back in the mail yesterday," I said as I handed her the large manila envelope.

"You mean this one has been rejected?"

"Yes."

"Well, I don't want to read something that has been rejected. Let me read the one you sold."

"I don't need any criticism on that one. Read this one first and tell me what you think and then I'll give you a copy of the other one."

She left with script in hand. I put Ann's visit out of my mind as the little ones were waking from naps and it was time for the boys to arrive from school. The next couple of hours were frantic as usual ... flutter, flutter, busy, busy, dinner on the stove, John's arrival, the boys bustling about almost busy as I was, helping to get the dinner from stove to table and the little ones entertained and out of the way of falling pots and splashing liquids. After dinner the little ones played on the back porch, while John and I talked to the boys about school and things in general. Afterwards, John headed to our bedroom for a two-hour nap. He got into the habit of napping in the evenings when he was going to school, and he was usually studying some kind of new material whether he was taking courses or not. He would wake up to help me put the little girls to bed by eight. I would follow to bed by nine o'clock, leaving John and the boys up shuffling papers.

We only watched TV on weekends. It was an ironclad rule. I was always too tired to watch TV anyway. I got up at four in the morning so I could have two extra hours a day to write before the baby woke at six. I think John was happy enough that I had something besides the kids. To him my stories seemed innocuous, I'm sure, but they weren't written for men, especially men like John. And I didn't really understand my own determination to crack the code of the confessions. All I knew was that I was learning something valuable to me, I was learning how to create a plot and bring it to a conclusion and this was so exhilarating to me I couldn't stop. When Ann brought the manuscript to me the following afternoon I was ready for her criticism. To my surprise she didn't have any.

"I think the story is just great the way it is," she said firmly when I pressed her for any changes I might make. "I don't understand why the editor didn't like this. You know what? I cried at the ending. I really did. Even knowing you picked the entire thing out of thin air it seemed so real I cried. It's good, I tell you. Why don't you send it off to some other magazine?"

After Ann left I got out the little note from the editor that had been attached to the form rejection slip sent back with the script. The editor had offered no criticism of the story itself except for the length. It was too long for their magazine, she said, perhaps I should try one of the magazines that used novelettes. On second reading, the note was encouraging. But I didn't allow myself to get too excited. Confession editors were softies, they didn't like to tell you that your plots were dumb as oyster and your writing ridiculous. But I sent the story out again, anyway, to one of the magazines that printed longer stories. But I didn't worry the thing because I was well into a new plot and I'd learned to send them out and then forget them. But I did notice that Ann began to make herself scarce around my house and that she was hardly ever home during the day.

Her little red sports car would leave relatively early during the day and ease back into the garage shortly before R.L came home. And Tommy, her four-year-old, was over at our house more often than not. Tommy was a big, sweet, husky, little boy, and he could reduce both Susan and Margaret Elizabeth to tears in three seconds flat. Tommy wasn't mean, just undisciplined. I couldn't understand either Ann's or R.L.'s method of parenting. They gave their kid everything but firmness. Out of necessity, I began to take up some of this slack. One morning after I hadn't seen Ann for at least a week Tommy came over to play with Susan and Margaret Elizabeth. A scuffle broke out immediately upon arrival, and I sent Tommy home with instructions not to return for the rest of the day. Later that afternoon, while the girls were napping I sat out on the back porch for a breath of fresh air. I was thinking about the story I was working on when I looked up and saw Tommy easing around the corner of the house like a hound dog puppy.

"Tommy, you go right back home," I ordered. "I told you that you can't play with the girls anymore today because you hit them, and you must learn to stop hitting. You can come back tomorrow and we'll try it again, but you have to go home now. Do you understand?"

His little face fell and he half turned as if to obey, and then suddenly he whirled about and came running around the corner of the house and flung himself, sobbing, into my arms. "I just came over to bring you a stick of gum because you're my best friend," he hiccuped as my arms closed around him. And then I saw the crumpled stick of gum in his hand. My heart melted. You poor baby, I thought, hugging him close. And smart, too. Best friend, huh? After a moment he recovered. We halved the gum and sat together and chewed happily in the cool afternoon shade.

"You know what I'm going to do, Tommy? I'm going to talk to your mama about sending you to playschool. I know your mama can afford to send you. She's rich, isn't she?"

"Yes'm. My daddy's rich, too."

"Well, would you like to go? There'll be lots of kids to play with, big boys like yourself."

"Yes'm. Can we wake your girls up now so we can play?"

We didn't wake the girls up, but I did call Ann that evening and she came over the following morning. We had coffee as of old and I explained in my superior maternal wisdom that Tommy needed the challenges of organized activities in a controlled setting to soak up his physical energies. Ann listened and pronounced the idea of playschool for Tommy a good one, but her mind seemed to be somewhere else. She didn't look well. There were dark smudges underneath her beautiful eyes and she was chainsmoking. Several days later when she came over to collect Tommy I asked her point-blank if anything was wrong. The kids were playing without mayhem for once, so she followed me into the kitchen where I was feeding the baby. We sat at the table and I poured what was left of the morning's coffee.

"So tell me what's wrong," I said.

"How do you know something is wrong?"

"I don't. Just a guess."

"I'm having an affair."

"Oh, Ann. No ..."

"Had you rather I had cancer?"

"Don't be silly."

"Why are you so shocked? You're on your third marriage yourself, aren't you?"

"So?"

"Can't women do the same things that men do?"

She is white-faced and defensive.

"Yes, they can," I answered. "If they want to be divorced. Do you want to be divorced?"

She slumped forward suddenly and leaned her head on the table. "Oh, Betty ... I don't know."

"Don't you love R.L.?"

She raised her head and looked at me out of dark smudged eyes. "I don't know that, either. I married R.L. because he seemed so strong, so safe. I felt sure he wouldn't die and leave me like my mother did nor turn off life altogether like my father did. I knew that R.L. was as solid as a rock. What I didn't realize was that he was also as inflexible as a rock. He's a young man on the outside, but inside he's old, and I don't mean old and wise, I just mean old and inflexible. It's like he's not capable of change, or even of hearing me. I try to tell him how unhappy I am, that I want more of his time, that Tommy needs more of his time, that we ought to do things together, as a family ... "

"Well, what does R.L. say for himself?" I asked, heartsick for my friend. Whatever she had done or was doing, she was obviously in torment.

Ann shrugged. "Not much. That he works hard all day and then he has to read these journals, and he's doing all this because he loves us and wants to provide well for us. Which is a lie."

"What makes you think it's a lie?"

"Because he loves his work. He would do it if he didn't get a cent for it, if he could manage such a thing. Just like you write volumes of stuff that nobody buys, but you don't give a damn, you write it anyway."

"But what will you do if R.L. finds out?"

"Just hope that he doesn't shoot me. Or my lover. Aren't you even curious who my lover is?"

"No. Don't tell me. That way if anybody asks I know nothing."

"What if I said it was your husband John?"

That strikes me as funny. John is even more of a slave to his work than R.L., if that was possible, and I could account for John's every waking and sleeping hour. I sniggered and Ann gave me a grim smile.

"See? You laugh because you know that isn't possible, because you know that John is as work-obsessed as R.L. and isn't any more interested in doing fun things with the family than he is. They're two of a kind, you know."

"Now, wait a minute. Just because you're mad with your ol' man, don't try to make me dissatisfied with mine. He's the first one I've had that was worth a tinker's damn."

"See what I mean? You don't even care that John is a workaholic. That's because you're one yourself. If you weren't you'd know more about what I'm talking about."

"Okay, but why don't you just leave R.L. rather than humiliate him?"

"I'm not trying to humiliate him. I've fallen in love with another man. A man who makes me happy."

"And who makes you smoke yourself into a coma, and keeps you awake at night, and puts dark circles underneath your eyes, and fills you with soul-destroying guilt."

"And even that is better than soul-destroying boredom. Your problem, Betty, is that you have never been bored. Every time you even feel the threat of boredom you have another baby."

I finished scraping the baby's dish of canned peaches and poked the last bite into Rose Mary's mouth. She smacked her lips appreciatively. "Is that what you are?" I whispered into her little pink ear. "Are you an antidote for Mommy's boredom?"

She giggled and I wiped her face and set her free from her high chair.

"I don't think that's true, Ann, but I do find kids interesting."

"And that's good for you. You make your own work to be obsessed about and it's the kind of work that doesn't threaten your husband. But I'm not like you. I'm not good with kids, and I wouldn't write the kind of stuff you do even if I could write, because I don't believe in it. As a woman in this male-dominated society I am a second class citizen, and I'll be damned if I'll say that I like it that way."

"And I do that in my stories?" I inquire stiffly. She is hitting me close to home now.

"Yes."

"I thought you liked my stories."

"I did before I started thinking about them."

"Ann..."

"I'm sorry, Betty. I guess we can't be such good friends anymore. But you won't tell my secret?"

"Of course not."

Ann took Tommy home, but she left me with a whirling head. And she had definitely hurt my feelings. Was my husband truly a workaholic? Yes, of course he was. I had known it since we were first married. But was I one, too? Well, yes and no. The work of raising a family had to be done once one had the family. And it was certainly true that John and the kids and I did very little together as a family except live together. But wasn't that enough? And unlike Ann, I had already been through two crazy, abusive marriages before I met John, and in many ways my present husband still seemed something of a gentleman. He wasn't a chummy kind of father to the kids, but he was interested in their progress, and he didn't differentiate between mine, and his and mine. In fact, sometimes I wasn't even sure he knew which ones were his and mine. And if he wasn't romantic or given to certain kinds of companionable intimacies, neither did he drink, batter, or zap any of us with cruel mind games. He wasn't a petty man. He had a largeness of spirit that I liked. No, thank you, Ann, I'll keep my sobersided, bookwormish, workaholic husband and thank my lucky stars. You can throw yours away if you like, but don't tamper with mine. And the important issues that Ann tried to raise that afternoon about women's work and women's place in society got buried beneath what I considered at the time to be her ungrateful and scandalous behavior. But I missed her just the same when she didn't come over anymore.

I missed Tommy, too. He was now in playschool for half a day every day and we didn't see him near as much. I started to go over several times and try to make friends again, but I couldn't figure how to do this, as she was the one who had discarded me. Maybe I shouldn't have been so condemning. Who was I to try to tell another woman how to live her life? I was having trouble enough with my own. Still, I didn't go. Instead, I found myself spending my odd free hours with Mrs. Thompson, the elderly widow who lived directly behind us.

Mrs. Thompson was an interesting woman. She was in her eighties and was born and raised in the area. The house she lived in was her dead husband's parent's house where she had been brought as a bride. She had a son in his fifties who lived with his wife in a modern brick house on the property and they looked after Mrs. Thompson, although both of them worked during the day. Not that Mrs. Thompson would put up with much looking after. She was fiercely independent and full of wonderful stories of old times. Her old-fashioned house was also full of fascinating relics of old times, antique furniture and clocks and wooden boxes and churns. She didn't cook much for herself anymore, and while her children kept her supplied with food, she particularly liked my homemade soups. So several times a week, whenever I put on a fresh pot of bean or turnip or tomato rice soup, I'd make an extra share for Mrs. Thompson. For my pains, I'd get to sit in one of her cane-bottomed rocking chairs and listen to how her father was lost at sea during a storm off the coast, and how her mother had repaired the fishing boat and in desperation, taken to the sea herself in order to feed her family. She told me of the deprivations they all suffered through the depression years, and how their garden and their mother's fish and the shell fish along the beach sustained them all, and then she would bring out her mother's lace and her aunt's embroidery, and I would admire the fine, ancient works of her female relatives. And then suddenly, out of the blue, Mrs. Thompson got sick.

She complained of weakness and took to her bed for a good part of the day. Her son and daughter-in-law were understandably concerned. They decided to move Mrs. Thompson to a nursing home not far from the village. That way they could visit her every day and they could work content knowing that she was well looked after. Only Mrs. Thompson had other ideas.

"I'm not going," she said defiantly the day I took over a bowl of fresh corn chowder. I sat the bowl down on her old scarred oak kitchen table.

"I can understand your not wanting to go," I answered. "It will be new and strange."

"Oh, not so strange. I know half the people in there. I just don't like the place. The building stinks of all that artificial stuff, everything is plastic and artificial. Nothing is real. Everybody just sits in front of the TV set. I ain't never had a TV and I ain't going anywhere there is one. And how would I live without all my things here?"

"Miz Lily, you better come rest on your daybed," a voice called out from another room. Mrs. Thompson ignored the voice.

"And they got Clara here to take care of me until next Friday when they're going to cart me off," she went on in a trembling voice. "And I ain't going. I declare to you, missy, I ain't going."

"Mrs. Thompson, your son and daughter-in-law just want you to have the best of care," I said gently. "You might like it there in the home, you know."

"I know for a fact I ain't going to like it there. And that's why I ain't going. But I thank you for the soup. It smells real good."

Clara, a middle-aged colored woman, came into the room and helped Mrs. Thompson to the table to eat the soup and I took my departure. It depressed me to see the poor lady so upset, but there wasn't much I could do about it. Thursday, the day before Mrs. Thompson was to be moved, started out in a particularly dismal fashion.

Joey woke up with a raw throat and a fever so I insisted he skip school and stay in bed. He was willing enough. What with sick room demands of hot lemonades and things to read, and getting an enormous pot of chicken soup on the stove, and tending to the little ones, I didn't even hear R.L. knocking until Joey shouted at me that somebody was at the door. When I saw R.L. standing on our front porch, I didn't know what to think. It was ten thirty. He and John rode in the same carpool to work, and R.L. should have been at work hours ago. But R.L. wasn't even dressed for work, he was wearing a crumpled T-shirt and running pants.

"Betty, I'd like to talk to you. About Ann," he said gravely.

My heart sank. "Ann? She's all right, isn't she?" I blurted.

"I don't know. I don't know where she is. I think she's left me." Sunken eyes behind the dark horn-rimmed glasses, skin stretched tight and fearful around the mouth.

"And Tommy?"

"She took Tommy, too."

"Come in. I'll get you a coffee."

Joey was pressed into service from his sick bed to monitor the little ones while I talked to R.L. in the livingroom. Ann had evidently left the night before. She left only the briefest of notes, telling him that she and Tommy were okay, and that she would contact him later. He had begun to suspect that there might be another man involved. Did I know who that might be?

"No," I answered truthfully.

He nodded. He looked down at his big hands, turned them over on his lap and stared at the palms as if he had never seen them before, as if he suspected that some alien entity might have come down during the night and stuck these ridiculous appendages onto the ends of his arms without his knowledge or consent.

"Think about it for a minute, Betty. Maybe there is some man she has talked about a lot ... you know, that she might have expressed admiration for."

"No, R.L. I'm so sorry. But maybe this is something that will blow over, something that ... can eventually be fixed."

He gave me a searching look.

"You do know something, don't you?"

"No. Not really. Ann and I haven't seen much of each other lately. But she did say ..."

"Yes?"

"That she wished you didn't work so many hours and had more time to spend with her and Tommy ..."

"That's a smokescreen, you know. That's not the real problem. The real problem is that she's always been bored with me, bored with her friends and relatives, bored with this town, bored with her life, for God's sake. Ann wants excitement. Well, I can't manufacture excitement for her. And what kind of woman is it who is always looking for excitement?"

"Maybe she just needs an outside job," I offered. "Or to go back to university."

There was a small silence. He turned his hands over again and studied their broad backs.

"Okay. If I had known that returning to school was that important to her I might have given it more thought."

"Well, can't you tell her that? When she contacts you? Surely she'll call you in the next day or so."

"I didn't say I would agree to her going back to school, at least not right away, maybe when Tommy starts to grade school."

Man, you are mad, I thought, feeling heartsick. Your house is burning down around you and you think you can bargain with the flames.

"R.L., however you and Ann work out your problems is your own business, but if you want Ann back, when she calls, I'd tell her that she can start to university tomorrow. At least I'd do that if I were you."

His eyes held mine for a long, thoughtful moment. And then he pushed himself up from the couch with his alien, awkward hands.

"I'll tell her," he said evenly. "When she calls. Thanks, Betty."

I saw him to the door and then tried to resume my routine. It was hopeless. Joey wanted to know what was wrong with R.L. I told him briefly. And then made him promise that he would never try to keep his wife from working or going to school. He promised, bemused, too sick to actually get into an in-depth discussion about it. I felt kind of sick myself. So R.L. was a hard nose, he was still a good man and I hated to see him suffer. And I felt worried about Ann. Even if she came back to R.L., by the time the gossips got through with her, she would be ostracized in the village. A scandal had already broken. Not an hour had passed from R.L.'s visit than I heard from another neighbour across the street, the mother of one of the boys Andy played with, that Ann had run away with a village man, also married, but childless, and at that very moment they were probably in the air, circling the Los Angeles airport. Whether or not R.L. was willing for his wife to go back to school had become a non-issue. I sent my good wishes along with Ann via thought control and hoped that her new man would impose a badly needed dose of firmness with Tommy, and that R.L. would find the courage to go on and the next time, be more sensitive to his woman's needs.

In the meantime, I damn sure wasn't going to be the one to tell him where his wife and son had gone off to. I had a headache but there was lunch and naps for the little girls and soup and aspirin and an ice pack for the patient in the back bedroom. I took an aspirin myself and lay down on the couch. I dozed a bit but was awakened by the postman's footsteps on the porch. Wearily, I got up and fetched the mail. Among the everlasting and assorted bills was a long envelope from a confession magazine. I opened it with trembling fingers. My story, the one Ann had cried over, was a winner. The editor wanted to buy it for seven hundred dollars!

A wild, unrestrained elation surged through me, wiping out the morning's troubles. Two whole year's work, finally vindicated. I could write, after all. At least I could write confessions. And that's all I wanted right now. I went in and broke the news to Joey. He was delighted. The money would mean a few badly needed new clothes. Then I called John at work. He was pleased, of course, but busy. While the girls were still sleeping I decided to take Mrs. Thompson a bowl of the chicken soup. After cautioning Joey to listen carefully for the little ones in the next room, I stepped out into the yard with the container of soup. And immediately spotted the long line of thick, black smoke hugging Mrs. Thompson's roof. I dropped the soup and rushed back into the house.

"Joey, get up! Quick! Mrs. Thompson's house is on fire!"

I called the fire department while Joey struggled into his jeans. Sans shirt and shoes Joey bounded through the back yard and over Mrs. Thompson's fence like a jackrabbit. When I caught up with him a few minutes later, Mrs. Thompson's house was engulfed in flames.

"Mother, I can't get in! The house is locked all around, even the windows!"

"Then break a window!" I yelled, horrified at the heat and fury of the flames. "Over there ... that one just fronts a hallway ..."

Joey threw a large rock through the window and immediately the flames leapt through the opening and from the smoke and crackling flames inside I knew Mrs. Thompson was a goner if she was in there. And then I saw what Joey was doing. He was busting through the back door with an axe from the woodpile. When I saw his intention my heart froze.

"Joey, no! Don't go in there! It's no use! She's dead ... please don't!"

But he didn't hear. Or refused to obey. Joey disappeared into the smoke and flames. I fainted. I think for the first and last time in my whole life. I swooned to the ground. But the faint didn't last long. I came to just in time to see Joey stumble out the back door, coughing explosively, hair and clothes smoking. I recovered from my faint and went to him. He was no longer smoking, but his face and arms were burned and his hair all singed off on one side. Suddenly the fire engines were there and people were congregating in the yard and Mrs. Thompson's body was being taken out on a stretcher. I knew she had done it deliberately. Maybe I don't even blame you, Mrs. Thompson, I said to her via my thoughts, if that's what you wanted, but you could have taken my son with you, damn your hide, you scared the living hell out of me. And remembering the little ones, I raced home.

They were still sleeping. Joey came home shortly after, his burns and cuts having been taken care of by the ambulance crew. Nothing terribly serious, but one could tell he had been in a fight of some sort. In fact, he looked terrible. Just as I got him back to bed, the little ones awakened, and it was while I was changing the baby that I heard the ambulance on our street. I ran to the window just as it was disappearing around the corner. And there were several cars around R.L. and Ann's house. I thought at the time that the ambulance contained Mrs. Thompson's body and the driver, for some reason, had cut down our street at the corner. Later that afternoon I learned via the same gossipy neighbour across the street that the ambulance had contained the self-poisoned and near-death figure of R.L.

By the time John got home I was a wreck. He was shocked at how close Joey had come to serious injury, shocked at his friend's attempted suicide, shocked that an old lady, rather than leave behind her precious house and memorabilia would lock all her doors and windows and burn it down with her in it. But most of all, I think, John was shocked that Ann had betrayed R.L.

"Well, she certainly acted like a tramp," John said in the privacy of our bedroom that night.

"Ann is not a tramp," I protested.

"I didn't say she was. I don't know her that well. But she's acting like one."

"You don't understand," I said wearily. "Ann tried to tell R.L. how dissatisfied she was. He wouldn't listen to her."

"Well, what was she so dissatisfied about? The man loved her and the boy and worked hard to give them everything ..."

"Ann didn't want so many things. She wanted R.L. to spend more time with them, take them places."

"Oh, hell. Maybe what she didn't understand was the enormous demands of her husband's work."

"I think she did. We both know how hard you all work. But women work, too, you know."

"You do. Ann didn't."

"She didn't work because R.L. wouldn't let her. He just wanted her to do women things she didn't like to do, and look pretty while she was doing them."

"Why didn't she like doing women things? She's a woman, isn't she?"

"Do men all like doing the same things? I don't see you running out to football games or hunting quail."

"Well ... those things are stupid."

"So are plenty of women things."

"Well, I'm just glad poor old R.L. pulled through. Good God! The man could have died. He's going to be damned embarrassed when he comes back to work, though."

"Embarrassed? That's what you're worried about is that he will be embarrassed? Because his pain came out and he was emotional for once?"

"Stop dramatizing everything so much. Everything that happens isn't a plot for a confession story. I don't want to fight. I'm just glad this hellish day is getting over. I'm tired and I've got ..."

"Lots of work to do," I finished for him.

I didn't want to fight, either. Neither John nor I could afford to allow ourselves to become alienated from each other. It took the most dedicated cooperation for us to survive socially and economically. But the issue of men's work versus women's work stuck in my craw in the days that followed. If men's work was the actual work of the world then women's work, like mine, must be play pretend. It certainly didn't feel like play pretend. Especially by the end of the week, when the girls, including the baby, started coming down with something very, very rotten.

It wasn't the same ailment that had struck Joey. That was a twenty-four hour bug that had allowed him to return to school the very next day in spite of his blistered face and arms from the fire, a hero of sorts. The little ones had high fevers, sore throats, and inexplicably, swollen gums. The baby, Rose Mary, wound up in the hospital attached to intravenous tubes and bottles. She was there for a week. John had to take time off work to tend to the family, while I stayed at the hospital. But at last the scourge was over, the girls were all pink cheeked and healthy again, everybody was back on schedule and R.L. had put his house up for sale.

The house sold immediately. R.L. also transferred to some other unit at work and John didn't see him anymore. I never heard from Ann again, either. I felt more confident of my writing now but when I sold another story several months later I didn't allow myself to get too happy. I no longer believed in God but I believed in the gods and I didn't want to call their attention to me in any way. The gods were too capricious, they gave with one hand and took away with the other. Go away, gods. I'm just a poor woman with a big family trying to survive. But the gods had me on a stringer and I would hear more from them in the future. But I must leave that time and come back to the present because our A-frame and ten acres in the Clayoquot Sound is now free and clear and this calls for a mortgage-burning party. Mike and I have invited all of our friends and neighbours to share in our good fortune.

These people are an individualistic bunch. They would have to be or they couldn't live as they do — on small islands or other isolated spots along the waters of Clayoquot Sound, where the usual kind of steady work is mostly out of the question. This type of life demands a lot of self-reliance and a willingness to embrace aloneness. It is early September, the weather is mellow and bright, and our guests begin to arrive in the morning.

Some have been in the Clayoquot Sound for many years, having raised families in the bush. There are also some young couples just starting out with homesteading; there are friends who live in the village of Tofino, along with a half dozen of Mike's construction buddies, men he works with in carpentry, and eight young graduate students from Germany whom Mike has befriended and who are working in the area for the season.

The German students of both sexes astonish me. They are so tall, and so knowledgeable. The four girls look like Amazons. The local men are enchanted. There is much commotion around the stove as the girls exclaim excitedly over the pot of boiling crabs, a little later they must be given instructions on how to open and eat the crabs.

Everyone who comes brings something delicious to eat. There is baked whole salmon, halibut and cod, great vegetable and potato salads, homemade rolls that are accompanied by the enormous tub of chili that Mike has concocted. There is pop and iced beer in a washtub by the side of the deck, rum cake and homemade cookies and donuts. Spirits run high. Later in the afternoon Mike brings out his guns and there is target shooting in the back which terribly annoys most of us older women, although several of the younger women take up the challenge. Still later the living area of the A-frame is cleared and tapes are brought out and the dancing commences. Which is great fun. And then some of us try to country dance which seems to be a combination of square dance and French Canadian step dance. Richard is from the village and he is the only one who knows the calls, and he only knows them in French, which causes some confusion. There is a right smart amount of stumbling about amid great peals and whoops of laughter, not all of it entirely sober. However, when the daylight filters down thin and pale, the gaiety subsides. The waters of the Sound can be as capricious as the gods. It is best to get where one is headed by dusk if one is travelling on the water. Mike is leaving, too, he must go back to Tofino. I go down to the dock and wave everybody off. When the last boat disappears around the bend of the cove I climb the steps back to the house and light the lamps.

There's not an awful lot to clean up. We ate most of the food and the guests helped clean up the paper plates for burning and the beer cans and pop bottles for recycling before they left. The other things I will wash in the morning. I am full, happy, and just ever so slightly tipsy as I fold out the sleeping chair downstairs underneath the skylight. I forgo the sleeping lofts upstairs most of the time and sleep right here. I love lying on my back and looking straight up out of the skylight into the night sky. Tonight the sky is crystal clear and peppered with stars. And then, in spite of my general sense of well-being, I begin to feel lonely. Most of the time I don't mind being alone, but tonight, I find myself minding terribly.

All of my life I have been surrounded by other people. Raised in my parents' house, married at sixteen, mother at barely eighteen, there have always been others ... if not in my arms, then at my elbows, or an arm's length away. I didn't know what it meant to be alone until I came out here. I am glad of the experience, but aside for certain psychological benefits my aloneness here reaffirms for me what I have always intuitively known ... that the family is every-thing.

By family I mean blood, for while my husbands have come and gone, the blood tie is constant ... my children, my mother, my sis-ter, my brother, my aunts and uncles, cousins, it is in these people that reside everlasting affection and concern for me and mine. Rela-tively speaking. I would have been more at home in a precontact society where one's clan was all and the relationship with one's hus-band the lesser tie. I think that the big lie of civilization is the denial of the blood tie in favor of the marriage tie. For upon what do our marriages depend? On sexual attraction, that most fickle of emo-tions. For one day one loves and is loved, the world is a happy place, one is carried outside one's self with joy and zest for life, but then one morning one wakes up and finds oneself out of love, or one's part-ner out of love, and then misery reigns, if one cannot escape the disappointment one may commit murder, or kill oneself. And on this highly volatile and unstable foundation we try to raise children to be healthy, happy and full of confidence. No wonder the world is mad.

But mad it is, I am convinced, which is why I am lying here in an A-frame located deep in the bush, isolated now from all fellow humans, gazing up at the night through the skylight, missing the departed guests, so full of energy and light, still feeling the echoes of the vanished bodies. I lie here alone, dammit. Which is the price one pays, I reckon, if one decides to rebel against the established order of things, the biggest risk the rebel faces is not that s/he will die alone, but that s/he will lie alone.

And then, out of my own aloneness and feelings of separate-ness, the magic of the Sound slowly seeps into my heart and sensibilities and the natural world closes in sensuously, banishing my loneliness, and I feel at one with the sea and the sky and the stars and the moon, and the Clayoquot Sound rocks me gently in her arms. And in this moment I know what life is all about, but it is unspeakable and full of glory. There are no words for this knowl-edge, it is spiritual but not religious, and rooted in an earthly mother. I think it must be akin to what all primitive peoples felt long ago, and here in the Clayoquot there is no fear in the awesome fact of nature. While one may not relish the idea of being chewed at by cougars, death is only an experience that those of us who are inhab-iting these particular bodies haven't experienced yet in these particular forms and the closer one can get to the natural world the less one fears death. And perhaps this is the strongest argument that can ever be made for saving old growth rainforests. However, if one loses one's fear of death then one naturally becomes a rebel. But I didn't deliberately set out to become a rebel. It just happened in the natural order of searching for a meaning to my life. And the real beginning of my search started with the discovery of the Unitarian Fellowship in Hampton, Virginia, not long after that horrible day when Mrs. Thompson died, and Joey nearly scared me to death, and R.L. tried to check out early. The Unitarians were my first contact with people, besides my husband, whom I felt to be in the same searching party I was in.

SEVEN

Unitarians have been called, among other things, atheists who can't kick the church-going habit. Actually, from
what I have learned, Unitarians started out as a traditional Christian sect, but turned so liberal in their thirst for
knowledge, their need to know, that they got sidetracked away from
theology into caring about the real world. They suited me just fine.
John even started going to the fellowship with me and the kids.
There was no minister, anybody could give a lecture if something
was on one's mind, but one must be prepared to defend one's thesis
as there would be many questions later served along with the coffee. I heard lectures from the lectern of that fellowship that would
have been sheer blasphemy in the deeply rural Louisiana culture
from which I'd sprung — lectures on civil rights, abortion, com-
munes, community planning, genetics, socialism, and even though
a smattering of the fellowship was in the military, on the evils of the
military. The list of engrossing, earth shaking subjects to be dis-

cussed was endless. My head felt to bursting with all these new ideas. It was like being a kid again.

Yes, at that point I became a child again, with an aching need to know. Christianity was a world view. Christianity had told me what I was doing here and where I would go when I died. If one accepted the Christian faith, it wasn't necessary to try to find answers to the troubling questions of abject poverty and obscene wealth. When I ceased being a Christian, I also lost my world view. I sorely missed having a world view. I knew many people, even most, could live happily without one, just as some people could live without grits and cornbread, but I didn't envy them none. I figured that the big and small things that happened on earth couldn't just be random happenings as there was order in the natural world if not the social one. The sun didn't rise sometimes in the west, gravity always pushed you down, it didn't sometimes suck you up, when I picked up a cup my hand reached forward and my fingers curled around the cup handle, my arm didn't flail out sideways occasionally, or my fingers try to turn back over my hand. I didn't want to hear mythologies anymore, religious or otherwise, I wanted to know what was. And the lectures at the Unitarian Fellowship while not necessarily providing me with tons of answers, were at least helping me to formulate the right questions. Unfortunately, by summer's end I was yanked away from the bosoms of my new mentors. John got a year's sabbatical to work on his doctorate.

We found a family to rent our house and then headed off to Blacksburg, Virginia where John and Joey both would be attending the Virginia Polytechnic Institute. Joey was still only sixteen, having completed high school early, but would be seventeen shortly after the fall semester started so was accepted by the Institute. We rented a big old farmhouse on the edge of town and hunkered down for a year of serious study. Susan started in the first grade and Margaret Elizabeth played school with Rose Mary ad nauseam. There were times when I walked through the house and every soul except me was bent over a piece of paper with pencil in hand, books at the ready. How wonderful. I lived in a house of scholars. I decided to take some university extension courses myself. This would fill up the void of the missing Unitarians. But these were creative writing courses and not anything particularly weighty, so I also entered into a correspondence with my Aunt Pearl's border, Mr. Kartus.

Aunt Pearl was the one who had helped me care for Susan when she was a baby and I was abandoned, and we had remained close. Eccentric, never married, she took in boarders. Mr. Kartus was a retired lawyer, Jewish, learned, mystical, and now very much into eastern religions. After hearing that I had fallen out with the Southern Baptists, he sent me some books by Shri Aurobindo.

I wasn't sure about this chap Aurobindo. He held that the downfall of humans was caused by desire, and that people must stop desiring anything, even the desire to be rid of desire, in order to set them-selves free from the wheel of countless reincarnations. I found this baffling. How could one possibly rid oneself of all desire? Wasn't desire simply life's longing for itself? After all, sexual desire made young people get up and start Juneing around. There was the desire to make babies and see them grow, to make other things, too, to do things, change things. How could anything be accomplished without desire?

I just didn't get it. And yet there was something about the idea of not being driven by desire that piqued my interest. All one had to do was look around and see the misery caused by frustrated desire. One was forever trying to control one's environment, influence events, persuade other people of the rightness or wrongness of thoughts or actions. What a relief to have done with all that. But what would take the place of desire and the struggles stemming from desire? Would the absence of desire be one big void? Or a sort of living death where one moved through the motions of living, looking neither right nor left nor up nor down, without heart, without soul, without consciousness? Or would the absence of desire be a deep, satisfying peace? Oh, mystery upon mystery! In sheer frustration I put Auribindo on hold and turned to other writers.

I decided to start with George Bernard Shaw. I had seen a couple of his plays, but had never actually read anything by him. But the book by Shaw that John brought from the library wasn't a play, it was a political book called *The Intelligent Woman's Guide to Socialism and Capitalism*. This was heavy stuff. I opened it with hesitation, even apprehension. Was I intelligent enough to understand these principles without assistance?

I suspected that the political lectures I'd heard at the fellowship hadn't thoroughly sunk in, that they were sitting on the top of my forebrain in an undigested state. I didn't really understand what was meant by the words socialism, marxism, communism, fascism, or even capitalism for that matter. I did associate, like every other

American that I knew, the word godless with almost every known "ism" other than capitalism ... godless communism, godless socialism, godless humanism, etc. And even though I had become godless myself, I wasn't sure I wanted everybody else out there to be godless, too. In the Southern society I knew the threat of hell served as a deterrent to some of the more serious transgressions against society. And yet when I thought about it, what people were more religious and yet more sinful than Southerners?

Politics, at least Louisiana style, was a farce, and the people seemed to actually delight in the corruptness of the politicians. Racism was part and parcel of the South. Southerners ate, drank, and slept racism on a daily basis. The double standard about women, both black and white, that I later came to recognize as sexism, was also part of the very air that one breathed. At the same time that southerners seemed irretrievably drawn to corruptness, they also loved authority, especially if it was in a form that could be based on some bizarre interpretation of the Bible and upheld in the Louisiana courts. And the state of Louisiana with all its patriotism, court systems, churches, the thousands of Bible-thumping ministers, the tons of potato salad and pecan pie and fried chicken churned out by the millions of dedicated church-going women, these forces never changed a thing to the good, not even when the entire state of Louisiana threatened, as it did, from time to time, to sink into the Gulf of Mexico under the weight of all that southern cooking dedicated to the gods of ignorance and superstition and nothing changed, ever, nothing important. Any improvement, bitterly opposed from the inside, had to be imposed from the outside. And the poor were still the poorest in the nation, rivalled only by Mississippi; the schools the most inept; health statistics the very worst. By almost any national measure that could be applied to monitor the well being of the American people, Louisiana usually came out on the bottom, again rivalled only by Mississippi and occasionally Georgia. Except for oil and oil products.

Oil was really the true king in Louisiana, country people just thought it was crayfish and hot peppers. Standard Oil ran Louisiana as far as I could see. But that was all I knew of politics. So I edged sideways like a crab into Shaw's book, ready to scurry at the first indication of danger.

But I needn't have been so shy. Old George was witty, charming, easy to read. And the message hit me like a field hand's hoecake.

Here, for the first time, somebody was actually explaining to me, in terms I could understand, why our society was the way it was, why there were a few people who were filthy rich, and on the other end, a lot of people who were dirt poor. This division of rich and poor meant there was a surfeit or an absence of things, material goods, in our society, and dividing people into two separate, distinct categories meant that there was a sub-species of people ... one group was elevated, as it were, up into the light of cleanliness, knowledge, leisure, beauty, spaciousness, travel, music, dance, art, in short ... heaven on earth. The sub-species was relegated to darkness, dirt, ignorance, poor health, cramped spaces, suppressed rage ... hell on earth for this unfortunate group.

I realized as I studied this book that there was a larger middle class in the United States than in the England of Shaw's day. And after all, John and I were trying to climb the rungs of that middle class ourselves. But Shaw's analysis of the capitalist system and his solution to the great disparity of income under capitalism, that grave injustice that had plagued me for years, had a simple enough solution. In a real socialist society that Shaw envisioned, everybody, even single living souls in the country, would have equality of income. There, wasn't that simple?

In Shaw's scenario everyone would receive the same income regardless of the jobs they held or even how well they performed those jobs. People who wanted to have more money or resources than their neighbours would just be flat out of luck as would be the people who would have been content with less. Just as no one would be allowed to have more, nobody would be allowed to be poor. Poverty breeds disease and degradation and thus threatens the entire society. We would have to change our priorities, we would have to learn to work for other reasons than individual accumulation and consumption. It would mean that individuals would have to reorient themselves toward working for the good of the community, the society, as a whole and at the same time, try to develop their own gifts, interests and aptitudes. Praise the Lord! In the beginning was the word. What a wonderful vision!

I thought of all the hours, days, years, that people everywhere struggled with money — the poor to have food and shelter, the middle class to keep from sliding down into the class below while trying to maximize their chances of a toehold on the bottom rung of the upper classes. And the capitalists, the real top dogs, they sweat out keeping a comfortable distance between themselves and certain upstarts from the classes below them who are always trying to muscle in. From the cradle to the grave everyone is preoccupied with money — how to get it, how to keep it, how much things cost, what they cost yesterday, what they will cost tomorrow, how much one owes, how much credit one has, how much money will be left over at the end of the month, will interest go up or down, will there be a safe pension or a pension at all, should women put something aside from the grocery money just in case. Marriages being what they are today, just a little more money and one could start buying food in bulk, but at the moment John needs a new suit for work, the boys need jeans again, the little girls new runners, I had hoped to have a freezer by now, we certainly need one for our size family, the station wagon needs new tires, oh God, there is no end to it, need, need, need.

Yes, out damned anxieties over money! Surely our primary purpose here is not to be preoccupied with money. To have lived a human life so preoccupied is tacky. I mean really tacky. Surely the human race could do better than that. So Shaw became my main man. We went together on a steady basis while he explained his systems to me. And before he turned me loose he introduced me to other thinkers concerned with human evolution for my further edification. And not the least of these were those two bugbears, Karl Marx and Friedrich Engels.

I started with *Das Kapital*. It might as well have been written in Sanskrit. I'm not sure who Marx was writing his book for, certainly not the working class. I wrote for the working class. I was the working class. And if I couldn't make my way through this ponderous stuff, then perhaps capitalism was safe forever. I asked John for help but he danced away with his own studies. Christmas, he promised. He would read *Das Kapital* and discuss it with me during the holidays. Downed but not out, I turned to the *Communist Manifesto*.

The *Manifesto* was easier going and a great deal shorter. After hoeing that row for awhile I cracked Engels's book *The Origins of the Family*. It was here that I began to get very excited about what I read. Engels was taking up in a direct and readable way the question Shaw left largely unanswered in his book, namely, exactly how did all this uneven distribution of wealth come about in the first place?

Engels told me. Not exactly, but more or less. It seems that all early primitive societies were communal societies. In these communities there was no concept of individual ownership, everything was shared — food, shelter, and skills. Of course, one's tools were one's own, the digging forks, personal clothing, hunting equipment.

When certain tribes began settling down and growing food instead of migrating back and forth in seasons, they also began domesticating animals. At first the animals and grains and vegetables belonged to the group as a whole, but as people got more skilled at farming and husbandry they finally reached a point where some serious bartering could begin. Engels thought that both farming and husbandry evolved almost exclusively under the hands of women, but, as the surpluses began to accumulate, the trading and barter was taken over by the men of the tribes. And this was the beginning of the long, slow, slide into social, political, and economic limbo for women.

Before men took over the trading, they didn't try to push women around because even aside from the bearing and raising of children, women's work was absolutely necessary to the survival of the group as a whole. Women's work largely fed the entire community. Early man knew what side his yam was buttered on, because if his day's hunting was futile, he could always go home to the steaming tubers and grain cakes of one sort or another at the woman's hearth. But when men started hogging all the grain and cattle and pigs that the women had raised, they weren't so generous to the women. And as men got more powerful they started bullying women, telling them what to do and how to do it, and then they invented religion to convince women they were supposed to obey men, because men were just this shy of being gods themselves. Engels was a little vague on the particulars of how this all came about as these whopping changes commenced before recorded history, but this theory certainly hit me where I hurt.

Didn't I know that women did all the poo work? And got blamed when things went wrong, while men got all the credit when things went right? And then Engels went on to explain to me how primitive communism evolved into feudalism and then into capitalism and how the logical outcome of this was socialism. By the time socialism became a worldview people would be so advanced they wouldn't need a state anymore to tell them what to do, and the entire apparatus of government would wither away. That part sounded like a dream but the rest got my vote.

For people had made the society we live in and, if enough people who didn't like the income disparity got together, they could unmake the present society and make another one more to their liking. This seemed to me a superior way of looking at the world than the religious view, particularly the Christian one. In the Christian world we are admonished not to fret about the poor because they will always be with us. Anyway, God will especially reward poor people after death if they have been meek enough in life. And if one doesn't trouble the waters with questions, one might eventually get a face to face interview with God about the matter of poverty, and why he doesn't forcefully intervene in mass starvation and slaughter of innocents. But then the doubting Thomases will be so chagrined at their own arrogance in even asking for some sort of explanation that they will whip themselves with rawhide or the heavenly equivalent for having so little faith.

So I studied and struggled to understand what these socialist writers were trying to tell me. From Marx and Engels I went to Lenin and then to some contemporary American and European leftist writers, and drifted off to sleep at night thinking about dialectical materialism and the class struggle. I was eagerly awaiting the Christmas holidays so John could go over some of this mind-boggling material with me. But tragedy struck the entire nation before Christmas rolled around that year, the Christmas of 1963. John Kennedy was assassinated in Dallas on November the twenty-second.

That certainly got my John's attention. It got everybody's attention. We watched, stunned, as the drama unfolded over and over again on television. What was one to make of it, the death of Kennedy and then Lee Harvey Oswald, and what to think of Jack Ruby? What forces compelled the participants of this ghastly drama, what was behind it all? Nobody knew. A sombre Christmas came and went and as soon as the school year was over the family headed back to southern Virginia minus one member. Joey had a job for the summer in Blacksburg and would continue at the university in the fall.

When we got home John and I decided not to disturb the renters in our house but to buy a larger house, one further out from the cities of Hampton and Newport News. The place we found that we all liked was a hundred and fifty-year-old house in the small rural community of Matthews, about forty miles from Hampton. The front lawn ran down to an inlet of Chesapeake Bay called Put In Creek, which the locals, in their own dialect, ran all together so it came out sounding like Pudding Creek. Whatever, we loved it. The water was unpolluted and eighty acres of virgin timber came with the house. And the house was enormous. Six bedrooms and a fireplace in every room. But the place was also terribly run down and neither of the two bathrooms had bathtubs. Because the house was built before widespread indoor plumbing, past owners of the house had simply added showers and toilets in two of the largest closets. However, there was a wide verandah in front with the traditional southern white columns just like Tara in Gone with the Wind and the expansive lawn rolled gently down to the water, and every window in the house looked out over the sparkling sea waters or the equally beautiful forests and lawns. The cost of the house and eighty acres was seventeen thousand dollars. I was tickled pink. We had definitely come up in the world. We were on a roll.

We sold some of the hardwood from the acreage to remodel the house. We sanded painted floors to reveal gleaming hardwood underneath, redid the crumbling stairway and paneled three of the rooms downstairs. Mike and Andy and I painted the entire house, both inside and out. Most of the houses on our side of the bank were painted the traditional white, or palest yellow. We opted for a deep slate blue with white shutters which shocked our neighbours a bit, and we became known as the people who lived in the blue house.

I liked Virginia. It was a beautiful state. Virginia had been a slave state way back yonder, with all the attendant attitudes that slavery must accommodate, yet the face of racism in Virginia seemed less crude and ugly than in Louisiana. There was more of an attempt to be liberal, maybe because so many famous politicians and statesmen came from Virginia or perhaps because Virginia's population was simply more diverse. We were not far from the heart of the military industrial complex, the shipyards, the naval bases, airfields, training bases, the National Aeronautics and Space Administration, plus a pig's throw away from the CIA and FBI. So the entire area was definitely right wing and militaristic. But because so many people were in and out from other parts of the country and the world, there was no way the state of Virginia could be born-again en masse the way Louisiana tried to do. And the Unitarian Fellowship, as usual, continued to educate me. I heard my first lecture on the background of the police action, as it was called then, that was going on in Vietnam. Curiosity piqued, I started to search for more material about that unfortunate country.

I learned more than I needed to know for my own comfort

level. I couldn't believe my country was actually doing this. The Vietnamese had been fighting various invaders for over a hundred years, the French most recently, and when the French couldn't impose their will on these incredibly determined people and were thoroughly routed, the U.S. moved in to take their place. It was horrible. The weekday no-TV rule fell by the wayside as I became a news junkie. The war images stuck in my brain, blurring the brilliant Virginia sunshine and stultifying the sweet sea breezes. John was equally affected and we made contact with several of the anti-war movements that had sprung up as knowledge of what the U.S. was doing in Vietnam circulated and opposition to this police action grew.

John and I felt we must try to do something to help protest what we thought to be a cruel, inhumane, illegal, unjust war against an agrarian people who had apparently done nothing to deserve such treatment except object to the invasion of their country by foreigners.

So our sympathies were definitely with the Vietnamese. Our hearts were also stirred by the young American boys over there fighting such a cruel war. As a mother of young men myself I suffered for the parents of the young men involved. And I felt guilty. My own sons were safe. Joey was in university and therefore in possession of a draft deferment. Mike would also go directly into university from high school. Young men of the middle class were protected by the universities. It was mostly poor, working-class young men of all races that became cannon fodder. Or more precisely, bazooka fodder, land-mine fodder, sniper fodder. My bitterness toward the U.S. military and toward President Johnson increased daily. And yet in spite of the Vietnam War, John and I retained some pleasurable excitement about our lives.

The house was finished and it was a thing of glory. I was selling more confessions and John was happy with his work. The kids were all doing well. Joey wasn't exactly thrilled with his second year of university, but he seemed to be surviving. Mike would finish high school early, too, and Andy was in the process of getting together a rock and roll band — the first of many bands, as music became his life's work. The little girls were sweet and clever, and we had a lovely shepherd dog named Jack, who played nicely with them and tried to herd them back to the house if they wandered too close to the gate that led to the road out back. And out of the final stand of hardwood at the rear of our property we decided to buy a boat, a real boat. Mike had a canoe he had made himself and we owned a little outboard motorboat, but this new boat was serious. It had a large cabin with a head and cooking and sleeping accommodations. I guess this qualified us as potential members of the local yacht club, because we received an invitation in the mail not long after this purchase. I couldn't believe it. Me, poor Louisiana country girl, and John, son of a sharecropper, invited to join the exclusive yacht club in the area.

We accepted the invitation to join and paid our membership fees, but as the months went by we couldn't seem to make it to any of the meetings or social events. The Vietnam War was heating up, I was pregnant again, and Joey was in the process of doing something so outlandish I almost had a heart attack. He called me unexpectedly from California to tell me he had dropped out of university and joined the U.S. Air Force. He hoped I wasn't too disappointed.

I was devastated. Even though his decision to join the Air Force wasn't a decision in favor of U.S. involvement in Vietnam, he was simply lonely at university and not doing too well and decided to see the world. Apparently, I had made the mistake of not trying to impress my son with our growing opposition to the war in Vietnam. The inter-family calls and correspondence had centered almost exclusively around family talk and studies. Joey actually knew very little about what was happening in Vietnam. And he was still only eighteen. I dragged around, my body heavy. There was another baby in my belly but there was a monkey on my back, a suffocating sense of dread. My son. My first born. Sensitive, intelligent with big, soft dark eyes and long, sweeping lashes, a calm child, thoughtful and contemplative, born hating dissension and violence. In the Air Force. Vietnam. I began to hate President Johnson and all of his consorts with a passion. When I saw their faces on TV I wanted to scream out at them, to hurt them in some way as they were hurting me. John and I started attending some of the anti-war protest marches.

I was involved in two marches in Washington, D.C. John joined me for the first march but on the second, which was the fourth of July, he went to one in Philadelphia that was being held simultaneously with the one in Washington. My own attitude was definitely hardening. Here I was, a thirty-six year old woman from the backwoods of Louisiana, pregnant with my seventh child, born and bred on religion and patriotism and yet somehow I was rapidly becoming an enemy of the state.

An enemy of the United States? Of Virginia? Of Louisiana? Of the southland? Oh, God have mercy on me, poor sinner that I am. How could I be an enemy of my homeland, of the south, of my parents, all my kin, the foot stomping music, the tantalizing food, all the funny, wonderful people I knew and had known ... no, it wasn't any of these things I felt to be the enemy. But I was becoming an enemy of the economic and military systems of my country.

This was happening because I was beginning to see that the capitalist system dictated policy to the government. And this had been so since the inception of government in the United States. The government apparatus was there, not to insure that democracy ruled, but to protect the rich from the poor, as the poor, in their practical wisdom have been known, from time to time, to try to even things up. It was the rich who declared and conducted wars and who profited from wars. It was the poor who fought and died in these wars, who gave their lives and limbs in the mistaken belief that they were fighting for democracy, for the homeland, for God, instead of dying for the capitalists' lust for more property, more influence, more raw materials and more markets. Even in times of peace, there were two classes of people, because the professional class that John and I had recently infiltrated was in the employ of the capitalist class even when the work was scientific government work, like NASA. Because almost any kind of government research is funded by taxes coughed up by the working people of the United States, when researchers come up with a new product, the taxpayers who funded the project don't whoop for joy and wait to take a cut in the profits. Oh, no. The taxpayers as a rule aren't even aware of the new discovery being paid for by them because once completed, the project is usually turned over immediately to the private sector for further developing and marketing. And profit taking. The poor taxpayer pays twice, once for the research and then for the product itself which has been co-opted by the capitalist class. I had to laugh at this realization. The capitalists are actually socialists. They believe in using public money for their own private good, while the taxpayers must remain capitalist, that is, the taxpayers must live and move and have their beings in strict competition, no socialist goodies for them. This is why the capitalists are so dead set against socialism. In real socialism, the taxpayers would also have access to public money and resources. The American capitalists not only plunder the purses of fellow Americans, they hog tie the third world by sucking up raw materials like they were sugar tits, while selling finished products back to the third world at world prices. John and I were having a wonderful life, not only because of our individual initiative, but because the third world had so little and because people in Vietnam were dying from our bombs and Napalm.

These realizations threw me into a deep depression. Because, of course, the Vietnamese were killing American boys, too. It was hard to tell how many. There were charges from opponents of the war that the military was inflating the figures of the Vietnamese dead while downplaying those of American dead. There were too many images on TV of young American boys being hauled onto helicopters, off planes, and out of hospitals in body bags. My God, one of them could be Joey! In a body bag, with an identification tag tied around his toe. And Mike. Would the war still be going on by the time he was eighteen? And Andy. There was Andy coming up behind Mike. This was madness that my sons should be taken away for such wicked, senseless destruction. I came out of my depression resolving that while the government had snagged one of my sons while I wasn't looking, they would get another one over my dead body. Literally.

And while I can still feel the heat of that time when I think of it, it was long ago, almost another lifetime. I am back in Cypress Bay now, the mortgage burning party over and the fall deepening. I have just received a letter from Victoria, from my youngest daughter, Marian. She has decided to take Open University correspondence courses for the year so she can come live with me for awhile. And my love affair with the Clayoquot Sound, my ordered, pristine, my private environment is about to get as scrambled as a hen hatching off a nest of duck eggs. The baffled hen and I want to do the right thing, if only we knew what that was. In the end the only course is to follow the ducklings down to the water, because they insist on going there, and hope for the best.

EIGHT

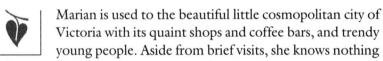 Marian is used to the beautiful little cosmopolitan city of Victoria with its quaint shops and coffee bars, and trendy young people. Aside from brief visits, she knows nothing about the life here, a good deal of which is about physical survival. But I remind myself that young women are not safe anywhere. Perhaps she is safer here, with me, after all, in the arms of the Clayoquot Sound. At any rate, she will arrive in two weeks and I await her coming eagerly. A week before she is due to arrive I experience the first storm of the winter season.

These storms arise suddenly in the Sound. One moment I am washing up the last of the summer's sea asparagus, which grows in profusion along the high tide level around the cove, and the next moment I am cowering underneath the stairwell of the house, shrieking in terror every time a fierce gust of wind goes shuddering over and around the A-frame. I had insisted that Mike install three large skylights because they bring the outdoors indoors, but now they are bringing in something I don't really want, a blow by blow, gust by gust, whirlwind by whirlwind account of the storm. Suddenly I know very well that I am going to be sucked up through the skylights, or blown out the big sliding glass doors and bounced way out over the bluffs. Or perhaps firmly impaled onto the jagged, rocks below, or tumbled over and over by the howling, screaming winds until I am engulfed by the wildly cresting surf. So I remain crumpled in the corner of the stairwell, whimpering, finding a sickening, trembling irony in the possibility that I will perish in a storm after having survived beautifully with no indoor plumbing or electricity and even managing to rise above the isolation and loneliness, the slugs and countless imaginary cougar attacks. Then after all this, to be killed by high winds seems somewhat silly of me, after all, I could have been killed by high winds back in Louisiana. Louisiana has plenty of high winds. They are called tornadoes. But wait! After what seems like hours I become aware that I am somewhat physically cramped by the cowering position I have assumed. I straighten up, leave the stairwell and move into the center of the room. The storm has not abated much, but familiarity breeds contempt after all, and the swooshing of the winds and the swaying of trees now seem not quite so terrifying. Besides, I'm hungry.

By nightfall the winds have decidedly slowed although the rain is still lashing the house in sudden sheets of fury. Emotionally exhausted, I turn in early. By morning all kinds of wonderful things have been washed up, or thrown up, on the beach. There are at least a half a dozen floats of various sizes, something that looks like part of somebody else's dock, a yellow dinghy, several good sized logs and an enormous uprooted tree. I can't do anything about the floats, the logs, and the tree, as they are all too heavy for me to deal with. Mike would certainly be interested in them, but he may not come again for several days, as sometimes it takes that long for the waters to calm down after a bad blow. But I rescue the dinghy and secure it to a large rock. Our own dinghy has disappeared, along with the canoe.

There is a strange unwritten rule out here about runaway or washed away small boats. It seems to be a matter of finders keepers. We could keep the dinghy washed up on our shores without troubling ourselves to find its owner, as could whoever might find our own washed-away small craft. Yet, because everyone knows everyone else, this seldom happens. Dinghies are returned to their recognized owners with only the expectation of a small gift in return for their trouble, usually a bottle of something alcoholic. Still, the canoe was borrowed. It will have to be returned or replaced. That afternoon the tide takes back everything it has landed on our shores except the secured dinghy and the enormous uprooted tree. The tree seems stuck in the entrance way to the large stream across the cove and may very well stay there until Mike can salvage it. In the meantime, Marian will be here soon and I must sweep the Blue Lagoon.

Marian brings with her all the refinements of the city. There is a tape deck and loads of tapes, trendy clothes, course work and school books, and she remembered to bring warm slippers and those indispensable items if one chooses to spend time in a rainforest, rubber boots and a sturdy rain slicker. Marian is tall and fair with the classical features of her father's side of the family, and she evidences a lively interest in all the flora and fauna at Cypress Bay. She has enjoyed her previous visits, but now she seems to be experiencing some sense of identification with the Bay, some feeling of responsibility for our being here. Everything is a delight to her and I rediscover it all through her fresh eyes ... all the mysterious beings that lurk on the shallow bottom of the cove, most completely unidentified, at least by me, the myriad of creatures that make their livings on and around the tideline, little crusty things that ring the rocky bluffs and cling desperately to the rocks, the marauding seal, the bears that appear unfailingly at low tide, all the air and water birds, the sounds we hear at night after we have packed it in for the day, all the rustlings and squeakings and squawkings at the forest edge as the night creatures come out and start raising hell, the wolf howls in the distance, the cougar tracks in the soft earth in the back yard that reveal themselves early in the morning, the skies and the mountains and the mists constantly shifting and merging patterns before our very eyes, and above all, the sounds of the gently lapping waves against the rocks and the wonderful, sharp, acid, salty smell of the sea. Solitude has its moments, but for sheer happiness, nothing beats sharing an adventure with someone you love. However, after a month of keeping steady company with me, punctuated only by occasional visits from her brother, I notice that Marian has developed a peculiar habit. Whenever she hears the sound of a boat motor she drops everything and rushes down to the beach to see if we have company.

And often it is. Word gets around. A single, pretty young woman can expect company at the ends of, and probably at the end of, the earth. The young men who come courting are Mike's friends and acquaintances, or the sons of neighbours. They are fisher people mostly and they come bearing a salmon or a clutch of crabs, a little shy, unsure of the situation. We offer coffee and conversation and invite them back. Fall is deepening. Pretty soon now the waters of the Sound will become more violent and the storms more frequent. There's not much time left for visiting for the sake of visiting. Soon some of the inhabitants of more remote parts of the Sound will be moving into the village for the winter. Marian and I will stay until after Christmas and then we will head south to visit my mother in Baton Rouge, Louisiana. But we plan on having a splendid Christmas.

We will invite some of the other homesteaders, mostly bachelors, who have no family around. In a freezer in Tofino we have salmon and some geese. I'll make cornbread dressing, a big tub of potato salad, and baked yams. Marian will conjure up her wonderful fudge and prized peanut butter and almond cookies. And after dinner, we will all sing Christmas carols. But we must practice.

No longer Christian, I change all mention of baby Jesus in the carols to baby Isis, the earth goddess of old, and remind myself and Marian that what we are really celebrating here is the winter solstice. It is unfortunate that we have no songs of our own for this, but I understand that the Christians stole the pagan celebration of solstice and dubbed it Christmas, so I feel no guilt in pilfering a few of their songs. It is a celebration and something must be sung. Practically everyone on my mother's side of the family sings or plays, or both. The few who can't do either are looked upon as deviants and as soon as they are old enough to recognize the enormity of this deficiency they must cast about for some other performing art that will let them off the hook at the frequent family get-togethers. I have one inadequately musical nephew who in desperation, turned to learning magic tricks. He became so adept at this that he helped pay his way through university by performing at children's parties. I learned to tap dance.

I never had any tap dancing lessons. I just learned on my own. Marian should have followed suit because her voice is almost, but not quite, as unmusical and off key as mine. However, in some strange genetic twist, we sound okay singing together, our individual off-tones are somehow reined in by the other's voice. But we still have a problem — I don't read music very well and Marian reads not at all; and the problem is compounded by the fact that Marian has been brought up on jazzy arrangements of Christmas carols and has no idea how most of them are properly sung.

But tonight we are off to a good start. The dishes are done and everything is tidied up for the night. The fire in the stove has mellowed to a warm, steady glow. We can hear the muffled throb of the surf, the darkened trees outside are swishing and swaying in the late wet wind ... but oh, we are so cozy inside! And for our further decadent pleasure there is a big bowl of warm popcorn accompanied by a pot of herbal mint tea. We are awash in the milk of human kindness. Ten minutes later we are screaming at each other.

The air is thick with hurled angry accusations. Marian insists that I am completely ignorant of music, totally devoid of natural rhythms, have no voice and am pitifully tone deaf. I try to explain to her, albeit at the top of my non-voice, that music has an order, is disciplined, that the purpose of the written notes is to explain how the composer wanted the notes to be sung. I take out a song book and open it to the carol we are fighting over.

"See?" I say. "The note goes down there so the voice must go down also."

She looks from the song page back to me with an icy stare that translated means "up yours, Mom" and then flops down on the couch with a mystery novel.

I am annoyed. The room is silent save for the burbling and hissing of the stove, but outside the wind is gaining force. I fetch my rag bag hidden within the stairwell. In this bag I have saved old shirts, pants, gowns, and dresses. I open the bag and start ripping up a well worn blouse. Marian ignores this activity for awhile. But then the silence seems to grow long and eerie and after a spell she peers over the edge of her book. Her tall, strong body is relaxed into the couch, but in the lamplight her face is soft and in spite of the scowl, painfully sweet.

"I thought you were finished with that rug," she says abruptly, her tones heavy with disapproval.

I glance down at the rag rug gracing our floor. It is a round, multi-colored, very large rag rug. Very attractive, really. I had meant only an accent rug, something of moderate size. Somehow the thing had gotten out of hand and now it covered the entire living area of the room. I wasn't sure how it had happened, only that once started, it seemed to grow of its own volition.

"Mom, if you add any more braids to that rug it will start running out the door. Or do you intend to carpet the entire area of the cove with one immense, stupendous rag rug?"

"I might," I snap, but inside I am somewhat shaken. This is the first time I've ever made a rug. Was such a thing possible? To get started on a project like this and truly not be able to stop? I remember a film clip I saw once about a man who lived in rural England somewhere, or maybe the man lived in Oregon, but wherever, this man started picking up a few rocks off his property to clear his land and then because he had the rocks, he began to construct a rock fence around his property. Then, because his neighbours knew he was building a rock fence, they began to bring in rocks from their property. Then people he didn't know and had never heard of began to haul up their rocks to his place and the man's fence began to wander off his own property and meandered down across some other people's land, across vacant fields and meadows. The last I heard, the fence was still going.

The fence had somehow assumed a life of its own, a will of its own, and obviously, a wanderlust of its own. My God, could that really happen with this rug? What if I simply couldn't stop adding braids to the thing? What if the same compulsive spirit that got into the man's fence was already into my rug, programming me to add to it without ceasing? Then the rug would indeed climb the walls of the A-frame, ooze out the front door over the deck, down the rocks to the beach and begin gradually to cover the entire cove. They would come get me, yes, they would, and lock me up and I'd never see my loved ones or the Clayoquot Sound again and all because of a damned rag rug ...

"Mom, are you really going to make that rug even bigger?" Marian asks, breaking into my terrified thoughts.

"Of course not," I answer stiffly. "I'm starting some pot holders."

"You don't even use pot holders," Marian says sternly. "I gave you some for Christmas last year and you don't even know where they are."

"That's why I'm going to make some more," I answer quickly. I've never made pot holders before, either, but I reckon it can't be too hard.

Marian sighs loudly, puts her book aside and swings her long legs over the side of the couch.

"Come on, let's sing some more," she offers. "I know you're not ripping up that stuff to make pot holders and if I have to watch you add one more braid to the rug I'll start swimming back to Tofino."

So we make up and sing and eat popcorn and molest the stove until far into the night. And then when we finally go to bed I can't sleep. The ghosts of Christmases past are upon me. When Marian is snoring softly in her loft opposite mine I get up and light a candle and try to pen down the elusive memories of all the Christmases of my childhood, and then the ones where I became Santa Claus myself to my own children. And the memory of one Christmas washes over me with such warm waves of sweet remembrance I want to weep, it was so unexpected and wonderful.

I was twenty-seven and newly divorced from my second husband. I was living in Phoenix, Arizona and the sole support of three little boys and a nine-month old baby girl. And that Christmas season started out to be really rotten.

We were just scraping by on the money I made as a waitress at the Adams Hotel. I was barely making enough to pay for the absolute necessities of life, and I depended heavily on my Aunt Pearl for baby-sitting while I worked. A week before Christmas I counted the money in the jar where I kept my tips that weren't immediately pressed into service for necessities. It was a pitiful amount. I called the boys for a conference.

I explained to the boys that we could either have our traditional Christmas dinner with turkey and all the trimmings and only a small token present for each of them, or they could each have a relatively nice present if they would settle for burritos and tacos and maybe a chocolate pie for Christmas dinner. To my surprise they opted for the turkey and trimmings. It was unanimous, too. Evidently the turkey and corn bread dressing and gravy, ambrosia and cranberry sauce and sweet potatoes and pecan pie was the most important thing to them about Christmas. Considering this, I suggested that maybe we should invite a couple of the boys from the orphanage in our neighbourhood to share our Christmas dinner. The children from the orphanage went to the same school as my boys and were friendly with them.

Joey, Mike and Andy greeted this proposal with enthusiasm and we all began to get the Christmas spirit. But it was Maria Hernandez, the Hispanic woman next door, who drew me into one of the most bizarre Christmas stories I've ever heard, much less borne witness to.

Maria was middle-aged and childless, warm, friendly, and devoutly Catholic. Her husband Russ was steady, mild mannered and highly thought of at the large bakery where he had worked for twenty years. Russ had a grown son by a previous marriage, but Maria's heartbreak was that she could not have a child of her own. So she borrowed mine from time to time, and I knew I could count on her to baby-sit for the odd times when Aunt Pearl couldn't. There was further excitement on the day I conferred with the boys about Christmas. That afternoon Maria came running over with a bundle in her arms and her face alive with joy.

A baby was wrapped in the bundle. A very new baby by the looks of the tiny red faced underneath the shock of straight, black hair.

"A boy," Maria breathed, proudly displaying the infant.

"Sweet," I said, assuming it was the child of one of her numerous relatives. "Whose is it?"

"Mine," she answered with a dazzling smile.

"Yours? Where did you get him?"

"God sent him to me."

I stared at her. Her countenance was indeed shining with a holy light.

"Maria ... "

"I know. You think I'm crazy. But I know God sent this baby to me. I prayed, you see, for many years, without fail. It was God who put the baby in Russ's car for him to find and bring home to me."

I began to hear alarm bells. Had Russ stolen the baby for his wife? But he wouldn't do such a thing.

"Maria ..." I began again.

"No, truly. That's just what happened. When Russ got off the night shift and went to his car this morning there was this precious baby in the front seat of his car."

"But, Maria, you can't just keep the baby," I blurted out. "He's been abandoned. You have to call the Children's Aid people ..."

"Oh, my God, no, never," she gasped, pulling the baby quickly back into the confines of her ample breasts. The infant whimpered and waved a tiny fist.

"There, you see?" Maria demanded as if the baby's whimper settled the argument. "Promise me you won't tell," she pleaded, her dark eyes filling with fear. "You must promise that you won't tell ... No, I won't hear it. Would you argue with God? God knew how much I wanted a baby and he has given me one. Will you argue with that?"

"Well, no," I answered slowly, thinking to hell with Children's Aid, what do they know of miracles? Maria's dazzling smile returned.

"Good. I need a few diapers. Can I have some of your Susan's? Russ is sleeping now but he will take me shopping tomorrow."

We plundered Susan's little chest of drawers for diapers, undershirts, gowns and blankets.

"Nursing bottles," I said as I put the clothing into a shopping sack. "And formula. Do you have formula?"

"Yes, yes. He came with two bottles and a can for formula. Isn't it miraculous? Tell me ... isn't it?"

I agreed that it was and put a couple of extra bottles into the sack. But I puzzled after Maria as she left. Who was the baby's mother? An acquaintance of Maria's perhaps? An unwed mother who knew about Maria, how warm and motherly she was, and how much she wanted a child? Or at least someone who had heard of Maria and Russ and thought they would make good parents? If this was a crime, it was a victimless crime. Oh, glory! Let's let our little lights shine. The following day I stopped by the orphanage on my way to work.

I was escorted into a large, cluttered office and offered a chair by a big boned, pleasant faced woman with iron grey hair. Her expression quickened and then softened as I bumbled through our invitation.

"You're very kind. We get several invitations like yours every year at Christmas time. But I'm afraid we must decline. We prefer to have our children all together on holidays. This is their home, you see. We're a family. Our children are not considered adoptable for one reason or another and most of them have been together for a long time. The other objection is that we don't like to play favorites. We don't like to see some of the children go out for special treats while the others are left behind. And we do try to give them all a nice Christmas. We have a very large tree, look for it as you go out the hallway ... that the children have decorated themselves and we plan to go caroling, and there will be plenty of turkey of course, and gifts. The service clubs are very good about gifts."

"I see," I said, pushing back an impulse to ask her if my kids and I could just spend Christmas with them instead of vice versa, being as how she had everything under such wondrous control. She thanked me for my interest and I went on to work wondering why

I felt so dejected. I decided it was because of the need to give. Mulling this over, I thought the need to give must be a far more common and powerful need than the need to take. Maybe that was one of the main reasons that being poor made people so miserable — it severely curtailed their opportunities to give.

The boys were also disappointed that there would be no guests at our table for Christmas. And the very next afternoon Maria came over without the baby, her eyes swollen with tears.

"They took him," she wailed, wiping her face with the edge of her apron. "They came and took him away."

"Who, Maria? Who took him?"

"The Children's Aid people."

"Oh, Maria, I'm so sorry. I didn't snitch, honest ..."

"I know," she moaned, wiping her face again. "It was my other neighbour. She came over and saw the baby and I told her about Russ finding him in his car, oh, what a fool I was, but I was so happy, I didn't know she would do such a thing, we had coffee together sometimes. I thought she was a nice lady ..."

Maria burst into loud, heartrendring sobs and I led her to the couch and tried to comfort her.

"If they can't find the mother maybe they'll let you and Russ be foster parents or something ..."

"No, it's impossible! Russ was in prison. Years ago. He tried to kill his stepfather for raping his sister. They won't let us be foster parents."

"I'm so sorry," I said, feeling really rotten at the way the miracle had turned out. "If I can do anything, tell me."

She made an effort to compose herself.

"No, nothing. I'll bring your baby clothes back tomorrow. I'm going home now. I want to rest."

"That's the best thing you can do," I said, patting her hand. She struggled to her feet and I walked her to the door. She turned.

"God is punishing me for something," she said matter-of-factly.

"No", I said. "That can't be."

"And why not?"

"Because..." I began and then hesitated, searching for an answer that would sound reasonable to Maria. She was a devout Catholic. Tell her that God couldn't be singling her out for punishment because I was having doubts there was a God? She would spit at me.

"Because you haven't done anything to be punished for," I said firmly.

"You don't know that either. In my dreams I do a lot of things."

"Maria, if God punishes dreams then we will all roast in hell."

"Maybe we already are," she answered, her voice weighted with unutterable sadness. "Goodbye."

She closed the door behind her and I went back to sorting the laundry. Was she right, I wondered. Were we actually in hell and part of the hellishness was not knowing that we were in hell? It wasn't a new thought. I'd read it somewhere. Part of eastern religious thinking. Maybe desire, after all, was the stuff that hell was made of — the desperate desire for what you can't have, or having something just within reach only to be snatched away. Just then I heard Baby Sue call out from her crib that nap time was over. When I went in she was standing on her head in the crib and I picked her up and her dark curls flopped across her forehead and her big dark eyes framed with long silken lashes gazed into mine and she gurgled her love and I buried my nose in her soft little neck and knew for sure, for absolutely sure, that I, at least, had four things I wanted and these were my children. And that was enough. For them I could endure whatever fate life could throw at me, but if the kids were okay, the rest could be hell, what did I care? But as it turned out, the rest wasn't exactly hell, either.

Aunt Pearl came to the toy rescue.

"Haven't you ever heard of the Salvation Army?" she asked when I told her we were having turkey instead of toys for Christmas. I stiffened.

"Charity?" I asked, wondering how she would have the audacity to even suggest such a thing.

"Not charity, you boob. I'm talking about the Salvation Army thrift store. They have lots of toys for sale cheap. We'll go in the morning before you go to work."

Aunt Pearl was right. As soon as we walked into the store my spirits lifted. There were bins and shelves and racks of used toys, all in pretty good shape and nothing priced over a quarter.

That was the beginning of my life-long love affair with the Salvation Army and Goodwill thrift stores. I became a recycler back when recycling wasn't cool. From necessity, of course. I took home a bright red scooter for Andy, cap pistols complete with studded holsters for Mike, a great looking football for Joey and six pairs of only slightly used jeans, two each for the boys, two baseballs and two bats, three gloves and a push toy for Baby Sue that played Pop Goes the Weasel.

"Why haven't I heard of this place before?" I asked as Aunt Pearl and I left the store loaded with purchases.

"You have. I tried to tell you about it before, but you were too busy trying to rise above it to listen."

I glanced at her. Aunt Pearl was a funny lady. All the Shivers were funny. Not funny ha-ha, but funny peculiar. Ill educated, if not downright ignorant, most of them fancied themselves to be philosophers. They were always trying to find the meaning of life. It was some kind of disease. I suspected I had inherited it, but I didn't want it. If one is a professor of philosophy at some university, or a learned psychologist, or a theologian or scientist, then there might be some advantage to being born with an innate desire to unravel the mysteries of the universe, an asset if you will, but, if you are a poor single mother, then trying to muck about in these muddy waters was only another burden, one I didn't hanker for. But my spirits were definitely lifting. That evening my brother Ray Allen called and said he and his new wife would be dropping in on Christmas Day with some presents for the children and they accepted my invitation to have dinner with us. And a big box arrived from Louisiana from my parents. But it was the following day that the real happies hit me.

I worked the breakfast and lunch shift that day so was home early in the afternoon. I had just put a load of laundry in the washing machine when there was a banging on the back door. I hurried to open it before the banging woke the baby. It was Maria. And she was carrying a bundle in her arms again and from the looks of the shock of straight black hair, it was the abandoned infant again. I opened the door and Maria stepped inside, reeling with joy. I stared, astonished.

"Maria ... is that the same baby?

She hugged the bundle close, her eyes glazed with happiness.

"Yes. The same. My own little one."

"Your own ... you are his foster mother now?"

"No. His real mother. I had to come and tell you."

"But how ... when ..."

"A half an hour ago. They brought him back."

"So the Children's Aid decided it didn't matter about Russ's criminal record?"

"It doesn't matter if they mind or not because Russ is the father. He went down to the Children's Aid and told them it was his baby and they investigated and that's what they found out. The mother already has three other children and can't keep this one. The Children's Aid was very angry with Russ for trying to pretend that somebody he didn't know just put the baby in his car, and he tried to explain that he only wanted to keep from hurting me, because I didn't know about this other woman who is the mother. But she signed the papers naming Russ as the father and giving the baby to him and to me. And my son has come back to me." She paused, gazing adoringly down at the infant in her arms.

"And you're not ... angry at Russ?" I queried.

"For what? For making me a baby? He should have done it a long time ago. I told him to go back and make me two more."

There was a small silence and then suddenly, as if on cue, Maria and I burst into explosive laughter. It was too bizarre. We couldn't stop laughing. We woke Maria's sleeping infant and then Baby Sue woke from her nap, too, and we laughed some more, all through Christmas, in fact. So as far as last minute reprieves from threatened rotten Christmases go, this one was outstanding.

But it has started to rain in earnest on the A-frame. The fire is dying out and a chill is seeping through the cabin. I blow out the candle and snuggle down for the night. But I still can't sleep, my mind has worked itself into a feverish state, still dredging up the past Christmases until it gets stuck on the one we celebrated in transit between leaving the land of our birth and immigrating to Canada. Ah, Canada. How I love you. It is within you we found safety from an insane war, it is within your borders that we stumbled across this rare and wild and wonderful place called the Clayoquot Sound. But it wasn't an easy transition.

NINE

When my son Joey graduated from the Air Force communications school he was shipped out, not to Vietnam, but to Italy. I was delirious with relief. But that didn't stop my anti-war activities. Nor John's. Other people's sons were still dying in that unhappy place, and the civilian population of Vietnam was being devastated. As I grew heavier with child the war intensified and I began to ponder why it was that parents were expected to care mightily for their sons, to kiss small scraped knees and elbows to make them well, to worry over enough milk and vegetables in their diets, to caution against too blatant a disregard for falling out of trees, riding bikes in the street, and challenging someone bigger and stronger to settle an argument with fists. And yet, at the magic age of eighteen, parents were supposed to willingly, if not happily, turn these same sons who had been so carefully nurtured to young adulthood over to the military to be sent to the ends of the earth to kill strangers and have strangers kill them. It was all very demoralizing, when one thought about it.

Because the state, or the government, seemed to me to take damned little responsibility for the rearing of children, except for providing a public school system. When I was a single parent I never applied for welfare, or mother's allowance, because even if I had been so inclined we couldn't have lived on the amount given to single mothers with children. The money I made as a waitress did manage to keep us afloat. I knew women who had resorted to prostitution because they had nothing in the house for their children to eat by the end of the month. In fact, I had been approached by pimps myself with stories of how much money was to be made in the trade and why was I working myself to the bone when I could have a much better, easier life. It seemed to me as I thought about it, that society considered women as unpaid raisers of children, and poor women, as prostitutes as well. Society not only turned a blind eye to the needs of children, in its general neglect the state actually became the enemy, withholding resources and exposing children to poverty, disease and degradation. And even if there were no war on, when a son or daughter finished school and went into the work force, the state claimed both sexes for economic purposes. Who is it that collects taxes from the children of the poor, who is it that makes tremendous profits from their labour? It certainly isn't the parents who have worked and worried and sacrificed all their lives to keep the kids fed, clothed, healthy and decent.

So I began to see that poor and working-class women not only produced goods and services for the economy for a mere pittance, they reproduced the work force itself for free. Great balls of fire! I was beginning to see the light. I joined a group of people who were refusing to pay their income tax on the grounds that the money was being used to feed the war in Vietnam.

I was summoned to jury duty. I refused to serve on the grounds that the world's respect for law and order was being severely undermined by the United States' conduct of an illegal, immoral war. I wrote a letter to the head of the local draft board asking him to search his conscience for his part in perpetuating the war. John also wrote letters, went on marches, and proselytized among his colleagues at work. And then one day his immediate supervisor called him in for a little confidential chat about his anti-war activities.

John was made to understand that enough was enough and that, if he persisted in his anti-war attitudes and activities, his security clearance might be revoked.

So one can't go around biting the hand that feeds one. Unless one is ready to take the consequences. Was I ready? Yes. Except for the fact that my baby was due in a couple of months. But I was beginning to hate my beautiful house and property, having seen it for the bribe that it was. If we would just shut up about the war, we could enjoy all the goodies we had, the space, the light and air, the natural environment, the boats, the gracious, roomy old house. The only hitch was that I might be asked to pay for it with my son's blood, for while Joey was temporarily safe, Mike wasn't. He entered college at seventeen but registered for the draft when he turned eighteen. He was attending the College of William and Mary and living at home, but there was so much confusion in our household, mirroring the turmoil of the society in general about the war that Mike began to loose interest in his studies and spent most of his time painting and making sculptures or wandering in the woods. I began to think about leaving the United States and immigrating to Canada. John was thinking about it, too. We made inquires, but it was impossible to do anything definite until after the baby came. Barbara Ellen finally put in her appearance on April 20, 1966. And I was so involved with the Fullbright Hearings on TV I almost didn't get to the hospital in time.

The Fullbright Hearings were congressional hearings, initiated by Senator Fullbright. He was just about the only U.S. senator who voted to cut off the military funds for the war. I had the greatest respect for him. He was insisting that the other congressmen take a hard look at what was happening in Vietnam and how it all began. This was enormously interesting to me. The hearings were televised for several weeks. I would stagger up in the mornings, get everybody off to school and work, and then stick my head in the TV set. On April the twentieth I advised John to stay home as the contractions I had been suffering for about a week had become particularly intense. He agreed and after the others left, took the little ones out in the yard. I settled down, as usual, to the Fullbright hearings. I was listening to a particularly pertinent point that Senator Fullbright was making when I became vaguely conscious that the contractions were entering a new, more meaningful phase. Still, I tarried. I hated going to the hospital too soon. And Fullbright seemed to be making some progress here. It wasn't until a contraction made me gasp with pain that I decided it was time. Just as I eased my bulk up off the couch my water broke. I called John. He quickly drove to the high school to bring Andy home to watch the little ones and then we were off to the Williamsburg Hospital. We made a brief stop by the doctor's office for an examination.

"My God," the doctor said. "You waited long enough. I'll follow you to the hospital in my car and John, if the baby's head crowns, stop, and I'll deliver it in the car."

We made it to the hospital, just in time for a quick shot before rushing into the delivery room. I hated those shots. I like to know what's going on and the shots always made me fuzzy. And I was definitely fuzzy by the time I got into the delivery room and hooked up to all the paraphernalia that the new monitoring systems demanded. When I saw the screen up above the foot of my bed I thought it was a TV screen with a lot of snow.

"You're on the wrong channel," I said in my fuzzied state. "Turn it, please. I'd like to watch the Fullbright hearings."

"You're not going to get any Fullbright hearings on that," the doctor answered curtly. "That's your blood pressure and pulse rate. One more push now ... good. One more. One more. And here's your baby. A little girl."

The other little girls will be happy, I thought as I inspected my new daughter. They wanted another sister. And she was darling. On the petite side, but chubby cheeked with a mass of dark hair, healthy and well formed like the others.

"You make beautiful babies," the doctor said to John when he was allowed in. John grinned in relief that the birth was over and successful.

"I had something to do with it," I reminded them.

"Naw. It's the father who gives the good looks," the doctor said, but he was kidding, and I was just glad that it was over, too, and that my baby was fine. I had worried so much during this pregnancy it was a wonder my new daughter didn't have two heads.

A couple of days later the kids welcomed us home and crowded around to inspect the newest addition. It took a couple of months to settle into a routine, but John and I were making definite plans to leave the country. I was being threatened by the CIA. They were threatening to arrest me and put me in jail for refusing to pay my income taxes.

I guess the government was really worried about a tax revolt spreading or they wouldn't have wasted so much precious time on me. The amount of money I owed didn't amount to a hill of beans. In the beginning the officers who came out were polite. Sort of. They came in pairs, dressed in suits even in the warm weather, and explained to me why I should reconsider and pay the income tax. I explained to them that I wasn't trying to withhold the taxes, as they weren't enough to quarrel over anyhow, but was perfectly willing to pay them into a fund that would be guaranteed not to go toward the war in Vietnam.

It was some sort of head game. The men would come, at first every other week, and then every week, and they would say the same things over and over, and then they abruptly changed tactics. Their politeness turned to studied harassment. They could seize the boats, they said. I answered no, they couldn't, because the boats were registered in my husband's name, along with the cars and the house. I had changed everything over to his name before I started my protest. Very well, they said. In that case, I would probably have to go to jail.

Well, now. My baby was only a couple of months old and I was nursing her. Would Barbara Ellen have to go to jail, too? And who would take care of all the other children? I called a lawyer. And I called some more lawyers. Finally, I was just going down the list of lawyers in the phone book, trying to find somebody, anybody, who would take me as a client. The words of explanation were hardly out of mouth before I was told, and sometimes less than politely, that my business wasn't wanted. I knew lawyers were a conservative bunch, but this was ridiculous. Finally, a woman in one of the protest groups who lived in another part of the state gave me the name of a black lawyer.

"Just keep nursing that baby," the lawyer said. "I don't think they will arrest you, at least as long as you have a nursing baby. Think how that would look. Mother of seven with a nursing baby thrown into jail and separated from her children because of her opposition to the war in Vietnam. Even the most hardened war hawk might give pause to that scenario."

He was right. The harassing visits continued in the weeks and months that followed, but as it turned out, there weren't that many weeks and months left for us to agitate the government, at least from inside the States. In early November Mike was called to report for his physical. One night, as we sat around the living room discussing how we could move the entire family to a foreign country,

Rose Mary, who was only five, suddenly burst into tears. Everyone looked at her to see what the matter was.

"I wish somebody would drop a bomb on the whole war," she blurted through her tears. I took her on my lap and tried to comfort her.

"That's what we're going to do, honey," I said. "Sort of. Because we're going to move to another country where the government isn't fighting a war in Vietnam or anywhere else."

And that's what we did.

But that was twenty-five years or so ago and immediately after our arrival all of our lives took unexpected twists and turns, a lot of them painful, but that's another story.

I have what I always dreamed of for my old age, a cabin in the woods, looking out over a cove, and the time to live a contemplative life. I have come to the wilderness of the Clayoquot Sound to retire, and except for the disquiet I feel about the clear-cut mountains behind us, I am enormously satisfied with my present life. Our homestead Christmas over, Marian and I are preparing for our trip to Louisiana when the Sound blesses our departure with a going away storm.

This is a whopper. Marian is a little agitated but the storms no longer unduly alarm me. I know their essence now. It is the outrageous, bellicose voice of nature stirring up the elements, cutting loose the dead wood, and infusing great gulps of needed oxygen into the natural world. But the following morning when Marian and I go for our beachcombing walk what we find is catastrophe.

There has been a landslide. A humongous landslide. All three streams are muddy, the cove itself is muddy as far out as I can see, and there are tons of mud and rock and tree branches just sitting on the beach, blocking off one of the streams entirely and smothering the shell fish on the beach underneath the slide. I have heard of the landslides around our cove but this is the first time I've seen one like this. The slides are caused by clear-cutting. The top soil is damaged by clear-cutting and as the top soil washes away, nothing grows back on the steep mountains and the rain becomes rivers washing deep gorges into the earth that in turn become mudslides. Marian and I walk around the tons of mud and rock, dumb in our disbelief. And then I feel that slow, hot anger begin to build inside my gut, the one that tells me I might do something foolish if I am not careful. This injury to the earth is so monstrous that I know the people who are responsible cannot be civilized. As we walk back to the cabin my heart is pounding and my brain whirling. These mountains have been raped and left to die. And there was no order in their destruction, no care, no intention to heal afterward, no respect, no conscience. There is nothing here but contempt, contempt for the earth, contempt for life. We leave early the next morning for Tofino, on our way off Vancouver Island. I make one stop in Tofino — at the government fisheries office.

The officer I speak to says that landslides are natural occurrences. I answer that the occurrences probably get more frequent and less natural in direct proportion to how badly the mountains are stripped. He is not interested. He says whatever, there is nothing he can do about it.

Marian and I go on with our trip, but when we return in the spring, we stop in the office of The Friends of the Clayoquot Sound and give a donation. There is going to be a blockade this summer. I'm not ready to stand up on a blockade and get arrested. I have come to The Clayoquot to retire and damnit, I intend to do that. I've earned that. I deserve that. Anybody who has raised eight kids deserves that. The young people can carry this show. Besides, there's this other thing ... I don't like to raise my hand against working people, even when I think they're wrong. I've cheered for the working class all my life, being in it myself most of the time. Loggers need jobs. John is a college professor in northern Ontario but he bought a little house in Ucluelet a couple of years ago where family members could hang out en route to Cypress Bay or for longer stays if needed. Ucluelet is a logger's village, more or less, located twenty miles of lovely windswept beaches from Tofino, the jumping off spot for our end of the Clayoquot Sound. Barbara Ellen, now the mother of a rambunctious small son, has opened a little ballet school in Ucluelet, and Margaret Elizabeth and her husband have come to stay. They all live in the house and I hang out in Ucluelet myself when I'm not at Cypress Bay. It's a folksy, friendly town, a bit rednecked, but nobody can touch the south in the redneck department. By the end of summer, I hear that a number of people have been arrested on the blockades. But at this point I am still trying to keep from getting sucked into the mess.

This year Marian and I are leaving early to go south. Marian has worked in Tofino for the summer and wants one last travel fling before returning to college. Mama and her younger sister Gladys have moved from Baton Rouge, Louisiana to Vicksburg, Mississippi.

Marian and I make stops in Lucadia, California to visit Joey and his partner Janice Lee, who live and work there; in Phoenix, Arizona to visit my brother Ray Allen and his wife Carol, and from there to Vicksburg. All this by Greyhound Bus. This is what we can afford. Anyway, I don't fly. We will wing by Toronto on our return swing and catch Andy, his wife Angie and son Aaron and Rose Mary and Susan and their families. I leave with a relatively light heart.

I feel sure that the NDP government will not allow clear-cut logging to resume in the Clayoquot Sound. As the new provincial government they are studying the situation and will surely realize that the Clayoquot Sound is one of the last viable rainforests in the world and that its value is above price. Also, The Friends of the Clayoquot Sound are bringing a lot of attention to the situation and there is a good chance the native people will press forward with their land claims and get an injunction to stop any new logging in The Clayoquot, at least until their land claims are settled. I feel confident that one of these possibilities will work out.

But none of them do. We receive a newsletter from The Friends of the Clayoquot Sound while we are in Mississippi informing us that logging in the Sound will resume forthwith. Marian is now co-owner of the property in Cypress Bay. Mike surrended to the wanderlust a year and a half ago, having completed the A-frame, The Raven Lady, the boat, and surprisingly, a book of poetry, and it has swept him in a northerly direction to the cold country. Marian borrowed the money to buy out his interest in Cypress Bay so what is happening there now has more than a passing interest for her.

"Oh, hell, I guess I'll go stand on the blockade and get arrested and go to jail," she offers after we've read the newsletter.

"Uhmm. Maybe I should go," I answer, thinking about it. "I'm a little old lady. They'll have to treat me nicer than they'd treat you."

"Maybe. But from what I understand, Mom, nobody really has to go to jail, just maybe for an hour or so. I mean people just sign this piece of paper, I think it's called an undertaking, and then you're free to go until your trial comes up."

"I know, but there might be some sort of criminal record involved. That could work against you in the future. Who cares if I have a criminal record?"

So go our speculations. Marian returns early to her job in Tofino but I continue east to spend a month with Rose Mary before the birth of her new baby and for a month afterward. Spencer, Rose Mary's eight-year-old son, is a big help to the household but I still don't get home until June. By the time I spend a few days in Victoria it is well into the first week of July when I arrive at the house in Ucluelet.

I am unpacking my travelling clothes and getting gear together to take out to Cypress Bay the following day when I turn on the TV to hear the evening news. What was new was the beginning of the summer's blockades in Clayoquot Sound.

I pause in my sorting and packing and watch the TV images. There are maybe a dozen people with their arms locked together standing in a line across the Kennedy River bridge in the Clayoquot Sound. One of the blockaders in Sven Robinson, an member of parliament from British Columbia. Damn. I had hoped not to get involved in this until I had a chance to do some repairs to the A-frame at Cypress Bay. But maybe it will be better to go ahead and get this over with first. I call the office of The Friends of the Clayoquot Sound and am advised of a meeting that evening at the Black Hole, a section of the forest that has been clear-cut and slash-burned and looks like Hiroshima after the bomb. Chris Lowther and Wayne Ross, a young couple with a jeep, pick me up and take me to the meeting. By the time I get home that night my mind is more or less made up. But I don't sleep much. I am treading in cold, swampy waters, I want to make sure I know what I'm doing. Because I have decided that once arrested, I will not sign the under-taking that will make me promise not to go back to the protest site. The Clayoquot Sound is crown land. Crown land, other than what the First Nations people claim, belongs to the people of British Columbia, to the people of Canada. I will be standing on my own property when I step up on that bridge in the morning, because every society, every tribe, every nation, every state, has the moral right to try to protect their property from a murdering, marauding invader. The Clayoquot Sound does not belong to MacMillan-Bloedel to finish raping and pillaging, to continue destroying the land with clear-cutting which pollutes the salmon streams and causes landslides that kill the shellfish and forest animals. And, if the gov-ernment of this province has given over our property in some legal hocus-pocus to these environmental monsters, then they shouldn't have. And they have, in effect, stolen one of the last re-maining rainforests in the world from the people of this country and are in the process of shipping it to Japan and the United States and Europe, and a lot of it goes simply for pulp and newsprint and toilet paper, magnificent old trees, hundreds, even thousands of years old, sacrificed for this. I feel the same refusal to comply that had slowly built up in my heart toward the government of the United States over the wanton brutality of the Vietnam War, and that had touched me briefly over the union ruckus way back then, and the insistence of the church that I knew back in Louisiana, of its pastor and members, that wrong was right, and that I must recognize and obey the wrong, because the wrong was the law, the majority and the will of God. That same hot anger washes over me again, bathing my innards and bitter-spicing my blood because I have witnessed the landslides, more than once now, I have lived with the body of the raped and beaten victim who tries to rise up behind the cove in the dry season but who is beaten back down under the torrents of rain in the winter, the outer skin of the mountain range so ripped away that she bleeds all winter long in the form of collapsed logging roads, crevices carved down to the bone by the rivers of gushing rain that grow deeper every passing year and the final falling away, the landslides that are the visible testament that the mountains are dissolving and melting into the sea.

Yes, I have seen it, lived with it, and, if this unconscionable destruction of life is legal, then it shouldn't be. So I won't sign the undertaking. I will have to interrupt my retirement. For I have come to the conclusion that while all the battlefields I've mucked about in have seemed to be different quarrels and that while in many ways Canada is more progressive than the United States, she, too, suffers from the same malady, and that is the unequal distribution of wealth in both countries and an unequal distribution of power.

I protest this disparity. And I reserve the right to try to redress this imbalance in any way that I can. I will break the so-called law, which in this case is simply a court-ordered injunction, and I will pay the price. I harbour only one hesitation. All my life I've suffered from a mild form of claustrophobia. Will I be able to tolerate being locked up in a cramped space behind bars for any length of time without going mad? I shall soon find out. I will be on the blockade in the morning.

TEN

Early the next morning I ride out to the Kennedy River bridge with Wayne, the same young man who took me to the meeting the evening before. The Kennedy River bridge will also be the scene of this morning's planned blockade. I have confided in Wayne that I plan to take part in the blockade and he seems to be somewhat nervous about this, concerned that I may have just gotten carried away by the excitement. He clearly does not want to be responsible for encouraging a little old lady to get arrested. I assure him that this isn't the case and that I was thinking about civil disobedience before he was born. Still, I'm not as confident as I sound, as I have never actually been arrested before. In fact, I feel like there is a spooked alligator stomping around inside my stomach, taking great bites here and there as he traipses about.

Wayne and I mingle with the thirty or so people who are milling about. Some are making coffee over an open fire and talking in hushed voices. I'm too nervous for the coffee. As the time for the first MacMillan-Bloedel logging truck to appear gets nearer, those of us who are going to put our bodies on the line that morning are asked to make the line across the bridge. There are twelve of us. An eagle circles overhead. The morning mist is beginning to lift. The mist is beautiful as it rises above the river and over the trees but I can't concentrate on the scenery as the alligator inside my stomach has gone berserk and I think I might be sick. But then people start singing and it is revival time again. I don't know the words to these songs, but they are compelling and repetitive, like gospel songs, and soon I am belting out with the rest, enjoying the solidarity, the unity of purpose with these people of all different ages and backgrounds whom I hardly know.

The logging truck arrives, but is turned back amid cheers. Shortly after, the RCMP arrive. We are arrested. At the Ucluelet jail confusion reigns. A couple of people sign an undertaking that allows them to go free until trial. We could all sign the same undertaking, but the rest of us think we will make more of a statement by staying in jail. We are obliged by the RCMP officers.

The ten of us who are left are all driven to the Nanaimo Correction Centre. We arrive late but are fed fresh fish and vegetables and then taken to our new quarters.

This is a men's prison and we four women are given the same packs of toothbrushes, toothpaste, razors, and soap the men are when we check into the plain but spacious enough building behind the high steel mesh fence topped with rows of tangled barb wire. We are also issued the same men's green pants and shirts. We are in protective custody. We will stay here until we have been sentenced, the men assigned to one side of the building, the women the other. There are two phones in the building and high on hysteria, we take turns informing loved ones of our whereabouts. I call John first, and then Margaret Elizabeth and her husband Andre. As I am talking to Margaret Elizabeth she hears the commotion in the background and when questioned, I find myself giggling. Margaret becomes exasperated.

"Mom, we've been so worried about you," she blurts out in an irritated voice. "And you're just ... you're just ... you're just having a good time!"

Well, not exactly. Two of the other women protestors are grandmothers like me, and because there are no nightgowns for females we sleep in the men's shirts and pants that have been issued to us.

Very uncomfortable business this. The men's pants are cut too narrow through the hips and crotch. I toss and turn, unable to sleep from information overload and the binding clothes. We can't just sleep naked as a flashlight is shown through our door windows every hour, so I lie awake, thinking. I should have called Wally, I decide. It would have been a little courtesy of sorts. Strange, how his opinion at one time was my guide line for everything, including breathing. How important his opinion was! I think of it now and marvel. And yet it was Wally who indirectly and inadvertently, led me to this place ...

John and I, with six kids in tow, arrived at the Canadian border November twenty-third, 1966. Joey, my oldest son, was serving a tour of duty in Italy, compliments of The United States Air Force. By the time the rest of us got through immigration and over the border I think we could all have benefited from a couple of week's stay, at least, in a psychiatric hospital. The kids were all trying desperately to understand this sudden turn of events and John and I were cruising on black coffee and nerves.

John and I didn't fully understand what we were doing, either. All we knew was that we were madder than hell at the U.S. government and wanted to punish the United States by removing our precious selves from her contaminated soil and become something else, something different, something better. But the price turned out to be very high. Had I known how high I might have considered turning around and heading back to Virginia. And yet even had I known I don't think I would actually have chosen to turn back. You don't get through troubled waters by standing on the shore, one might as well wade right in and stir up the mess some more and see what happens. And that's what we did.

From Fort Erie, Ontario, where we were accepted as landed immigrants, we headed straight for Toronto. Even though we had temporarily lost one member of the family and now numbered only eight, John and I were aware we might have some difficulty finding immediate accommodations in the city. But the very first evening of our arrival we lucked upon a three bedroom and den apartment in Scarborough. It was in a high rise, on the top floor.

From the freedom of eighty acres to roam around in just by stepping out the back door, now the children couldn't even reach dirt without going down a dozen flights in an elevator. And when they got there it wasn't dirt, but pavement. And my God, we all had to be quiet! There were neighbours, not eighty acres away, but eighty inches away. John started looking for a job somewhere, anywhere, where there would be some room to spread out. And the first response he got was from a college in Kirkland Lake, Ontario. They needed a math and physics professor. So shortly after Christmas we all mushed north.

I don't know what I was expecting from the town of Kirkland Lake. At least a lake, I think. But Kirkland Lake was an old gold mining town and the lake, if there ever was one, was now a sinkhole of old pilings. The sign that welcomed us to the town limits read Welcome to Kirkland Lake, Hub of the North only some joker had crossed out the H of the word Hub in black paint and written a huge P over top so that the sign actually read Welcome to Kirkland Lake, Pub of the North. I didn't like the ring of that for truth is often spoken in jest as someone obviously noted long ago. It was midnight by the time we found our destination. The faculty housing consisted of a long row of two-storey townhouses and, when we pulled up in front of the one assigned to our family, I was immediately struck by the height of the piles of shovelled snow that lined the walkway to the apartment. But it was still snowing and the wet flakes on my eyelashes were probably blurring my vision, I thought, numb as I was, with fatigue.

Strange. So strange. And so horribly cold. The swirling wind cut to the bone. We hustled the little ones inside to the warmth, but an ominous disquiet was settling over my southern soul. There had been snow in Toronto, and cold, and I hadn't liked that, but this was much worse. This was serious cold. This was a Mother Nature I didn't know, forewarning me now, of a cruel and unforgiving kind of natural world I had never experienced. Why, even the blazing deserts of Arizona were not totally unrelenting, an animal, or a human being, lost there, even in the driest, most scorched areas could expect to find some moisture in the cacti, some mercy in the cool evening desert breezes. But the frenzied frozen wind cutting through my woollen jacket as I hurried the little ones inside knew nothing, I could tell, of mercy. Still I didn't realize how cold it actually was until the following morning.

I quietly straggled out of bed at eight o'clock, dressed, and went downstairs. The others, worn out from the long haul of the day before were still sleeping, even the baby who usually activated at six-thirty sharp. The apartment was littered with boxes and odds and ends of furniture, mute testimony to the day's work ahead. After a bit of puttering, I found the box with the coffee pot and breakfast things. Leaving the coffee to perk on the stove I wandered into the living room and hesitantly poked a finger through the blinds to see what I could see. What I saw was astonishing to me.

The pathway to the townhouse was no longer visible and the mounds of shovelled snow were almost as high as the apartment building. My God, were we at the North Pole? And then, as I stared at the winter wonderland outside, the school children began to drift into the street.

At least I surmised that the stuffed-and-wrapped-to-the-eye-balls, roly-poly figures walking and sliding and even skating down the street were school children, for I was hard put to know for a certainty what they were or where they were going or even how they could see where they were going through the mounds of scarves and masks and mufflers. But going they were. Trying to stifle a strong surge of panic, I went back to the kitchen and turned on the radio. Exactly how cold was it?

It was forty below, that's how cold. That's what the radio announcer said. I couldn't believe it. It couldn't possibly be that cold. I had never heard of any place being that cold except maybe the north and south poles. Panic spilled over into the kitchen. I raced to the back door, flung the door open wide and stepped out on the back porch. I took one deep breath and almost fainted. My southern lungs were not prepared for such a blast of icy air, there was nothing in their evolution that could possibly have prepared them for such cold. There was an immediate searing pain in my chest and both lungs threatened to collapse on the spot. I staggered back inside and slammed the door shut. Leaning against the door jamb for support, it took a few minutes to convince my lungs to start functioning again. Had the hair in my nose actually crackled and froze? Oh, my God! What had we done?

At least the apartment was warm. Trying to hide my dismay, I had oatmeal and toast and jam and hot chocolate ready by the time the others straggled downstairs. But that very first day I could tell that John was not depressed by the cold and snow as I was, he was in fact, somewhat exhilarated by it.

It was his Norwegian ancestry, he explained, when I later voiced my own worries about surviving such a climate. While my ancestors were from northern Germany on my father's side, this dubious northernness was evidently counterbalanced by my mother's Cajun French ancestry, he went on. I would have to acclimatize. So I set about to overcome my distaste for the snow and the cold. I told myself that with such a large family I would be too busy anyway, to set around and brood over the climate. The kids all had to be enrolled in school. There was only one high school but there were two elementary schools, one French and one English.

It seemed to me that we might as well take advantage of this situation and send the girls to the French-speaking school. It would be a good thing for them to become bilingual, after all, there were two official languages in Canada. And then I was told that the French-speaking schools were also religious schools. The children would be given regular Catholic instruction. This struck me as outrageous. We were led to believe at the point of immigration that one had a choice about French or English schools, when, in fact, there wasn't really a choice. We were not only not Catholic, we were not religious at all, although we considered ourselves Unitarian. The nice thing about being a Unitarian is that you can be an atheist and still be a Unitarian. So it seemed to me that the Catholic Church owned the French-language schools in Ontario, and wasn't that somehow unconstitutional?

As I inquired into this odd state of affairs, I found an even odder one, at least to me. Canada didn't exactly have a constitution. It had something, sort of, but whatever it was it was in the Queen's care in England and didn't even reside in Canada. Pierre Trudeau was instrumental in fixing this glaring discrepancy later, but back in 1966 there was no clear separation of church and state in Canada the way it is laid out in the American constitution. So after enrolling Andy in the local high school and leaving him to the unfamiliar terrain and the cruelties of teenage cliques, I walked the girls down to King George School, the English-speaking school. And before registration was over, I learned that here, too, the girls would have two periods of religious education a week along with all the other children in school.

"Wait a minute, I don't really understand this," I protested in the principal's office. "This is a public school, isn't it?"

"Yes," the principal answered calmly. Grey-haired and well on the other side of middle age, I understood that he had been the principal there forever.

"Then how can you give religious instruction?"

He blinked at me.

"I don't understand your question," he said.

"Well, I don't like my kids being taught something that I don't believe is true," I blurted. "For instance, the theory of evolution is just that, a theory, and that's the way it's taught even though its based on observable phenomenon, while Christian dogma is only a belief, and not based on anything but a belief and yet you're telling me that this is what is taught here in this school as fact. I strongly object to that. And I know that this isn't done in Toronto."

"Well, that's the way it's done here. We're a long way from Toronto. I'm sorry you're displeased, but you can always have the teachers allow your children to leave the room during the religious instruction periods."

"Do any of the other children leave the room?"

"Not at the moment, no. It has been done, though."

I left, horrendously disturbed. My God, had we jumped out of the frying pan into the fire? But I had an even more immediate problem than religious instruction in the public schools. I was having trouble remaining upright in my boots. They were leather and I had worn them for years, which was the problem. They had become somewhat slick-bottomed from wear, and even when new had not held the foggiest notion of packed snow and long, slick stretches of solid ice. I cut through the school yard and headed toward the town center. If I hurried I had time to buy a pair of boots worthy of the name before Mike, who was at home babysitting Barbara, had to leave for a job interview.

As I crossed the street that led to the main shopping centre I vaguely noticed a tall, bareheaded young man wearing horn-rimmed glasses and a dark overcoat crossing just behind me. When I stepped up on the curb my slippery boots gave way and after much flailing of arms, I landed on my back. The young man stopped and assisted me to my feet. Close up I saw he wasn't a kid, he was in his late twenties or early thirties. Not that I cared. At least not then. I thanked him, rattled and embarrassed. He acknowledged my thanks politely, and as he turned to go was greeted by another man passing by and the two stopped to chat.

I hurried on down the street, looking wildly from right to left, trying to spot a shoe store. I knew I could go down again at any moment. Every step I took now was a half slide and I could feel myself lurching about like a Cajun Saturday night drunk. When I glanced briefly behind me, I spotted the same young man who had officiated at my fall, and he was gaining ground one me! Oh, he strode so purposely, so confidently in his thick soled fur bound boots! How I envied him. But please Merciful Goddess of the Winter Snows, I prayed, forgive all the bad things I've said about you so far and just don't let me fall again before I can find a shoe store, not in front of this same man. I'll just mosey over to this furniture store and look in the window and wait until he passes ... slip, slide, wham! I'm on my back again. And of course, here is Sir Galahad, Johnny-on-the-spot with his sturdy boots and horn-rimmed glasses. I am once again assisted to my feet. This time I catch a glimpse of large, intense blue eyes behind the glasses before I turn away, mortified.

"Are you all right?" he asked.

"I'm perfectly fine. Thank you."

He hesitated as if to say something else but thought better of it and went on his way. I was walking safely behind him this time when I'll be damned if he didn't meet another friend, a portly woman this time, and pause for an exchange of words. Which meant that if I continued down the street he would probably wind up behind me again and oh, horror of horrors, have to pick me up a third time. This was just too nutty! But I had to get on with my errand. Mike would miss his appointment if I dallied too long. And the sidewalk up ahead looked as though it had been sanded. I barged forward with an unsteady sail and in the middle of the next block I saw the sign. A shoe store up ahead! But alas, now I suddenly found myself in an unsanded stretch of sidewalk. Fearfully, I looked behind me. Sir Galahad was indeed gaining ground!

Not a third time, I begged the Nordic Goddess, no, please, this is a small town, this man whoever he is obviously knows people, I will get a reputation for being crazy before I even have a chance to show my good side, whatever that may be, but my feet were doing weird things again.

I went into a slide, a wildly spiralling slide but sheer determination kept me upright and I made an abrupt left turn and slid right into the glass door of the shoe store with a loud thump that almost knocked me flat. But I saved the situation by a desperate grab for the door handle. I paused to collect myself and noticed the woman at the desk inside staring at me curiously through the glass door. Had she seen my embarrassing slide? Probably. No matter. I was the victor here. I had not gone down for the third time. Gathering my composure, I opened the door and stepped inside. I left that store in a pair of boots so warm they could have melted a rattlesnake on the rise, and so sturdy they could have been used as icebreakers in the Arctic seas. I fairly scooted home and just in time for Mike to make his appointment.

I don't remember where I thought Mike was going for an interview, but when he got home I was shocked to learn that he would now be working in a gold mine.

"You're what?" I demanded.

"Going to work in a mine, Mother. It will be an adventure."

"Adventure, my foot. Men get killed in those mines. Is that what we came here for? For you to get killed in a mine?"

"Mother ..."

"We'll talk to Dad when he gets home."

John didn't like the idea, either. Mike stubbornly persisted and went off to work the next day in the mine. He went there for three and a half weeks until his working partner was hospitalized. The partner was hit by falling debris and Mike took another look at the mining business. He came home that day quite subdued.

"Mother, I've been thinking."

"Yes?" I asked, handing him the baby so I could stir the soup pot.

"We're all kind of stuffed into this apartment "

"And you want one of your own."

"No. I'd like to go travelling."

"Where?"

"Out west. See something of Canada."

"Good idea. Stay out of the mines."

"Good idea."

A couple of weeks after Mike left there was a party. A faculty party. It was held in the college club house. I met some of the other faculty wives that didn't live in the same long row of townhouses we did and John introduced me to some of his colleagues. When he brought over the tall young man with horn-rimmed glasses fronting intense blue eyes, I immediately recognized Sir Galahad. I saw the flicker of recognition in his face, too, but he gave no indication that he had ever laid eyes on me before. I didn't bring the matter up, either, and, after chatting briefly, he went to greet some people just coming in. Sir Galahad turned out to be Wally Krawczyk, head of the math and physics department at the college. And John's immediate boss. On the way home I remarked to John that Wally seemed very young to be a department head.

"He is, he's only twenty-eight. He was just in the right place at the right time. Not that he isn't a sharp fellow, he is. Likable, too. And at least knows something about the political situation in the States. Maybe we'll have him over for dinner one evening."

There weren't many people that John wanted to ask for dinner, ever, I usually had to do all the inviting, so I knew Wally had made an impression on John. John did invite Wally for dinner about a month later and I found that I liked Wally, too. He was good at general conversation. He was very well-read and unusually witty. He made me laugh. And in the weeks that followed John talked about his work and his colleagues, when he talked at all, and he usually mentioned Wally. Something Wally had done or said, and even though I saw Wally several times that spring at various get-togethers, I didn't talk to him much. Anyway, I was worried about Andy.

After Mike left Andy was my only big boy at home and I didn't like the noises he was making about getting his own place. Not that he wasn't big enough. Not yet seventeen, he was six foot three and still growing. And, however hard basketball coaches tried to entice him onto the basketball court, Andy had only one love. Music. He played piano, organ, keyboard, guitar, drums and the saxophone, mostly by ear. He had already formed his own group and they practised until the wee hours of the morning in a church basement, which caused no end of stress and worry in the household. If he moved in with a friend would we help him financially as long as he continued in school? After much debate, John and I decided to comply. We discovered that in Ontario a parent could not stop a kid from moving out once s/he reached sixteen. Andy was so talented he was employable already as a musician, it was only a matter of time before he hit the road. I just wanted to keep him in school as long as possible. He was a good student, and John and I both hated to see him chuck school for a band job as he was now talking of doing. So we agreed to his moving out and settled on a living allowance as long as he stayed in school. Our family was shrinking alarmingly. We were now down to the four little girls. Not that John noticed much.

John was extremely preoccupied with his new job. At NASA in Virginia he had been a research scientist. Now he was a professor and this new thing seemed to be more stressful somehow, more demanding. He spent most of his time in the evenings with papers and study plans. And my own typewriter was silent.

I had been writing confessions for over ten years, selling ten or twelve a year in the confession markets ... *True Story, True Confessions, Modern Romances, True Romance* and the lesser lights in the confession world, *Secrets, Real Confessions, Uncensored Confessions* and at least a half dozen others.

I loved writing confession stories. They dealt with the nitty gritty of the working-class woman's life and I understood that life very well. The stories weren't always about romance. About half of what I wrote dealt with the social problems of poverty and racism, and the difficulties of being wife and mother in the modern world. But after enlisting in the anti-war army I found I couldn't write these stories anymore. One can't really write what one no longer believes and I no longer believed in the American dream. My heroines could no longer, at the end of a story, simply realize that they had been approaching a problem from the wrong angle, and that by shifting emotional and psychic or intellectual gears they could make things right, that the underpinnings of society were inherently okay, it was they who had to grow and develop. I just didn't believe it anymore. So I couldn't write it.

But after awhile I began to write other things ... letters to the editors of newspapers in the province of Ontario, the states of Virginia and Louisiana plus the *New York Times* and the *Washington Post* about the continuation of the Vietnam War, a brief to the minister of education of Ontario advising him of the captivity of the French language by the Catholic Church, the truly awful situation of having one's children sit through religious education when one is profoundly irreligious, yet not wanting them to be excused from the class as this invites retaliation upon the dissidents by students and teachers alike. And I started a novel so bizarre and depressing that, the other day when I stumbled across the script and read it with fresh eyes, I can't even conjure up the pitiful state of mind I must have been in to have conceived such a plot. In reality, in addition to a deep, pervasive cultural shock, I was suffering from SAD, the Seasonal Affective Disorder that even strikes some members of the Inuit, at least to a certain degree, as they have a special name for this condition that means "polar hysteria".

I had polar hysteria in spades. For me the disorder seemed to have more to do with all the snow and cold rather than the total amount of sun-lit days. Louisiana had plenty of rain and overcast days, yet I maintained a cheerful disposition there. But if the Inuit knew about SAD then they were the only ones. It hadn't yet surfaced into Western medical thought. All I knew was that for the first time in my entire life I had trouble getting up in the mornings.

I had been blessed with high energy levels at birth and mornings were my best times. Now I had trouble just getting dressed. Dismayed at the way I was feeling I tried to throw off the depression by more engagement with the outside world. I began to look about for other women to be friends with.

Our townhouse block was full of faculty wives so I managed to pull myself out of the lethargic morass I was mucking about in and make a special effort to get acquainted. But while I found the women congenial enough I was still operating, when I operated at all, in the crisis stage of such a burning rebellion against the destructive might of the American War Machine that I wasn't really fit for casual afternoon coffee. I had lost the knack of ordinary female conversation. Or at least what passed for ordinary female conversation back then. And I missed dreadfully the Unitarian fellowship where one could discuss issues until one collapsed on the floor in a dead faint and still not be thought strange. Kirkland Lake, in spite of sporting a college, wasn't exactly what one would call a progressive town. At least not in those days. And there was too damned much drinking going on.

Kirkland Lake seemed indeed, to be the pub of the north. There was a lot of public drunkenness and rowdiness, lots of racism, lots of poverty and a lot of churches. Pubs and churches abounded on every corner. If it hadn't been for all the snow and ice on the ground and the fur hats and boots and the lack of anything interesting to eat, as far as social attitudes were concerned I might as well have been brooding in the backwoods of Louisiana. At least I would have been warm.

Even at faculty parties the booze was always the main thing, and John started partaking of the substance more than he ever had before in my presence. And even though I would take a drink or two myself during an evening, I have always feared alcohol like a hungry swamp alligator. I knew first hand that alcohol had the power to turn relatively reasonable men into staggering idiots and violent maniacs, and women into weeping, self-pitying victims. I didn't like John when he drank. He had a tendency to get impossibly self-righteous and accusatory. So I found myself avoiding the same social situations I had originally reached out for. And my depression deepened.

Now it was only the children who could jog me out of my fog ... their physical care, their food, their clothes, skating lessons, their school work. And then a funny thing happened. I began to look at John and wonder who he actually was.

I knew John very well intellectually. And I admired him intellectually. But it slowly dawned on me that I didn't know this man emotionally at all. Back in Virginia our house and property had been so large that John and I almost had to make an appointment to talk to each other. And we could hide behind our roles so successfully that either he or I could have been suddenly replaced by someone reasonably similar and equally role conditioned, and neither of us would have noticed much, except for the political part. John was a southern man and he made most of the money and most of the decisions, and my main job as a southern woman was to transform his money and decisions into tangible goods and services. But these roles didn't really fit anymore. At least I didn't feel they did. Crammed into a far from spacious townhouse where John's body or books or papers or clothes was always at my elbow, I began to wonder who he really was. What inner person dwelt behind those probing green eyes and deliberate considerations?

It was weird. It was almost as if I were living with a strange man who looked vaguely familiar. In spite of all that we had been through together, and the odd kind of mutual admiration that we held for the other, I had to admit I had no idea who this man was. I found this a deplorable state of affairs and I set about trying to remedy the situation.

But just because one partner decides s/he would like more intimacy doesn't mean it will automatically be forthcoming. I think true intimacy is the most difficult thing to accomplish between a man and a woman, and has only become possible relatively recently in human, history growing up alongside the possibility of economic and social equality for women. And although John gave lip service to all kinds of equality his head wasn't programmed for the equality of wives. Not then. And I don't think mine was, either.

I thought that first winter in Kirkland Lake would never end and that spring would never come. Actually spring never did come. At least anything that I recognized as spring although native northerners may have recognized some slight deviation in the slant of the nightly snowfall or some minuscule rise in the temperature. The snow and ice blanketing the world outside was still an affront to any semblance of order and decency as far as I was concerned. But the kids actually seemed to be enjoying it.

I dutifully took the girls for skating lessons and watched them skim across the ice, often on their rears. I had tried skating myself at first, thinking it must be similar to roller skating. I found to my chagrin this was not so and forthwith contented myself with watching my little ones wrestle with gravity, as their childish rears were much more flexible than mine. Sometimes we would get to the rink before the big boys finished practising hockey. I hated hockey. So violent. Worse than the football I refused to let Mike play in high school. But if hockey was too violent for my tastes, curling simply mystified me. It does so to this day. But the little girls were happy enough with their school and their friends, and Andy, true to his word, was attending school every day, too. I think the two most frustrated people in that non-existent spring were me and the baby, Barbara Ellen.

Barbara Ellen was a year and a half now and stayed busy trying to train the cat that had been fostered off on us by a neighbour child. Barbara Ellen wanted the cat to ride in her baby buggy, dressed, no less, in her doll's bonnet. There was lots of trouble about this. The cat certainly didn't take to this activity and protested with tooth and claw. When the tooth and claw business brought down stern disapproval from me, the cat simply hid when he saw Barbara Ellen bringing out the doll buggy. So Barbara Ellen spent most of that pitiful excuse for a spring looking for the cat, and I spent it trying to create, if not locate, a non-existing intimacy with my husband. Neither of us succeeded. But school was finally, over and while spring never did come to Kirkland Lake, one morning in early June I was thrown pell mell into a hot, bright summer.

It happened overnight. I swear. I went to bed with it still colder than ole Billy hell outside and snow still slathered all over everything and when I got up the next morning and opened the back door, summer had arrived. The snow had turned into singing water and it burbled and bobbled, sassy and sun-kissed, as it formed little riverlets carved out by its own passionate need to reach some far

away sea in order to begin the cycle anew. And the trees were dancing in their brand new bright green shimmering dresses, and the
birds were yelling themselves silly, and the pungent air announcing
the imminent arrival of uncountable, unspeakable things bursting
into life almost knocked me out.

I could feel the depression lifting from the soles of my feet and
then begin to work itself upward through my body until it was coming
out of the top of my head and I felt so light and buoyant I had to
hold onto the back porch railing to keep from rising bodily into the
air. After my metabolism settled down a bit and I could let go of the
porch railing without fear of ascension, I rushed back inside.

"Get up, get up!" I sang to the lay-about children. "Good morning, good morning, good morning, the sun shines above us today!
Let us play while we work, let us work while we play, that's the way
to be happy and gay!" A little kindergarten song, before gay rights,
that my children especially loathed, and that I only used when I was
serious about their getting up.

"Go away, Mom, please," the girls moaned in unison.

"No, no, no! We've got to go! Mommy says so," I sang back.

And we did go. Sort of. We all went to Montreal for Expo and
camped out in a beautiful little private park for three days and when
we got back home we made two day-trips around the countryside.
And then the blueberries ripened. I was fascinated with the prolif-
eration of blueberries in the area. Blueberries surrounded the town
on all sides, holding it captive for several weeks of the summer, but
one needed a car to get to the best places, especially with four small
children in tow. The girls and I loved blueberries better than any
bear, but we couldn't get John to take us blueberry picking.

I had given up driving six years before after that harrowing move
across country from Louisiana to Virginia when John first went to
work for NASA. When we finally arrived in Virginia and I struggled, trembling and incoherent, from behind the wheel of that station
wagon that had transported six kids, one of them an infant, and a
dog just to further complicate things, across thousands of miles, I
had vowed never to get behind the wheel of a car again. It was
probably time to rethink my position on this, but the berries would
surely be gone by the time I practised a bit and got my driver's
license. And John's attitude about berry picking didn't sit right
with me.

"Look, we've already done some family things," he pointed out defensively when in sheer exasperation I finally got his attention by pulling a book he was reading from underneath his nose. Something new, I could tell by the title, on quantum theory. There was a definite danger, when John sank deeply into these books, that he might never surface again. In fact, sometimes I thought that was the main reason he married me was to make sure someone was around who cared enough, or was hungry enough, or worried enough about the bills, to drag him back to reality when he wandered too far into the abyss. If a book was really absorbing, he could go for days without sleep, refusing all nourishment except a few crackers smeared with mayonnaise and a bit of yoghurt washed down with pots of black coffee. At such times he responded to inquiries with only unintelligible grunts and head shakings.

"Five days," I said. "You have given us exactly five days of your time this summer. Are you saying that's it?"

"No ... no. We'll do something else later on. But you have to understand that I need to learn more about what it is I'm supposed to be teaching here. And this is an extraordinary book ..."

"I don't give a damn!" I yelled at him. "You will never get all the books read. There will always be extraordinary books waiting for you, are you trying to tell me we should all just go away until you've read all the frigging extraordinary books you want to read?"

"No, but what I'm saying is that I need some time this summer to consolidate things I've already worked on ... "

"The girls and I want to go blueberry picking. Soon."

His eyes held mine for a long moment. He was measuring, I could tell, the amount of hysteria he would have to suffer if he didn't comply. He decided it was more than he wanted to contend with. He sighed heavily.

"All right," he agreed in his most put-upon voice. "We'll go tomorrow. Give me back the damn book."

I gave up the book, satisfied.

"We'll go early," I said. "I'll make a picnic."

He mumbled something in reply but at that moment I didn't care that he wasn't enthusiastic. We were going blueberry picking. We would be out in the country, way out in the fresh, open air. For a little while, it would seem like we were back in Virginia.

And it *was* fun. We filled great buckets of blueberries, had our picnic lunch with a minimum of fuss and then went to an outlying park where there was a playground. After the girls were totally exhausted from the day's activities, we packed them into the car. Barbara Ellen was already asleep. I got into the back seat with her and Rose Mary and Margaret Elizabeth while Susan scrambled into the front seat beside John. Before starting the car John adjusted the rear view mirror. Our eyes met in the glass and I smiled at him.

"See?" I said. "Didn't we have fun? Aren't you glad you came?"

Instead of an answering smile, a decided frown creased his forehead.

"Well, it was kind of a waste of time as far as my getting any studying done," he answered. His voice wasn't especially curt or accusing, simply matter-of-fact.

Strange. John had said things like this before. He was a total workaholic and always had been. Back in Virginia and before that, Louisiana, I was able to accept this because I was so busy myself I hardly knew which end was up. But suddenly workaholism seemed unnatural to me, even bizarre. What was a family about, anyway? Were relationships really supposed to be subordinate to studies of matter and mathematics? Was work the most important thing in the whole world? Must one regret stolen moments that were squandered on sheer being? Something inside my psyche began to shift and tilt dangerously. Except for the kids, I didn't like anything that was happening in my life, and that included this strange man frowning at me in the rear view mirror who regretted the perfectly wonderful day we had just experienced because it was a day lost of his man's work, his important stuff. Being with me and the girls obviously wasn't important. To hell with it, I thought. To hell with it. And from that moment on I felt myself to be alone.

Being married but feeling alone is a painful state to be in. And dangerous. But in the weeks ahead I tried to overcome these feelings. After all, the sun was bright and warm after the impossibly long winter and I had the children. Joey was stationed far away in Italy, but at least he wasn't being killed in Vietnam or forced to deny his humanity by killing other people, and Mike was safe on some sort of communal pig farm in British Columbia, and Andy, while still living with friends, came over often to visit, and the little girls absorbed a lot of my time. Anyway, who said a happy marriage was necessary to one's mental health? A lot of women suffered more than mere workaholism from their husbands. I would force myself to try harder to connect with the community and I would continue with my own education, even if I couldn't write confessions anymore.

But I had been knocked off my emotional base that afternoon in the blueberry patch and I couldn't find a new one. As the summer waned and the long winter loomed large before me, I actually began to fear for my mental stability. This time even John noticed my lethargy.

Perhaps you should get out some, he suggested. French classes were starting up and did I still want to take an evening course in conversational French? He would watch the girls a couple of evenings a week if I would get them ready for bed before I left for class. All right. I knew I should get out, do something. I actually realized at this point that the climate was not good for me, but I had no idea this misery was compounded by the fact that I was in mourning ... that I was grieving deeply for the loss of the south, for the familiar forests and streams and wild woodland animals that I knew, for my friends, relatives, an entire way of life, grieving, too, for the confession stories that I would now never write, and most of all, for the notion that I had a satisfactory marriage. And in spite of a heightened sense of reality about some things, it seemed to me that I had lost touch with reality. It was scary. I felt I could no longer trust myself to form realistic assessments about the universe. At least taking a course would force me to think of something else, to learn something new. It was a week later that I accidentally ran into Wally Krawczyk at the post office.

It wasn't much of a meeting as far as meetings go. We only exchanged a few words. I was struggling to enter the post office building with Barbara Ellen, Barbara Ellen's stroller, and several assorted packages I was mailing to relatives. Halfway through the post office door I accidentally rammed the stroller handle up against the midsection of the man behind me. When I turned to offer my apologies I saw it was Wally. In an attempt to be funny I made some stupid remark about never knowing whom one was going to run into with a stroller.

"Yes, and on government property, too," he said, smiling good naturedly. As I looked up at him I noticed that the blue of his eyes was actually quite beguiling and decided that I very much liked the way he held his slender, raw-boned body. Straight. Proud. And there was something in the way he acknowledged my presence that was pleasing to me. In some unspoken way he admitted his awareness of me as a woman as he smiled and helped me and my bundles and baby inside the building that bounced off my emotional void but didn't roll quite far enough away to be beyond recall. Something definitely stirred in me that afternoon. Looking back it was as though I caught some sort of virus from this brief encounter, some manner of insidious germ that sank unbidden and unrecognized into the cells of my primitive brain and incubated there. When it showed itself eight months later full blown in feverish, hallucinatory behavior, my husband didn't know what to make of me. Neither did anybody else. I didn't know what to make of myself. For the first time in my whole life I had fallen madly, senselessly, passionately in love.

How very, very, long ago that was, I muse as I turn over in my bunk for the hundredth time. This is the sixth time the flashlight has shone on me in my little cell room so it must be getting close to morning. I must try to get some sleep. I do eventually drift off, but we are routed at six-thirty. I feel surprisingly refreshed from so little sleep. Perhaps I'm still cruising on dramatic hysteria from the day before. Whatever, I am a prisoner now and I can hear voices rising excitedly just outside my door.

ELEVEN

Some of my fellow protesters want to have a "circle" before breakfast and are trying to get everyone up and organized. There is an argument with the guards about opening the back door to the basketball court outside this early, but by the time I have washed my face and brushed my teeth and braided my hair the argument has been settled and the back door opened. The circle is forming outside on the basketball court.

I've not been in a circle before so the others have to teach me. We hold hands and share feelings and thoughts, chant, sing, and do some physical exercises. It's relaxing and invigorating. The morning air is sweet and pure. We can't get off the court as it is surrounded by a high wire fence and topped with the same clusters of barbed wire as the front fence but we can see through the chain link fence to the trees sloping down the hill to the edge of a large lake. Over breakfast I get better acquainted with the other two grandmothers, Inessa Ormond and Judith Robinson. Our other partners-in-crime are mostly young, impossibly young, and sweet and high-minded and energetic. After breakfast we have a strategy meeting to discuss our options. We will be taken to court that morning to enter our pleas and each of us has to decide how we will plea. I decide to plead "not guilty" as I was standing on crown land at the time of my arrest, which, other than what the First Nations People claim, belongs to all the people of British Columbia. If this is my land how can I be made a criminal for trying to protect its destruction?

The courtroom is full of supporters singing softly and this touches me. Most of the others also pleaded "not guilty" and from the courtroom we are all taken back to our new home at the men's correctional centre in Nanaimo.

There is a routine. We are not just left to our own devices. We have chores to do. Lots of cleaning. And we do our own cooking. Most of us are vegetarian so the cooks in the main building give up and just send over crates of raw vegetables, fruits, cheeses and some grains. It's good enough. There are a couple of creative cooks among the men and I do my thing with enormous pots of soup. We are getting to know each other. And then our numbers begin to wax and wane.

Some of the original arrested ones decide they would rather be doing something else and sign the undertaking, but as new arrests are happening every day, new people also come in all the time. It's very interesting. Because so many people are being arrested I feel confident that the clear-cut logging in the Clayoquot Sound will have to stop relatively soon. So I leave the press reports and most of the letter-writing to the young ones, and when my chores are done for the afternoon or the evening I head outside to the basketball court.

The country school I attended in Louisiana didn't have a basketball team or anybody resembling a coach, but it had an outdoor court of sorts. When I was about thirteen I somehow got the hang of shooting baskets and eventually became even better at it than most of the boys. It was because I practised more than anybody else. I liked just dribbling down the court by myself and shooting first at one end of the court and then the other. This rather aimless activity somehow settled my mind and calmed my usually overheated imagination. And astonishingly enough, in prison I found that shooting baskets still had that same calming effect on me, so I spent most of my free time connecting with that sort of chubby thirteen-year old who still lived on in some mysterious spot inside my brain and bones who loved to run up and down the court dribbling a basketball. But one evening after dinner, when we had been at the correctional centre about a week and a half, instead of heading out to the basketball court I went in to the hallway where the telephones were and began to wait my turn. I had put it off long enough. I had to call Wally and tell him I was in jail.

He already knew. Someone in Sarnia had seen the first arrests on TV. We didn't have much to say to each other. He seemed rather uncomfortable with the call so I hung up after a decent interval and went to my room. I felt upset. I couldn't talk to Wally the way I could now talk to John or any other man even vaguely interested in social justice. The most trivial conversation between me and Wally had to turn into a tug of war, as though we were sibling rivals in some sort of mortal combat for the affection of the universe. It was too crazy. Just the telephone conversation had given me a headache. I lay down in my bunk with a wet cloth over my forehead. How had Wally and I got into this state of armed verbal combat? When the major thing, the biggie, the incredible, wonderful, marvellous thing that had drawn me to him in the beginning was that I could talk to him. Lord have mercy, how we had talked in the beginning!

The talking started in French class. John, true to his word, let me out on Tuesday and Thursday evenings to go to class. I didn't know Wally would be taking French, too, but there he was. However, he and several others got bumped up into an advanced class as they weren't rank beginners. I was disappointed to see him leave as he had sat next to me and joked about my trying to speak French with a southern accent, like bon jour, y'all. He made me laugh. When I ran into him in the hallway before class a couple of weeks later he asked about my lessons.

"It's okay," I said. "I think it goes a bit slow. I grew up in Cajun country, listening to Cajuns jaw-jaw. For me the class could go a little faster. How's your class?"

"Good. Listen, why don't you speak to my teacher? We're not terribly advanced, either. Maybe you would get more out of my class. Madame would let you sit in with us, I'm sure."

"Oh. I'll think about it."

He smiled at me and I noticed the sweet curve of his mouth. Soft and vulnerable, like a child's mouth. He walked on down the hall and I went in to my own class. But during the week I thought, why not? I'm a quick study. If I work hard I can probably catch up. So the following week I did speak to the teacher of the advanced French class, a large, elderly, good-natured French woman. She welcomed me to the class as there were only four other students in it besides Wally. The other four were all women. But after my first advanced class I thought I had probably bitten off more than I could chew. I said so to Wally as we walked home from the school through town. Wally lived in an apartment building about three blocks from the faculty townhouses. The town wasn't large, one could walk comfortably from our area to almost any other spot in the village.

"Well, you know best how you feel about it, but perhaps you shouldn't give up so soon. Why don't you give the class a couple of weeks before you make up your mind? Maybe you were just a little nervous about it this evening."

"Maybe," I answered, smiling up at him. There was a light snow falling, melting against his glasses and settling atop his fine, sandy colored hair. Two other students in our class walked just ahead of us, teachers, both in the public school system, youngish, single, both attractive, one engaged. They turned as we approached a coffee shop.

"Anyone for coffee? Hot chocolate?"

Wally looked down at me. "Do you have time?"

"Uh ... yes. I think so."

We four found a booth and drank several cups of coffee each and talked and laughed, and all of us women flirted with Wally. It was fun. It was harmless. But the next day when Barbara Ellen was down for her nap, and it wasn't time yet to think about dinner, I found myself looking rather searchingly in my bedroom mirror. I hadn't looked at myself, really looked at myself for years. I was thirty-eight years old. Ten years older than Wally. And my body had endured seven pregnancies. Yet I was still relatively slender. Mama had blessed me with her family's fine, smooth-grained skin, but unfortunately I had also inherited some features from my father. The one outstanding physical feature that he and all five of his siblings shared was that they were all completely white-headed by the time they were forty. And my own hair was turning fast. Underneath the Lady Clairol I had great wings of white at each temple. However, I *had* discovered Lady Clairol a couple of years before and my long hair was thick and now skilfully colored the nice, soft light brown of my girlhood. And people often expressed surprise that I had such grown up boys, in spite of a work-worn life and seven kids I could just as easily have passed for a matronly thirty-one as a youngish thirty-eight year-old. But maybe I should buy some new makeup, I thought as I peered into the mirror. And then I blushed at my thoughts. What was the matter with me? My preoccupation with my reflection was arrested by a muffled "ping ping ping" sound on the stairs. I recognized the sound immediately. The cat had found Rose Mary's cache of marbles and was in the process of rolling them, one by one, down the stairwell.

The damned cat was a fanatic for rolling marbles around the house. I had told Rose Mary, and told her, to keep her marbles hidden where the cat couldn't find them. That "ping ping ping" was enough to drive anybody crazy. Thoughts of makeup fled from my mind as I wrestled the marbles away from the cat and Barbara Ellen woke up and it was time to think about dinner. Still, I found myself eagerly looking forward to the next French class.

In the weeks that followed I hung on in the advanced class by the skin of my teeth, determined not to leave because the class had now become a bright spot in my life. Wally was extremely entertaining. He had read a lot of the classics that I had, Dickens, Thoreau, and William and Henry James and some of the French writers, Hugo and Balzac. And he knew a lot of writers I didn't know but had heard about. So we talked before French class and after French class and in the coffee shop, usually with one or two of the other students, but occasionally Wally and I would go for coffee by ourselves. And once, with a couple of others we stopped in a bar for a beer. That seemed a little daring so I made an effort to tell John the details. But his head was off in outer space and if I hadn't come in until midnight, I'm not sure he would have noticed. But whatever rage I felt toward John for not meeting my needs for intimacy, I still respected him. And I began to be wary of gossip.

I was beginning to think that Wally felt for me much the same attraction I felt for him. I worried that we were too obvious in our happiness at being in each other's company so I tried to make an effort not to talk to him so much, not to look at him so admiringly, not to laugh at his jokes so readily. But we simply had too much to talk about. His grandparents were Polish immigrants and he told me all about being raised on a farm outside Hamilton, of being the first of his family to go to university, of his love of books, music, poetry. Ah, we were indeed kindred spirits. I was so infatuated that I didn't notice then that he did most of the talking and that the burning questions of poverty and injustice that had plagued me all my life were not really burning issues with him. But he was young. His reading was bound to eventually bounce him off onto the same path I was on. And he was absolutely the most charming companion I had ever imagined. He could have stepped full-blown right out of one of my confession stories.

In fact, I think that really is where Wally came from. From my own imagination. I needed someone desperately at that point and Wally was it. I superimposed on him all the qualities that I needed, or thought I needed, and years later when I found an obvious discrepancy in the reality of the thing I was astonished. But in French class, Wally was the king, and I was his most loyal subject. Then the classes were discontinued for the Christmas holidays.

Much to the cat's disgust Barbara Ellen got an even bigger, sturdier doll buggy for Christmas. Susan didn't want anything but clothes. Old looking, expensive clothes that the high school kids were wearing. She would soon be twelve and had taken to rocking and rolling upstairs for hours to the blaring music on her tape deck. "Jeremiah was a bull frog!" What a song. If I could have found Jeremiah, I would have knocked him in the head, cut off his legs and fried them in olive oil with a little garlic. I hadn't had frog legs in a month of Sundays. That's what I would have liked for Christmas, some frog legs and crawfish bisque and jambalaya. And turnip greens. Fat chance! At least Margaret Elizabeth and Rose Mary were still little girls and were happy with little girl presents. John and I didn't exchange presents. We never had. He just wasn't into Christmas much, except for the dinner. But we all got a present from Wally.

It was a large, beautifully bound and illustrated French dictionary and while the card was addressed to the Camp family, I knew for whom the present was intended.

"We should ask him over for dinner again when he gets back," John said after we had all admired the present.

"Oh? Where did he go?" I asked with studied indifference.

"To his parent's place. He has a girlfriend there I think."

My heart froze. Wally had never mentioned a girlfriend. But then why should he? It wasn't as though I meant anything to him,

I chided myself. Not really. He probably just enjoyed my company and felt flattered by an older woman's admiration. And if I thought otherwise, well then maybe I didn't have a lick of sense. Christmas was ruined for me nonetheless. When classes started up for the new semester, I was determined not to be glad to see Wally again.

But my heart leapt and did a jig and I couldn't help grinning at him like a mule heading for the barn. That evening when the others, after coffee, headed toward their apartments Wally ignored his own turnoff and continued to walk with me in the direction of the faculty townhouses. It had snowed almost non-stop for the last month and everything, streets, sidewalks, yards, and alleyways, was hardpacked and crunched loudly when stepped upon. But this night the sky was clear and the stars where showing off, and a crisp half moon was just beginning to rise. I didn't even ask Wally about the girlfriend. I could tell by the way he acted when he first saw me that evening that if he had one he didn't love her. He walked me to the top of the hill, within a block of the townhouses. The hill was so steep I usually just slid down it on my rear, if I tried to walk down, I ended up in the snow banks anyway. I turned to tell Wally goodnight.

"I'll wait until you get down the hill," he said.

"No, don't do that. I'm fine."

"Is there any reason you don't want me to see you go down the hill?" he asked, his voice lightly teasing.

"Not if you go down with me," I yelled and grabbed his arm and we were tumbling down the hill rolling over and over and laughing and acting like moon-struck children. When we got to the bottom Wally helped me up; we were still laughing and brushing off the dry powered snow. And I reached up and kissed him on the mouth. And then I ran. I didn't even give him a chance to say anything, I just ran home. I rushed into the foyer and slammed the door behind me and stood in the doorway to the living room for a moment, trying to get my breath. The house was quiet. The kids were evidently in bed, if not asleep. From the living room couch John looked up from one of his everlasting books.

"What's the matter with you?" he asked, frowning at the interruption.

"Nothing. I just felt like running. Do you want some coffee?"

"Sure."

But of course everything was wrong with me. Several months

later Wally and I did more than kiss. We had sex for the first time. We played hooky from class and went to his apartment.

"I don't know what to do about this," I said afterward as I was dressing to go home. I was sitting on the side of the bed pulling on my red and black wool tights. Wally was standing by the chest of drawers, buttoning his shirt. "Do you love me?" I asked point-blank.

"Yes," he answered without hesitation.

"I mean really. Love, love ... you know."

"Yes I do know. And I do. Do you love me?"

"Yes. I think you know that."

He smiled at me in the semi-darkness of the room.

I reached for my slacks. My best slacks, I had worn them for the occasion. They were all crumpled now, in a heap on the floor. I picked them up and carefully straightened them out.

"I have to tell John," I said firmly, tasting the words as they left my mouth. "I can't do this behind his back. I won't make a cuckold of him. At least no more than I already have."

"I agree. Tell him."

I looked up at him. "You do understand, don't you, that I have no means of support other than John?"

He came and sat down beside me on the bed and put his arm around me.

"I will take care of you," he said.

I nodded. "But there are my girls. I won't leave them."

"I don't expect you to."

"You could lose your job, you know. There could be a big scandal."

"I've already faced that."

I rested my face in his shoulder. There was one more thing.

"And your parents. Have you faced that?"

He pulled away. I knew how proud his parents were of him, what high hopes they had for him. Prime Minister, at least. I also knew they were Catholic.

"That will be the hardest of all, but they'll just have to try to understand."

A sudden thrill of terror washed through me.

"My darling, are we sure ... are you sure?"

"Sure? I don't know ... how can one be sure of anything? I just want to be with you, that's all, and I'm willing to do just about anything to bring that about."

"But the kids? What if you don't like the kids?"

"I don't think that's possible, that I wouldn't like your children. I've seen you with them, how you take care of them. I'm sure that part of it will be fine."

Calmed somewhat, I went home and told John I was in love with Wally and wanted a divorce. Yes, I expected him to be upset. Yes, I expected his pride to be hurt. Yes, I expected him to bully and threaten me. I no longer believed that he loved me, but he was used to me, used to my being there for him. I expected him to raise a bit of hell, but I didn't expect him to go out and buy a gun and threaten to shoot Wally. And in the process so upset the college which was getting ready for year-end exams, not to mention my children who stared at me with wide, worried eyes, that we all descended into hell for three whole weeks.

At this point Wally and I decided to run away, taking only the children and a few clothes with us. There was no question in my mind where I wanted to go. In his letters Mike said the southwest coast of British Columbia was a lot warmer than anywhere in Ontario. So one morning after John had left for work I packed a few things for the baby and the older children, called a taxi, met Wally who had rented a car in another town and was waiting at an appointed place, and then went by the school and collected the girls. I felt bad about leaving Andy but he had launched out on a life of his own. He wasn't the only one who could leave home. John would have all of his time to himself now and I hoped he was satisfied with it. But I was somewhat surprised at the girls' reaction about leaving John. After all, he hadn't been what one would call a doting father.

But kids know what they want. They were used to their own daddy, he was always home when he wasn't at work, he might not pay much attention to them but he was always there, he could be counted on in an emergency, he was often comforting, he made them feel safe. The girls cried and complained bitterly to me and about me to each other halfway across Canada. But somewhere in Alberta they began to cheer up a little. Wally tried to stop in motels and hotels that had swimming pools and play grounds. And Wally was very patient. He took their rebuffs gracefully. By the time we crossed over into British Columbia the girls had started letting Wally read to them in the evenings when we stopped, and he could tell stories, too. In fact, he was a damned good storyteller. And by the time we got to Vancouver, Barbara Ellen would let Wally pick her up and carry her back and forth from the car and the others had become interested in the new surroundings. Unsure of where we should light, we took the ferry over to Victoria. Wally and I just wanted to get out of John's way for awhile until he had time to cool down so that he wouldn't do something horrible and unfixable. It was from the manager of the hotel where we stopped in Victoria that we first heard about the Clayoquot Sound. He said it was a remote and beautiful area with fantastic beaches. Mike's communal pig farm was in a small town outside Vancouver and I didn't want to run into him for awhile, either, so the following morning we headed north up Vancouver Island.

It was April and there had been no snow in Vancouver and Victoria, in fact, flowers were already blooming everywhere. Immediately I pledged my allegiance to the west coast. But as we drove up past Port Alberni toward Tofino and Ucluelet, my bubbling anticipation turned to outright terror. There was no highway going in this direction, only narrow logging roads. When we met another car we had to stop. The girls and I hid our faces in our hands, unable to look over the abyss, deep, steep mountain sides where the pitiful road seemed to extend into thin air. What a way to end our journey! All dead at the bottom of the mountains. Ah, how the gossips back in Kirkland Lake would smile and say to each other, yes, of course, *they* may have deserved it, but what a pity about the poor children ...

I begged Wally to turn around and go back. He agreed and when we found a lookout point that was wide enough to turn around we stopped. But we met an Australian couple there who had paused to take film of the incredible drop-off. They told us that we were already over the worst part of the road and that up ahead lay unimaginable scenery. We decided to go on. And our Australian friends were right. Once on the road to Tofino we turned off at Long Beach for a rest break. When I actually stepped out from the foliage of the dense woods onto that beach I stopped in my tracks, rooted in astonishment.

I was familiar with some well known American east and west coast beaches but I had never seen anything like this before. I tried to take it all in with great gulps of fresh, salty air. Miles and miles of wide, hard-packed white sandy beach. The foamy, surging surf splashing and breaking against the giant boulders that ringed the shore line. Old growth rainforest then crept down from the mountains to the very edge of the sand. And as we stepped forward to explore, still stunned from the heart-stopping beauty, we found an incredible abundance of sea life right on shore — clams and mussels and enormous barnacles just underneath the sand or attached to the rocks. We were the only humans on the beach but life was everywhere and everything was breath-takingly beautiful.

And it was warm. Evening was coming on and the air was still warm. Lagging a little behind the others I knelt down and kissed the sand. Oh, merciful Goddess of the universe, thank you. Thank you for giving Canada at least one warm spot where I can survive and for making it so unbelievably magnificent. Thank you. Thank you.

We found a motel just outside Tofino and settled in. The motel was a two bedroom structure and Wally paid for a week. I hauled out my typewriter which I had taken with me at the last minute. I thought I might need it. And I did. Wally and I were both concerned about money.

Wally had enough savings to support us for three or four months. If I could sell a few stories we could maybe extend that to six months. Surely in six months John would have calmed down from a blazing fire to a slow simmer. And then we could talk about the kids, visitation privileges and all that.

After the first week in Tofino we rented a small house. And we had to get about enrolling the girls in school.

It wasn't much of a school, one building and a trailer in back. As I remember, there were only three teachers and one of these was the principal, but they were all very nice and friendly and seemed competent enough. The other kids, half of whom seemed to be native, welcomed our daughters as something of a diversion. In spite of the worry over John's state of mind, that spring and summer flowed over me, around me, and through me like a lovely dream from which I hoped never to awaken. After so many years of study and work and intellectual worry I was now cruising in a state of pure being.

I wrote confessions, politics be damned, took care of the kids, made love to Wally, and communed with the rocks and the trees and the sea and the sky and all the living creatures therein. Almost every afternoon, as soon as the girls were home from school, off we would go to the beach with a picnic or something to barbeque and stay until we could no longer see a thing. And then school was out and the berries were getting ripe and I made pies from a berry I had never heard of before called salal and the waters of Kennedy Lake, unlike the open ocean, were warm and inviting for swimming. There were hiking trails and a little beach called Shell Beach, where we collected countless unusual shells. We ate salmon and clams and Wally and I took turns telling the girls stories and Wally read Treasure Island, Tom Sawyer, and Wind in the Willows in the evenings. I felt myself at home. I never wanted to leave. But the outside world intruded.

John found us. I knew he would eventually, from the girls' school registration records. He raised hell for three days but finally left on the promise that I would send the three older girls to him for Christmas. But not Barbara Ellen, she was too little. And there was another intrusion. Even though I was selling some stories, by the end of October our money was definitely getting low. Wally took a temporary job working with a roofing gang, but it certainly wasn't what he was trained for and the work was sketchy at best. He began applying for teaching jobs in Victoria. He found one almost immediately. A high school math and physics teacher had dropped dead in the classroom from a heart attack. Could Wally be there next week?

We went down to the beach for the last time. It was early evening. A very red sun was setting out over the water. The girls played in the little makeshift driftwood beach houses that the university students had left behind at the end of the summer. I felt so overwhelmed by the beauty of sea and sky and sand and forests and the knowledge that we must leave it all that I started to weep. Wally held my hand, trying to comfort me. It was no use. How can one be comforted for the loss of paradise? But after a bit I consented to discard my shoes as the others had done and Wally and I, with Barbara Ellen riding on Wally's shoulders, trailed after the girls into the shallow water of the outgoing tide, heading toward the small island that was sheltering the dark, sleek animals that appeared to be seals under the multicoloured sky.

"Come back," we yelled and the girls turned, reluctantly, so drugged by the overwhelming magical sway of sounds and smells and colors they must have temporarily thought themselves seals, too, or something near, their excited voices transmitting their longing to plunge into the sea and become one with it all.

Margaret Elizabeth and Rose Mary cried, too, the next morning when we were all packed and had to leave behind our great treasure box of seashells, I even saw Susan, big girl that she was, brushing back some tears. We each took a few of our favorite shells. It was raining when we left, to match our sad mood.

In Victoria, we started all over again.

Victoria is a lovely city. But the girls and I didn't really like cities, and their new school wasn't so friendly and instantly welcoming, either. But we found a well kept, interesting old house to rent and bought second hand furniture. It seemed we had no sooner arrived than Christmas was upon us.

"I think I should go ahead and file for divorce and get temporary custody of the kids before we send them to John for Christmas," I told Wally as the time was nearing for the girls to go.

"I don't know about that. I think I'd say no. If John feels you're trying to take some sort of advantage about the kids, he might dig in his heels and become even more intransigent."

I agreed, but I should have gone with my intuition. Almost as soon as the girls got off the plane John filed for divorce, asking custody of all the children including Susan who wasn't even his, and also filed suits against Wally for "Alienation of Affections and Criminal Conversation," whatever that was, for an outrageous sum. Wally and I were in trouble.

We spent an enormous amount of money on lawyers. We were advised that we would have a better chance of regaining custody if we moved back to Ontario. Wally started sending out resumés all over the province of Ontario. He had excellent credentials but the problem was that he had left his college in Ontario without notice just before final exams the year when we ran away. And the president there wanted to let all who inquired about Wally know the pertinent facts about our great dash for freedom, never mind that up until that point he thought Wally so reliable he appointed him department head at the ripe old age of twenty-seven, that his students loved him, that he was admired by almost everyone who knew him. But Wally had been prepared for this and just kept applying. A bit desperately. I was pregnant now with Wally's baby. And Barbara Ellen kept asking about her sisters.

Barbara Ellen and I went to Kirkland Lake on the bus to see her older sisters and big brother Andy. It was awful. Just awful. Andy wasn't speaking to me and John threatened me about trying to steal the girls. And I would have, too. Except that John had put on such a poor pitiful face to Susan and Margaret Elizabeth and Rose Mary that they felt now they should stay with him because he was alone and Wally wasn't their daddy, anyway, and didn't have any business taking them off in the first place. So we all cried together, every day for a week. And then Barbara Ellen and I went back to British Columbia.

Strange business. What did John know of raising kids, girls at that? Why, he didn't know diddly-squat about their clothes, their food, their hair, or their schoolwork. So he held little conversations with them, yes, and questioned them from time to time about their doings, but who would have thought these little attentions would have been so important to the girls? I had seriously misjudged how much they cared for John and identified with him. I knew then that I had been out-manoeuvred by John, but I was determined to fight it out to the bitter end.

Wally finally got a job teaching in the math and physics department at a college in Sarnia, Ontario. Our baby was born six weeks after we arrived, a big healthy girl with blue eyes like her father and a fuzzy blond head. We named her Marian Theresa, after Wally's mother and sister. Trying to appease, I guess. Wally and I were both bogging around in swamps of guilt. The final divorce and custody hearing took place in Sudbury barely two weeks after Marian put in her appearance.

I was nursing Marian so she had to go to Sudbury with us. We hired a nanny to take care of her in the hotel room while we were in court. I hadn't regained my full strength after childbirth, and this was one had been tremendously stressful. I felt ill and faint. By the time John's lawyer got through emphasizing what a paragon of virtue John was, I wondered myself how I could have left such a wonderful husband and father.

Why, this poor man had given up everything, including an extremely promising career as a research scientist to move to Canada at my request in order to protect my son. He slaved to provide for me and the children. We were his life. He was faithful, industrious and kind and had never given me the slightest reason to wantonly betray him, to make a cuckold of him in front of the entire world. And this was all very true on the surface. It was even true at some deeper levels. But on that innermost gut emotional level, where we all live after basic external needs are satisfied, John had taken a hike. And because there was no way to even talk about this particular kind of unfaithfulness, at least not in that time and place, at that moment I hated John. He knew very well all the times I had tried to turn to him for comfort and intimacy and been rebuffed. He knew very well the times I had reached for his hand and he had drawn his away because he didn't want to deal with my emotional neediness. He hadn't had time; he was too busy with the real world and didn't want to be drawn into what he considered my fantasy one. Well, we were both dealing with the real world now. And so at that moment I hated him. And I hated the judge, too, who was definitely showing signs of sympathy for John's position. My hatred also extended to both of the lawyers, for no particular reason except what a hell of a way to make money, off people's heartbreak. I stopped just short of hating Wally, too, for giving me such rotten advice about not filing for custody of the girls before they left British Columbia. But then, no, I couldn't blame Wally. He didn't know John like I did, he didn't know what a bull dog fighter John was when he was aroused. And I wasn't surprised at the judge's verdict.

I was guilty. Oh, yes. John got custody of all three of the older girls, including Susan. I got custody of Barbara Ellen, but the judge let me know his decision about Barbara Ellen was based on her tender age, had she been older, she would have gone with her father, too. But having split up the children in this way, he then had to allow very lenient visitation on both sides. That was something at least. I had almost unlimited access to Susan and Margaret Elizabeth and Rose Mary as John did to Barbara Ellen, but we lived at opposite ends of the province and this ruling didn't assuage my worry about the girls' daily care. I understood that John had a cleaning woman come in once or twice a week, but that he and Susan were doing the cooking.

Neither John nor Susan had ever cooked anything before that I knew of. Susan was an extremely gregarious girl. She wasn't into cooking or sewing or cleaning or any activity that pertained in the slightest to domesticity. Her home was primarily where she came to eat and change clothes in order to rush back outside with her friends where there was music, dancing, softball, skating, tobogganing and snowshoeing. Try as I might, I couldn't conjure up an image of what sort of meal she and John might put on the table. Sandwiches? Scrambled eggs? Frozen TV dinners?

"Stop worrying," Wally admonished after we got back to the old farmhouse. "I'm sure they won't starve to death."

But I worried just the same. And grieved. I'd lie awake at night long after Wally had fallen asleep and wet my pillow with tears of longing for my absent children. But this state of affairs began to change soon enough. After John got a good taste of what constant unrelenting childcare was about he began to soften his stance and become quite cooperative about the older girls' visiting times. Susan and Margaret Elizabeth and Rose Mary were anxious to come down and see their little sisters. When they came to spend the summer, Rose Mary received permission from John to stay with me and Wally until Christmas. At the Christmas break we were all together again and this time Margaret Elizabeth stayed behind when Rose Mary and Susan went back to Kirkland Lake.

This movement back and forth began to form a pattern that was actually fairly successful. At least it relieved my greatest worries having each of them a good part of the year. But there was something about the divorce trial and custody hearing itself that hung around in the back of my throat and brain and refused to locate a spot where it could comfortably settle down. I found myself regurgitating this experience at odd moments and chewing on it for a spell like a cow at cud. I kept trying to find a slot that I could fit this experience into, but somehow it just stuck out there all by itself like a lost mole without a hole. Then one day, I don't remember how, I found a book in my hands. *The Second Sex* by Simone de Beauvoir.

I can't recall who gave me this book. A friend, or perhaps I checked it out of the library myself. Whatever, this book changed my life. Drastically. But not all at once, the change was gradual. I was still having trouble with climate depression and I remember opening the book first on a fall evening when day bumps abruptly into the night with nothing in between, nothing like Henry Longfellow's poem *The Children's Hour* which so beautifully describes that wonderful time between darkness and daylight that occurs in more reasonable climes. The first sparse snowfall outside was trying to make up its mind whether to get serious or knock it off entirely. The little ones were in bed, Margaret Elizabeth was practising the piano and Wally was in the kitchen grading papers.

Wally had a room upstairs that was set aside just for his office but he rarely used it. At first we had fought over the spare room. I wanted it for my writing room, a place to put my typewriter and papers so they wouldn't scatter all over creation. No, Wally said. He needed an office worse than I needed a writing room.

So now nobody used the room. It sat empty with old newspapers scattered about on the floor that Wally refused to clean or to allow me to clean, but when I tried to claim the room again Wally put up the same arguments and then continued to do his work on the kitchen table. I concluded that he just didn't want me to have the room on general principles. But on this particular evening I had settled down on the couch to listen to Margaret Elizabeth practice and to get acquainted with Madame de Beauvoir.

I was still reading after everyone else in the house retired. I was fascinated by Simone de Beauvoir, but finally went to bed around one or two, mindful that we all had to get up early. But I couldn't sleep. Madame de Beauvoir was still talking to me. And she continued to talk non-stop in the weeks and months that followed.

This had happened to me a few times in my life before, when a book would have such a profound influence that the computer files in my brain would start grinding and then come to a complete stop while awaiting further, more complicated or different instructions. I had heard of feminism before, certainly, but it was out there somewhere, not anywhere inside me. But as I read and reread *The Second Sex*, my brain files began to reshuffle, all of them. As this book described the condition of women in general, I began to see how women, through the institutions of patriarchy, came to be regarded as chattel, and how they have remained that way to a certain degree to this day. Certainly there was a double standard between men and women that had always irritated me.

Hadn't I just come through a lawsuit where I had been considered one man's possession, and the law gave the man who possessed the right to sue another man for taking his possession away? Hadn't I just seen that John was awarded the older children not by proving that I was an unfit mother, to the contrary, in court John testified that I was indeed a good mother, my crime here was not how I treated my children, but consisted instead of what the court decided was my lack of loyalty toward the man who had legally possessed me.

And that was only the beginning. I began to understand how females were conditioned from birth, how it was just assumed by my parents and those around me that I would marry early and have children, so of course I did, how years later when I was working as a waitress to support my children when my prize of a first husband, who turned out to be a bobby prize, refused to support his children unless he could sleep with their mother, how a lot of men looked upon me as meat they should be able to order with their drinks and got offended when rebuffed, how men controlled everything I had ever personally come into contact with, including having babies, a man was there when the baby went in and there when it came out. Good God, was there no relief from man-controlled things?

I began to remember all the admonitions concerning religion and sex that I was taught so early and how even when the religion went the prohibitions about sex remained, conditioning me to think of men as powerful and women as frail, to think that a woman without a man was a pitiful being, that women had to have men to tell them what to do and show them the way. This in spite of the fact that it was men who wreaked most of the mayhem in the world, who killed and abused women and children, who were self-centered and egotistical, who cared only for their own children, if they cared at all, who expected another whole sex to fight for the chance to serve them, who made whores out of women and children, who collectively had just about all the power and money, but used it largely for more things and access to more women for themselves, and even good men, as John and Wally both certainly were, felt they were entitled to a certain subservience from women.

Marriage was, after all, an institution like the other patriarchal institutions, only more powerful, because this one, like a mud catfish, lurked around at the bottom of the others that gave rise to racism, militarism, the oppression of women the world over and the horrendous unequal distribution of wealth. Patriarchy ruled over these conditions and had created them in the first place. I began to toy with the idea that marriage was bad for women and a lousy way to raise kids, but what then? If not marriage, then how else could society be arranged? This question loomed large in my mind in the months ahead. I turned to Wally for discussion. Wally wasn't having any, thank you.

"But honey, won't you just read the book? Then we can discuss it rationally."

"I'm too busy."

"But you read everything."

"I don't want to read about what a son of a bitch I am. I know that already. Just ask my boss. He'll tell you."

That was a tactic that Wally used to avoid any issue he didn't want to discuss. Which was patently unfair. Still, I didn't want to be too hard on him. He was young and he had picked out a long row to hoe in the first place by throwing in his lot with me. He was trying to become a traditional family man. Could he help it if I had tangled up with some new ideas about family life that were not only foreign to him, but scary as well? For Wally, too, while much more interested in daily family life than John had ever been, also believed in his heart of hearts that a woman's needs must be subordinate to the man's needs. Of course, he wouldn't say this. But it was there. After several years of marriage I was ready to face up to the fact that Wally picked our friends, decided which movies to see, what functions to attend, when to make love, when to take our nature walks in the woods behind our house, and most importantly how our money was to be spent.

In spite of the fact that Wally was ten years younger than me, and that the union would have benefited from some of my wider experience in life, including extensive childcare experience, Wally was the man and considered himself the expert, even in things like child feeding which he knew beans about. But I had put the children through so much misery to be with Wally, and had given up so much myself in terms of being there all the time for the kids, that I desperately wanted this marriage to work. So I more or less decided to keep my own council about the matter of Simone de Beauvoir, which I did until that fateful day the article about women's rights appeared in the *Sarnia Observer*, the local newspaper. That day was a turning point in mine and Wally's relationship. A small event, that article, but one that eventually led me totally away from the concept of traditional marriage and set my feet upon a path so emotionally rocky there were times when I wasn't sure I would survive.

But survive I did. And here I am still, although languishing, in this Canadian equivalent of the Birmingham Jail, trying to prove my love, love of nature, love of the natural, love of the feminine principle. Proving that love to myself, if nobody else. Headache better, I get up and fasttrack toward the basketball court. But night has lowered and the guard is closing the back door. Later, we are allowed to watch the news on TV.

More arrests. It truly is only a matter of time, I think, before the clear-cutting will stop. The next day we learn that the first groups arrested will be taken to Victoria the following day for a court appearance in which the trial date will be set. But I wake up with an earache and swirling dizziness. It is an infected inner ear. I've had it before. The prison doctor orders some antibiotics but we have to leave for Victoria before the medicine arrives. And nobody tells us that we three grandmothers are to be flown over until we arrive at the airport.

I protest by insisting that I am a non-flyer, which I most sincerely am, but I grit my teeth at Judith's and Inessa's urgings, and am half-pushed and half-pulled into the small rickety-ass plane. The entire proceedings are made unbelievably complicated by the leg shackles and handcuffs we are forced to wear. Three grandmothers in leg irons for protesting the demolition of one of the world's last old growth rainforests! Lord have mercy on us and thunder and tarnation! I am finally seated but my stomach knows very well that this is a risky business and threatens to revolt all by itself. I am handed a paper bag, although all I heave into it are tears of humiliation. Had I known what awaited me at the city jailcells in Victoria, I would have backed up and flat refused to get on that pitiful excuse for an airplane.

TWELVE

Dear friends and gentle people, whatever you do, try to stay out of the city of Victoria's jailcells. At least if you are a woman. These cells are a pox on that fair city, a veritable Dark Ages nightmare, a dank dungeon of sunless stale air, cheap torn plastic mattresses, and severe shortages of towels, shampoo, clean blankets, and pillows. There is a drunk tank in line with four other small cells, all with open toilets but no sinks; the only sink in the place is in the back room which is inaccessible when prisoners are locked down for the night. The building is ancient and the ventilation practically nonexistent. The cigarette smoke is overpowering and there is nowhere to go for a breath of fresh air. And oh, the food.

All from the depths of the fast food bowels of A & W. Fried hamburgers, chickenburgers, or a small anaemic iceberg lettuce salad for lunch, the same for dinner, except a few French fries and a fried apple pie thrown in for good measure and I do mean thrown. I am not well. I take to my bunk, feeling snake bit and damned to die.

But no, I am taken to see a doctor. In the waiting room of the private clinic there are stares. While the officer has removed my handcuffs before entering the clinic, I am obviously being escorted by a sheriff. I am almost overwhelmed by the urge to rise in my seat with clinched fist and should "Long live the ancient forests of Clayoquot Sound!" But I am afraid I will be taken away without the medicine that I sorely need. But back at the cells I find a further complication to life and sanity. Belinda arrives.

Belinda makes quite an entrance, kicking and screaming profanities at the male officers who are trying to wrestle her into a position to be searched by the matron. Belinda is a big woman, with powerful arms and shoulders. On the face of it, I will put my money on Belinda. The officers and matron in charge of getting Belinda through processing and into the cell block with the rest of us must not use excessive force, and Belinda is all excessive force. But finally she is subdued and locked into an individual cell. Much to my personal relief.

But not for long. Under the matron's urgings Belinda soon simmers down and promising to be a good girl, is released into the common area with the rest of us. She stares straight at me and Inessa and Judith. We, like rabbits mesmerized by an unblinking, hypnotic rattler, stare back.

"What the hell are you old ladies doing in here?" Belinda demands.

We try to tell her what we are doing in here.

"So you're tree-huggers," she concludes in a menacing voice.

"Umm ... yes," I admit, wondering if I can outrun her around the common room. Or perhaps I can persuade the matron to lock me down in my own cell.

"Well, I don't think you have any business in here cluttering up my space," Belinda answers, the scowl on her broad face deepening.

I smile. A nervous smile. An old southern girl device, when faced with danger, flash the pearlies. But Belinda is not softened. It is Inessa who defuses the situation. She suggests we have a circle and invites Belinda to join us. Belinda declines. She's not having any of this garbage, she says. But when we start singing softly she changes her mind and comes into the circle.

Belinda has a hog-calling voice that grates the ear but she is an energetic singer. I can't figure her out. I've already met a fair sampling of "junkies" and she doesn't seem to be that, nor does she seem to be drunk. The way she hops and rocks around she just seems manic, and later I learn that is exactly what she is.

Belinda is well acquainted with the city jail. Periodically she inexplicably stops taking her medicine and then trouble automatically ensues. She was brought in this time for raising a ruckus with her ex-landlord about an unreturned damage deposit. Later in the afternoon Belinda confides in me that this was the third time she tried to get her damage deposit back and the third time she'd been arrested for her efforts.

"You'd think the son-of-a-bitch didn't want to give me back my damage deposit, wouldn't you?" she asks rather wistfully.

This time I try to hide my smile but don't quite succeed.

"You think that's funny," she says threateningly, giving me the fishy eye again. "Just wait till you see dinner."

She's right. Mostly vegetarian now, the thought of a greasy hamburger or imitation chickenburger on buns made of paste makes my stomach quiver like a frog leg in a frying pan. So I order another anaemic iceberg lettuce salad. Along with this comes a few French fries and a little fried apple pie. Louisiana people, until just recently, would fry most anything that flies, swims, crawls, stands in a field or just leans against the side of the porch in a provocative manner. My mother's generation didn't know way back then that all that fried okra and fried green tomatoes and fried pork chops and chicken and grits swimming in gravy made with fat back or salt pork, and hush puppies made with lard and fried along with the catfish would stiffen your arteries and shorten your life span. But even the most rural country people have got the message now that frying everything one puts in one's mouth isn't healthy. But the Victoria city jailcells have somehow not gotten the word. Or else they don't give a damn. Suspecting the latter I turn in early wishing desperately that I could get away from all the cigarette smoke.

Inessa is suffering from the smoke, too, and complains bitterly. She writes poetry and feeling the need to compose requests pen and paper. She gets neither. But I am so exhausted I fall asleep immediately in spite of the bright lights, cigarette smoke, endless chatter and swearing from the other more typical inmates, the metal bunk, the crummy mattress, not enough pillows as I have to sleep propped up because of the ear infection, and not enough blankets. Oh God, what misery! I would have been more comfortable in an open field with corn husks for a mattress. But sleep catches up with me before

I can turn over twice, which is a good thing, because Belinda is up at four-thirty, rallying the troops.

"Get up, you tree-huggers!" she hollers in a voice that would surely be prized even among the most particular hog growers in the south. "Get up and get out there on the road! Those MacMillan-Bloedel trucks are rolling!"

The matron tries to appeal to Belinda's sense of fair play, but Belinda's medicine hasn't totally kicked in yet.

"Come on, tree-huggers! Let's roll. You gonna lay here and let those trucks go through? Let's get cracking!"

I want to crack her head. But she is only an hour and a half early as we have to get up at six anyway for a court appearance to ask for a postponement of the trial. Sheila Simpson, one of our number, decides to go ahead with her own trial and is sentenced to six months in prison. The rest of us are taken back to the Nanaimo Correctional Centre.

Tonight I lie awake, too tired and confused to sleep. I think about my past experience with civil dissent and how regardless of where I go or what I do some big ole mess of one kind or another seems to float right up on my doorstep, bellowing out my name like a lost heifer looking for its mama. But the other conflicts seemed somehow easier to grasp. This one is as slippery as a revival preacher's fistful of tithe pledges.

In the first place, the NDP government is obviously in a position of conflict of interest. The provincial government is the single largest stock holder in MacMillan-Bloedel. They bought additional stocks shortly before the government brought down the ruling that MacBlo could resume clear-cutting in the Clayoquot Sound. And if that isn't enough, this same government that I voted for, that I have always voted for since I was allowed to vote in Canada, takes over the cost of prosecuting the trial.

There is also something very rotten in the woodpile when most of the forty-odd accused people do not have lawyers of their own but are depending on a pool of volunteer lawyers who are constantly shifting, none of whom seem to know what the others are doing. How can any sense, never mind justice, come out of a mass trial like this? Maybe Sheila was right, just go ahead and get it over with and take whatever. Still, I have cast my lot with the others and will stay till the bitter end.

On the twenty-sixth of July we are all taken back to Victoria from Nanaimo for selecting a trial date. The date is set for August thirty-first, not nearly enough time for the lawyers to bring forth a presentable case. At the end of the day there are only three of us who refuse to sign the undertaking, Inessa, Judith and I. The three grandmothers. The Clayoquot Grannies. We three are sent to the women's prison in Burnaby, B.C.

Our initial processing takes several hours. This includes showering and washing one's hair with anti-lice shampoo. I might have been horrified at the suggestion of lice had I not spent the last five days in Victoria city jailcells. Had they told me that I had contacted leprosy there, I wouldn't have been surprised. After processing, we are taken to our cell block. Housing sixteen or so women, we each have a room of our own. The rooms have real doors on them and although the doors are locked at night and only the matrons have keys I don't care, the doors are not bars. The building is relatively new. Everything is clean and bright. I can see grass from the window and green fields, and I am allowed to call my children. My spirits lift but I retire as soon as I am allowed to do so. This living in the fast lane is wearing me down.

After breakfast the following morning Inessa and I are sent to the sewing room. It is here the prison greens are made. I am to help make them. Very well. At lunch there is a message for me. My daughter Rose Mary wants me to call her immediately.

From Ontario Rose Mary tells me that Susan is in the hospital in Washington, Pennsylvania. Susan's left eye has inexplicably closed. The doctors think it may be an inflamed muscle. I don't like the sound of this. But Rose Mary promises to call again tomorrow morning which will be Friday.

But she doesn't call and I have to go to the sewing room with the others. The mistress of the sewing room says she can't use us until Monday and to report back to our unit. There are chores to do there but I manage to hang around the phone waiting for Rose Mary's call. The call comes after lunch. Rose Mary tells me in a shaken voice that Susan's pulled eye muscle has somehow turned into a brain aneurism. Susan is being flown from Washington, Pennsylvania to Pittsburgh for an emergency operation. The world comes crashing down around me.

I must get out of here, immediately. I must go to my daughter. I inform the officer on duty that I will sign the undertaking and leave as my daughter is very ill. The officer understands and contacts her supervisor. While this is going on I remember that my wallet is in transit from Nanaimo Correctional Centre. When we were processed into Burnaby we were told it might take a few days for our personal possessions to arrive. My wallet holds my credit cards and my identification, both necessary for flying across the border. The officer inside the glassed-in office hangs up the phone and comes to the door again. She's frowning.

I remember her as being youngish, concerned, and somewhat flustered at having to deal with my growing anxiety.

"There seem to be some problems associated with the undertaking. The main office isn't sure they have one to sign. And even if they find one you can't just sign it, I mean, you have to sign it before the proper authorized body ..."

"What are you talking about?" I demand in a strange, thin voice that seems to be coming from somewhere outside my own body. My hands and legs are shaking. "I have to get out of here," I go on. "Do you know where my wallet is?"

"I'll see if I can locate it for you."

The officer turns and goes back to the phone and then Inessa is at my elbow leading me in my highly agitated state to the table outside the office door.

"I don't understand this," I mumble as I fold my trembling frame into a chair.

"Just sit here," Inessa says soothingly. "I'll get you some juice. As soon as the officer hears anything I'll come tell you. I'm right here."

She moves away and Judith comes and offers money, she can borrow it, she says, from relatives in town.

"But even if I have money for a plane ticket I don't have any identification without my wallet. I can't get over the border."

The officer appears again in the doorway. The concern on her face has deepened.

"I'm sorry, but there is no undertaking here for you to sign," she says.

I start to rise from my chair. It is like trying to swim up through a barrel of molasses, but I make it.

"But can't they get one?" I shriek in panic-stricken tones.

"Yes, but the problem is not just anybody can bring it over on the ferry. A sheriff's deputy has to do it."

"Well?" I demand, trying to keep from screaming. "Tell the sheriff's department to bring one."

"I did, but it's a holiday weekend."

"What holiday?"

"British Columbia Day. The sheriff's office is short of deputies. There may not be a deputy available until Tuesday."

I stare at the officer wildly. Inessa gently forces me back down into the chair.

"I'll call the lawyers," she says firmly. "One of them is bound to be able to figure some way out of this." She heads for the phones on the side wall where the prisoners are allowed to make calls at will, but only local or collect calls.

"Please let me call the hospital," I beg the officer. "I have a credit card."

"I'm so sorry," she answers, her eyes softening with pity. "The phones in here don't accept credit cards. The only way you can call long distance is collect."

"But the hospital won't accept a collect call from me. You can understand that, can't you?"

"Yes, and I'm terribly sorry."

I will go mad. Susan, my black-eyed Susan, my sturdy, healthy little girl with wild, dark curls, learning to walk, ride a bike, climb a fence, wilful, headstrong, loving, a young matron now, with a husband and two little girls of her own, Carla and Sarah, who are equally dark-eyed and headstrong and loving. What will become of them if Susan dies? I can't stand it. I break into wild weeping.

"Call some of your other children," the officer suggests. "They can call the hospital for you and then call you here."

Good idea. I pull myself together enough to go to the phones but I can't get ahold of anybody. Nobody answers at Rose Mary's place, John's place, or Susan's house, and I can't get either Margaret Elizabeth or Andre to answer in Ucluelet. My God, where is everybody? Has Susan already died? After a million years Inessa comes back from the telephone.

"I talked to one of the lawyers. He's going to do what he can. He's making some phone calls."

My chest is hurting. Am I having a heart attack? "I can't breath ..."

"Come see the nurse," Judith entreats in a soothing voice. "Maybe she can give you something."

I follow her small, neat figure down the hall and out of the unit. I find myself in a bleak, bare, walled-off waiting room. Judith is not allowed to wait with me. Finally the nurse comes in, a thin faced, cold eyed woman of indeterminate age. I tell her about Susan, and how I don't know what is happening, and how I can't go to her because there is no undertaking to sign and it may be Monday before one can be brought over, and I have chest pains and difficulty in breathing. Sitting across from me she has listened quietly. When I finish she reaches over and lightly pats my hands.

"You're just suffering from anxiety," she says, smiling a little. I don't like this woman's smile nor the smug expression in her eyes nor the coldness of her touch. I stare at her.

"Just anxiety?" I ask dumbly.

"Yes. I know this is hard for you but at times like these there are also opportunities, opportunities to turn to God for help. He is the only one who can really help you, God and His Son, Jesus Christ. They will help you through all this."

I have stumbled into an insane asylum. I get up and leave without further ado, hoping that, as much as I dislike this woman, it is as she says, about the chest pains at least — that they are the result of acute anxiety. But how does she know without examining me; she is only guessing. I am sixty-five years old and older people have heart attacks all the time, from acute anxiety, too. No wonder the woman advises turning to Jesus Christ for help, as there is certainly no help forthcoming from her department. When I get back to the unit there is news. Of a sort.

The lawyer is trying to contact the attorney general of British Columbia and find out if there is any sort of humanitarian release that will allow me to leave the correctional centre. But it may take awhile. I call Margaret Elizabeth's number again and this time Andre answers. He tries to comfort me and says he will stay on the phone to both Rose Mary's and Susan's numbers. Dinner trays come down but eating is impossible. I go up to my room and stare out across the fields.

I am a prisoner. Now I know what prison is. If you know you can get out anytime by signing a piece of paper you may be incarcerated but you are not imprisoned. But now I am definitely in prison. I cannot get out. My daughter may be dying and I can't go to her. There is no freedom anywhere.

My Suzie-Q, how I long to be with you, to hold your hand, to touch your live flesh ...

The pain in my chest grows tighter. Dinner is long over. Sounds of inmates talking and moving about float up from downstairs. Someone is playing their in-cell radio just below my room. I struggle up from the bed and wash my hot, swollen face with cold water. Just as I finish there is a knock on my door. It is the evening duty officer. There is a long distance call for me. I fly downstairs to the little side office where inmates receive incoming calls. The officer leaves and shuts the door behind her so that I have privacy. And then I turn to stone. I am afraid to pick up the phone. What if it is bad news? Are they calling to tell me that Susan is dead? But I have to pick up the receiver. I can't refuse to pick it up. That's not allowed. The universe doesn't allow that sort of thing. Time does not, will not, stand still. I pick up the receiver with such shaking fingers I can hardly bring the instrument to my ear, and over the roar in my head I hear John's voice.

"It's okay," he says without preamble. "She's going to be okay."

His own voice is badly shaken and I know he has been weeping.

"She's okay?" I repeat mindlessly, brain reeling.

"Yes, she's going to be okay. I just got through talking to the doctor. He said the operation went very well and barring anything unforeseen he expects a good outcome."

My shaking legs can no longer hold me upright and I collapse into the chair by the desk.

"She's okay? She's really okay?" I ask again.

John laughs but I can still hear the weeping in his voice.

"Yes, she really is."

"Oh, my God! How wonderful! I was afraid ..."

"Me, too. But we're all very lucky. A surgeon who specializes in this sort of thing just happened to be in the hospital in Washington and he flew her to Pittsburgh and into the operating room before the blood vessel began to leak seriously or erupt ..."

"Oh, my God! It's over and she's really okay ..."

"Yes. She's fine. The doctor says they expect her to come through now without complications ..."

I find myself trying to explain to John the administrative nightmare I am enmeshed in, but it is difficult as I am crying and laughing at the same time. Oh, my God! She's okay, she's okay, she's living, she's breathing, she'll hold my hand and smile upon me again. For this blessing, oh Mother of the Universe, for restoring my daughter, my life is yours. Do with me what you will; of course you will do that anyway, but there is a difference between simply taking and having something freely given ...

"Maybe you ought to just relax now and stop worrying about trying to come here," John is saying. "Joe's parents have the kids, and I'm here to spend night and day in the hospital if need be, and besides, Joe is with her, too. She's his wife, you know ... I'll keep you updated. And as soon as she's able I'll have her call you and I'll send her some flowers from you, too, okay? You don't need to go anywhere, but you do need to stop worrying, right now. Promise?"

What a wonderful man, I think as I hang up the phone. Our friendship has survived ignorance, marriage, sickness, social unrest, war, hurricanes, floods, fires, jealousy, psychological torture on both sides, divorce, rearing children between two different households and the willingness, nay the eagerness, to explore contentious issues to the very bloody end and let the chips fall where they may. A friend indeed. I don't know how we reached this place, this cool, shady place of friendship, but we had, years before.

I head back to my room, the weight of life and death gradually lifting from my chest. I can breath again! Hugs and congratulations from Inessa and Judith and smiles from the others as I make my way upstairs. I sit down gingerly on the edge of my bunk. Yes, I can definitely breath again. There is a hollow ache in my chest where nothing much was going in and out of my lungs for awhile, but I can feel the oxygen start to seep into all the spongy crevices again. Yes, and I can see normally, too, and hear and smell. But my stomach is growling. It's because I haven't eaten lunch or dinner. I get up and wash my face again and then go back downstairs to the kitchen where there is always toast and peanut butter, and people who want to hear the particulars about my daughter, and I don't care that some of them have killed their lovers or boyfriends or pimps, or tried to transport a truck load of dope, or held up a service station with a knife. They are women, after all, and concerned with family relationships.

It is Sunday evening and Susan calls. I can't believe it! She was at death's door on Friday and here she is chatting at me, a metal clamp in her skull, her voice a little wan and weak, but her infectious chuckle the same. I ask her if she wants me to sign the undertaking tomorrow and come to her.

"No, Mom. It's too late. All the action is over."

"I can help look after the kids."

"The girls are fine at Joe's parents. And Dad's here. I don't want to be responsible for causing you to give up your protest. I'm going to be fine, Mom. And if you can help save some rainforest for the kids to come visit then that's the very best thing you can do. So you just hang in, okay?"

THIRTEEN

I hang in. But my thoughts are rarely far from my recuperating daughter in the days and weeks that follow. They hover around her and her little family, rooting around like a wild hog in a turnip patch, worrying every possibility to death, searching through a maze of complicated questions of health, both mental and physical, such as ... how does one go about raising healthy daughters in such a woman-hating society?

How can a mother like me give a daughter something she herself never had, something she herself was deprived of in her own childhood, a healthy sense of self-esteem? How can a mother encourage a strong sense of selfhood in a daughter when that very daughter sees her mother's daily round of duties in diametrical opposition to independent selfhood? The mother must become selfless in order to rear her daughters in such a hostile environment. Besides the children, there is usually an outside job and a man of one sort or another to pacify, too. It's too much. It's too hard. And if the mother really gets into the history of women's oppression then the man, because he is the man closest at hand, must answer to some of this garbage, one way or another. He's a man, isn't he? He's a member of the male society that has bullied women about for all recorded history, isn't he? Well, and what does the hapless fellow have to say for himself about all this?

Sometimes nothing. If he's caught off guard, the way Wally was when I discovered Simone de Beauvoir, the man may simply retreat. But a woman mustn't mistake this for surrender. Oh, no. The man just goes underground and turns into a guerrilla fighter. Too clever by far to stand up in a pitched battle and run the risk of verbally losing his head, my own Wally went out of his way to pacify enemy territory. On the surface. Underneath, he waited for opportunities for lightning strike ambushes, and then quickly, before the opponent could recover, would do a fast fade back into the jungle, leaving the dense foliage behind to cover all traces of the attack. And Wally was decidedly quick on the draw.

At first the ambushes were confined to parties or other get-togethers. Wally would amble over to where I would be in deep conversation with at least one other person about some issue raised by some book I'd just read. Wally would inform everyone within earshot that the writer of the book hadn't really said what I said he or she had said, that he or she had actually said or meant something else. Then he would pat me on the head like I was his pet goat and wander away. Back at home, when I would confront Wally with this outrageous behavior he would rewrite history. He really hadn't said what I was accusing him of saying, he had actually said something else. But the worst was yet to come.

The worst came in the form of an article in the *Sarnia Observer*. It was about this new movement called Women's Liberation. Women's Lib for short. Women's Lib somehow was less threatening to everyone than saying Women's Lib-er-at-ion which was kind of scary. Women's Lib was kind of cute. The article was cute, too and so were the three women interviewed. Upper class women, all. They all three said, oh no, no, no. We don't need any women's rights here. We like our privileged positions.

So I sat down and wrote a letter to the editor saying well, maybe not these three women, but run some of those women's rights by me. And I included a phone number for any other woman who might feel the same.

Well, the phone fairly rang off the wall. Us, too, a couple of dozen women out there yelled in unison. Lay some of those women's rights on us, too. There were twenty women for a first meeting and twice that many wanted notification of future meetings.

How exciting! I'd been to one country fair and two goat ropings and I'd never seen anything like this! In the weeks and months that followed our numbers increased daily. We formed committees and spread out into the community like a swarm of killer bees. The school system first felt our sting for objecting to textbooks that showed males forever dashing about in charge of earth-shaking events while women were largely ignored or shown as victims or pitifuls.

Next we stung the chemical plants in the area for not opening up some of their high paying jobs to women. Then we drew a bit of blood from city council about the inadequate daycare program. The churches in the area felt our stings, too, especially the Catholic church for its stance on abortion and its tendency to blame all society's ills on women. And then we honed in on the local politicians for their general lack of sensitivity to women's needs. What energy! What devotion! And an entire new group of young feminist writers began to barge into women's consciousness like late stompers at a country dance, tying together loose ends of old arguments and stirring the already agitated waters with new ones — Germaine Greer, Gloria Steinem, Kate Millett, Robin Morgan, Evelyn Reed, and a clump of others were taking Simone de Beauvoir and Betty Friedan's place in the goat wagon and were riding hell bent for glory. But I couldn't persuade Wally to read any of these books.

"But how can you call yourself an educated man if you know nothing of the historical oppression of women and refuse to read any of the literature that is lightning striking this country?"

"The same way you think of yourself as an educated person even though you know nothing of math or physics and have never darkened a university door."

That was a low blow. And not entirely true. I *had* taken some university writing courses in extension, graduate courses at that, from the University of Oklahoma. The undergraduate degree was waived as a prerequisite if one was already published. Which I was. And there were other courses — I had taken Canadian history courses and the bloody French course and college English courses. But that didn't amount to much of anything in his eyes or anybody else's. But I resented his using my lack of formal education as a weapon.

However, his favorite weapon, and the one that produced the greatest body count on my side, was Wally's fantastic memory for details.

For me, reading is a little like eating a jar of salt mackerel. I am keenly interested in the taste, smell, and texture of the mackerel and only after I have finished eating do I bother much with names and titles and places of origins of the mackerel. In fact, I most often don't bother at all unless the mackerel has made a wonderful impression on me. Ah, but Wally is the opposite.

Before Wally even opened the damned jar he would go straight for names, titles and places of origin. He wanted to know where this mackerel first sucked in it's water oxygen, where it was abiding when abducted, who his (I say his because Wally rarely read books by women, feminist or no) mama and daddy were, when he first moved out of his birthplace to go abroad, when he first mated, who all of his subsequent mistresses were, who his friends were and what he did for amusement. And at some function a week or a month or a year later Wally would trot out these little details about a mackerel he may never even have tasted, leaving me sounding like a fool as I tried to explain the texture of these same mackerel that I had feasted upon. It was maddening.

And Wally's aversion to feminist literature was puzzling. This man read a lot of pretty obscure stuff, and even as time went on and feminism threatened to become mainstream, Wally still refused to crack a single feminist book. Paradoxically, John *was* reading feminist literature at a voracious pace and we began a rather clandestine correspondence about the literature.

John wasn't trying to lure me back. He had given up on that when we divorced. Besides, he had a new woman who was warming his cold feet at night. But John and I had these years behind us of mutual reading and discussion, at least about political trends and events, and with this new thing of women's liberation that had crawled on board we had lots to discuss. When John called about the girls' ever-shifting schedules or grades or music lessons, he would usually mention, in a rather furtive manner, as he didn't want to be accused by Wally of feeding me subversive literature, some new book or new article that I should see.

Peculiar. But maybe not. Because John had reason to start thinking in feminist terms. He still had children, at least part of the time, but he no longer had a wife.

John and his new love weren't actually living together. So John had to be his own wife and act as mother and father to boot when the girls were with him. These experiences had moved his soul wonderfully. He had suddenly gained an almost instantaneous and abiding insight into women's unpaid, unrecognized, and largely unappreciated role as caregivers. The man could now relate. There was at least one male convert in the land.

But I certainly hadn't given up on Wally. I loved him still. He was a decent man, respected by his students and colleagues. He was also a very sweet father for the little ones, attentive and imaginative in his care of them. When he was asked to run for the NDP in 1974 in the federal election I actively encouraged him.

I thought this was a great idea. When we first arrived in Canada, I had latched onto the NDP like it was a tar baby because there was nothing like the New Democratic Party in Ku Klux Klan land. I was a great enthusiast for the NDP. Had I known then that, the first time I was in a province where the NDP actually came into power, they would arrest me for protesting their forest policy, I might have been a tad less light-footed on the matter.

Wally didn't refuse whatever assistance I could throw his way. After all, women's rights had become part of the NDP platform, so it didn't look too shabby to have a wife who was active in the local women's movement. Not that Wally had a snowball's chance in hell of winning, Sarnia was, after all, a Liberal stronghold in those days. But I appreciated Wally's courage for putting himself on the line, and I loved his speeches, and found the general bite and claw of a Canadian election sort of interesting, even if it wasn't as funny or entertaining as southern elections. That is, none of the candidates, including my husband, gave their speeches dressed only in overalls with no shirt and with their fancy ladies hanging over their shoulders. Or sang their own made-up country songs, usually very badly, while accompanying themselves on the guitar. Canadian temperaments were somewhat milder, having cooled over the centuries with all that ice and snow. But while the election had its bright spots, the things that were wrong with me and Wally kept getting wronger.

For one thing, every winter my ole SAD syndrome came back to claim me for its own. In the depths of Ontario's dark, grey, cold winters I would dream longingly, both asleep and awake, of the Clayoquot Sound. I could feel the surging tides of Long Beach calling me. It was out there, I hadn't just dreamed it or imagined it, I could actually see the eagles soar in my mind's eye, I could smell the myriad smells of the sea and rainforest. The yearning inside me was worse than any longing for a lover. The urge to return to that unforgettable, unbelievable place was so strong at times that I could feel an incomprehensible sorrow swell up inside me that was physical as well as emotional. At the worst times I pleaded with Wally to consider relocating back to the west coast. I only succeeded in irritating him.

"Look, after our last mad dash westward I'm lucky to have a job at all. We're here, we're settled, and I'll remind you that your ex-husband also lives in Ontario, which makes it relatively easy to transport the kids back and forth. Everybody can't live in Lotus Land. Forget about Vancouver Island and let's make our lives here."

Easy for him to say. He was born around Hamilton, his parents lived in Waterdown, it was all home to him. But he had a point about the kids. For them it was definitely easier to stay put. But in spite of my new resolve every year to totally busy myself with the kids and my women's group so I wouldn't notice the weather so much, by fall's end the inevitable depression would descend, deepening as the snows began, fostering the distinct sensation in my gut and brain that the world was dying. Snow and ice covered the entire earth, smothering it, and me, too. I couldn't breath, there was no oxygen, the life-giving leaves were gone from the trees, replaced by death-dealing ice and snow and Arctic winds.

Ah, yes, this black depression would settle upon my spirit like an evil, suffocating blanket, numbing my brain and blurring my eyesight. My limbs, no longer swift and light became slow and stupid. No more singing and dancing around the house, clunk, clunk, my leaded limbs blundered from room to room searching for an unoccupied spot to collapse. And Wally, unable and unwilling to relieve my suffering, but unnerved by it nevertheless, sharpened his tongue against my leaded armor, usually in front of other people. The separations began.

There were at least a half dozen leave-takings. I would move, taking the kids, from Wally's house to another house somewhere in and out of Sarnia, then back to Wally's house, then away from Wally's house again, to a neighboring town. Then as the years passed, the leave-takings began to carry me and the girls further and further away, like some capricious, westward wind and it was harder and harder to get back. Finally we blew all the way to California to see Joey, my oldest son.

By this time Susan and Margaret Elizabeth and Rose Mary were young women in college. When we left California some months later, Susan and Rose Mary returned to Ontario, but this time, recognizing that my relationship with Wally had become all sink holes and hollows and anyway, had long ago grown cold enough to start killing hogs, I decided to go home. Not back to Louisiana. The countryside I knew there as a child had vanished. Margaret Elizabeth and Barbara Allen and Marian and I headed straight up the coast to Vancouver Island. The call of the wild was thundering so loud inside my head I couldn't have heard Gabriel's horn calling us to glory had it sounded. Damnit, I was going home. To the Clayoquot Sound.

FOURTEEN

 But it took awhile to make it back to the Clayoquot Sound. There were school and work opportunities to consider for the girls and I needed a job myself, so we settled temporarily in Victoria. And Mike, my second son, was newly arrived in the area, too. Mike was a teacher, an artist, and a house- and boat-builder, but he was particularly a wilderness man. Which his wife didn't appreciate at all. His wife was a lovely woman, but a city girl, and the way nature throws together such ill-matched people is a crime. But nature cares only for the offspring of such unions which in this case was Jason, a beautiful, intelligent boy.

Aside from hating cities and loving the wilderness, Mike was determined to stop teaching art, which was what he had been doing, and start *doing* art and take the financial consequences, which is a revolutionary act that always tempts total damnation from society, fate, and the universe at large. The summer following our move to Victoria, Mike and Jason and I, Jason being on loan to us for the summer, went up to the Clayoquot to look around for some cheap land.

And we found our ten acres in Cypress Bay. As soon as Jason returned to Ottawa, Mike moved out to the property and started building an A-frame. I went up every chance I got. Three years later, after Margaret Elizabeth went to explore Toronto, where her brother Andy and his wife and son lived and moved in musical circles, and after Barbara Ellen decided to move into her boyfriend's apartment in Victoria, and Marian, in college and trying to break the apron strings, decided to take the smaller apartment across the hall from Barbara and friend, I decided it was the perfect time to head for Cypress Bay.

The land of my dreams. Paradise on earth.

The mountains behind our place were dreadfully clear-cut but no logging was going on at the moment. And I was just delirious with joy to be back in this magical place. Later Marian, having inherited the wilderness gene, too, and discovering the Open Learning University, came to Cypress Bay to keep me company. But as the fall deepened, we learned that all was not well back in Victoria. Barbara Ellen was pregnant, ill, and wanted to leave her partner.

I couldn't bring her to Cypress Bay. Her pregnancy was a complicated one. Marian and I went to Victoria shortly before Christmas and stayed until Barbara Ellen's son Julian was born. A perfect little boy, in spite of all the worry. I had been looking for a house in Tofino which was the nearest village to Cypress Bay, but the prices there had blown up like a mule let loose in the corn field. Tofino was becoming trendy. Ucluelet, the next closest town, was decidedly not trendy. It was a working-class town that had disfigured its own mountains with clear-cutting and a lot of the town's loggers hated Tofino's environmentalists and hippies. But being working-class myself, or whatever the Louisiana country equivalent is, and decidedly pro-union, I didn't turn up my nose at Ucluelet. Besides, it had a larger population than Tofino, thus more kids, which is what Barbara needed for her plans for a little ballet studio when she was ready to go back to work. Besides, the houses in Ucluelet were decidedly cheaper.

John, who was also worried about Barbara Ellen's situation, sent me the money for a down payment and we bought a little two story clunker of a house right across from the elementary school. Margaret Elizabeth hadn't cared much for the Toronto scene, but she had found a man she liked, Andre Sperling. He and Margaret Elizabeth married, moved to Ucluelet, too, and occupied the top part of the house while Andre set about making much needed repairs. Barbara Ellen reconciled with her partner, Michel, so her little family took over the bottom half. Satisfied that this was a good arrangement, I went back out to Cypress Bay. And eventually to the blockades.

But Barbara Ellen was still unsettled. The baby was thriving like wild poke salad, and Barbara Ellen did get the ballet school off the ground, but the reconciliation between her and Michel didn't stick and Michel moved out. Barbara Ellen married someone else some months later, and she and her new husband decided to relocate in Vancouver. They were looking for an apartment about the time the trial started and I mentioned this to Inessa as we were being transported to the courthouse for the first day of the trial.

"Tell her to call me," Inessa said when we were settled in the courthouse cells. It would be at least an hour before we would be taken upstairs to the courtroom. The waiting in the courthouse cells was an agonizing business. One bunk to sit on. Open toilet. Prisoners allowed to smoke.

"Call you?" I asked, unsure what she meant.

"Yes. I've decided to sign the undertaking. I can't take those Victoria city jailcells again. My body just won't take the cigarette smoke. I'm allergic. Besides, I think I can probably do more on the outside. And I'm going to be moving out of my apartment to a smaller one. Barbara Ellen can come look at my apartment if she wants to and if she likes it I'll give her a recommendation."

"But you're leaving us!" I wail.

"Yes. I think it's best for me."

I hug her and tell her of course she must do what she thinks best, but I will miss her sorely. That leaves only me and Judith incarcerated. So I will just have to work harder at this, whatever this turns out to be.

We are finally escorted upstairs into the crowded courtroom. I think I am actually hoping for a glimmer of justice in this mess. But when the Honourable Mr. Justice John Bouck enters and bows before taking his seat, before he even utters a word, my hopes are put on hold. This elderly man of a stocky build with his pink-white face and white white hair bears a striking physical resemblance to my father.

My father has been dead for twenty-five years, but there was so much anger and confusion and personality conflict in our relationship that a judge looking this much like my father is most certainly a bad omen. By the time the day is over my intuition has been confirmed. Judge Bouck is definitely not on our side.

I don't mean that I think he should be on our side. He shouldn't be on anybody's side, he's supposed to be the judge. And yet he has already forewarned us that for him the issue is a simple one, did we disobey a court injunction by standing on the logging road at Kennedy Bridge blocking a MacMillan-Bloedel logging truck? And if we did we can expect to be charged with contempt of court, possible criminal contempt of court. My own personal opinion is that we are already condemned in this man's eyes. Still, hope springs eternal in the human breast, and, if we can present good enough arguments, then perhaps the judge will be moved. Even in murder cases, motive carries a lot of weight, and surely Judge Bouck will consider our motives.

And then that night, back at the loathsome city cells, I receive the most unexpected, marvellous present. Around seven-thirty a group of supporters appear on the top railing of the parking arcade outside holding lighted candles and they begin to sing. They are serenading me and Judith! My heart leaps in gladness. What a stupendous thing to do! I jump up on a chair and try to see through a slit in the frosted-over window. I can't see clearly through the slit but I catch a glimpse of Valerie Langer's slender figure and long, dark, curly hair. Valerie, although a young woman, acts as the mother of the Friends of the Clayoquot in Tofino, the group that made the blockades possible. Later, Inessa tells me that she was there, too. But the serenade is definitely making the matron and the male jailers nervous.

Several officers are hanging around our cell block, checking the doors and windows as if they expect the singers outside to storm the Bastille. I want to respond to the singers outside, tell them how much this means to me. How to do it? A note? Yes. I hastily scribble a note and slip it outside the tiny crack in the window, hoping it will be seen when I drop it. But before I can drop the note a young man leaps onto the ledge outside the building and runs to the ledge beneath our cells.

Suddenly the matron and guards are going nuts. Now there are a half dozen cops opening the big door that leads to the outside ledge and Judith and I are unceremoniously locked down into our cells. Well, so much for a moonlight serenade. But I can hear a commotion outside. The singers are being made to disperse. I am sorry I tried to slip the note, the young man might have been hurt, or arrested. But I will never forget the singers.

The following morning I find I have a lawyer assigned to me. However, as the days progress I see that there are distinct advantages to defending oneself as a lot of the others are doing. If one is one's own lawyer, one can object to things being said in the courtroom and cross-examine witnesses. After the first week I inform the court that I will represent myself. And even though Judith and I are still incarcerated and must sit apart in the jury box under guard instead of down in the courtroom proper, lawyers Robert Moore-Stewart and Ron MacIsaac see that we get most of the information that is floating around among the others. But the first week is largely taken up with showing videos of the arrests.

We see ourselves standing on the blockade at Kennedy River bridge and being arrested. These videos are interesting to me because I was hauled away in the very first group and didn't get to witness any of the other arrests. Some of them are very moving. The videos of the Harrises, George and his young sons, Tyson and Adam, are especially stirring, as are the ones of Sheila Simpson, that fey little Irish person, whose name is listed on every legal document that passes into my hands, MacMillan Bloedel Limited verses Sheila Simpson, et al, how this makes me smile, and then there is the awesomeness of the silent arrests.

But I am having a contentious time in the city cells. The ear infection is trying to return and my mouth is covered with fever blisters. Job is beginning to seem like a piker compared to the pestilence being heaped upon my head by the Victoria police department. But there has been one improvement from the last time we graced these cells. The authorities have started giving us a piece of fruit a day. But an apple or an orange is not enough nourishment to stave off the dietary toxification of a steady A & W diet, the lack of sunlight, the general bedlam and disorder of the cells, the lack of cleanliness, and most of all, the lack of fresh air. There is also the little matter of "pepper spray."

The men's cells are directly below ours, and, when the prisoners down there get quarrelsome, they are sprayed with what has been dubbed "instant manners." The pathetic ventilation system that just a few moments before could not be bullied or cajoled or reasonably persuaded to deliver a whiff of fresh oxygen upstairs suddenly kicks into high gear right smartly and with unprecedented efficiency rushes the pepper spray upstairs to us women. We all share equally in this, men, women, and matron. About the only time the big doors on the other side of the bars are opened to the balcony is when the matrons are choking on pepper spray. But while the pepper spray is temporary, the cigarette smoke is not.

There are usually three or four and sometimes eight or nine women in our tiny cell block puffing away. In court I appeal to Judge Bouck to move us for the duration of the trial, but he refuses, saying it is not his business, and if we don't like the city jail we can sign the undertaking and get out. But Inessa has give a newspaper interview describing the conditions in this hell hole, and Dr. Ron Aspinall, fellow arrestee and well-known west coast physician and environmentalist, has taken up the cause. In the meantime, I'm trying to hold on to sanity.

It isn't easy. By the middle of the second week of trial my nerves are skittering around like hush puppies frying in hot fat. I've always had good concentration, the knack of being able to shut out background noises and movements. I'm not sure whether one is born with this capacity or if it is developed by circumstances. Certainly my own ability was honed by the noisy business of raising eight kids. If I wanted to think an issue through, or develop a story idea, I had to program my mind to respond only to direct appeals from the children, or threats to their physical safety. We could spend long hours outdoors by a small stream or wading pond, while the little ones fished with a stick and a piece of string or built imaginative rock and mud houses or bridges. Entire afternoons would pass this way and by the time we came back to the ole humdrum world I would have formulated a letter or reviewed a puzzling book or started a story. Other times I focused my entire attention on them, but when they were busy amusing themselves, I'd learned to take a mental stroll.

This ability to block out background static has proved extremely useful in my life, including the situation I find myself in now. If I concentrate on my own thoughts, the mental reviews and forward winds, I hardly notice the prison rules back at the correctional centre, the way we're herded here and there like a bunch of sheep, the confinement, the million and one irritations of incarceration. So far I have also been able mentally to conjure up my own little cove at

Cypress Bay. But in spite of this, as our tenth day in the cells turns to darkness, I can feel the Victoria city jail wearing down my psychological protection. I don't know how much more I can take.

For exercise, I try to do some stationary running in my cell but then desist for fear that I am damaging my lungs more by breathing in more cigarette smoke. Mike calls from Prince Rupert. He has read the paper with Inessa's interview and is worried. I tell him not to be, that his ole ma is a survivor. Then I tell him of hearing that his sculpture, The Raven Lady, sold only a short time before to a Ucluelet business man, is flying yellow ribbons. Yellow ribbon has become the logger's symbol up island for solidarity. Mike, true to his twisted funny bone, thinks this is amusing. I don't. I love The Raven Lady. The very idea of this most beautiful and graceful symbol of the wilderness being used to further the cause of clear-cutting just ticks me right off. And even though I assure Mike that I am doing fine, it is that very evening after talking to him that I loose my cool. I crack like a Sunday chicken's neck and the reverberations are heard up and down the chain of command. And all over a spinach salad.

Several days before I had been given, instead of the anaemic iceberg lettuce salad for lunch, a fresh, crunchy spinach salad. It tasted wonderful. I devoured it. I ordered a spinach salad again the following day. This perked my spirits right up because with this and an apple a day, plus the vegetarian sandwich we were graciously served in the courthouse cells for lunch, I just might survive. But this evening when I give my order to the matron she tells me that I can't have any more spinach salads as they are not in the A & W contract and the others have been served by mistake. The jailers will not let us have access to our own money or even let us have the fruit and vegetables our relatives and supporters bring. We can eat only what they give us and nobody, not even the worst offenders, should have to eat garbage day in and day out. I have been pushed to the limit. For a moment I am out of control. I yell at the matron, demanding to speak to the chief of police. She replies that she can't bother him with such a trivial thing, and that if I persist in my demands she will lock me down. But I know I *must* be allowed to speak to a lawyer. It's the law. So I lower my voice to a more reasonable pitch and tell the matron that I want to speak to my lawyer and that I intend to tell him that I am going on a hunger strike and that he is to inform the press why. The matron seems to be looking up the number for Robert Moore-Stewart in the little cubby hole on the other side of her desk where the tea things are, and then I hear her talking to someone on the phone. But when she comes back to her desk I am informed that the chief of police is out of town but the acting police will be down shortly.

When the acting chief comes I shake hands with him through the bars and explain the situation. Judith and I are not good friends anymore for reasons that I won't go into here and as she has asked me not to speak for her in any situation or confrontation, I carefully leave her name out of my complaints and comments. I tell this man on the other side of the bars, who seems pleasant enough, that I have already been here for a week and a half and might be here for a month or more if the trial lasts that long, and that the rotten health conditions in his jail is at least alleviated somewhat by the spinach salad, considering that we aren't even allowed to take our own vitamins.

The acting chief replies that for the time being I can have the spinach salad but when the real police chief comes back the final decision will be up to him. I ask him to emphasize to the real chief that, if I'm not allowed the spinach, then I'll be forced to go on a hunger strike and I will try to make it as public as possible.

At this point the acting chief tells me not to threaten him and I reply that I am not threatening him, I am threatening the real chief of police and would he please just deliver the message. His eyes snap and his mouth tightens but he controls himself. I thank him for coming and he leaves. As soon as he is out of the cell block all pandemonium breaks loose. The six or seven women occupying the cell block with me who have been silently watching the confrontation with the acting chief erupt into great whoops of laughter and a couple of them start mimicking me in an exaggerated way ... "Call my lawyer!" they cry. "I'm going on a hunger strike! Call the press!" The matron tries to calm them down with the promises of cups of tea but for the rest of the evening I am a cause celebre. Two days later I am yelling again, this time at one of the male jailers.

It is after the evening's A & W version of dinner and I am lying on my bunk trying to collect my thoughts about the ongoing trial. Again, there are half a dozen or so women in the common room which is just a long narrow room attached to the cells, when a new prisoner is brought in. She has been brought over from some other facility in the company of two officers, one male and one female.

While the new prisoner is being processed one of our own in-house jailers starts trading smut talk with one of the prisoners already inside. This is really raw stuff. I try to ignore it. I don't want to hear this, I don't want to get in an uproar again, but the unspeakably obscene banter between our friendly jailer and the girl inside finally breaks down every barrier I have erected between me and this filthy place, and I throw down my court papers in a rage and fly into the common room and grab the bars that separate me from the jailer.

"Who do you think you are?" I demand of the offending officer. "We are prisoners here, I know there are rules and guidelines about how women prisoners are to be treated, and I also know that we are to be treated fairly and impartially and with a certain amount of respect, and you are certainly not doing your job."

He is somewhat astonished and asks petulantly if I heard what the female prisoner said to him, and I yell "It doesn't matter what she said to you! You are supposed to be in authority here, and you're job is not to trade sex talk with the female prisoners, and I am in these cells, too, and there are other women here who are not prisoners, the matron and the female officer — are we all supposed to stand here and listen to your vulgar talk that serves to humiliate all women, even if some of the female inmates do enter into the verbal exchange willingly?"

My head is swirling with rage, I feel dizzy. I am tired of these male guards and jailers who feel they can, with few exceptions, say what they please to any of us. They have no consideration at night when there might be some possibility of sleep — they take this opportunity to sing and whistle and laugh loudly as if they delight in keeping prisoners awake, and they aren't above throwing the rotten A & W food on the table like they're slopping hogs. The matrons are generally reasonable, they even bring in a few goodies out of their own pockets, but the matrons aren't running this place or setting policy. The offending jailer backs off and I sit down at the rickety table and try to compose myself. I realize that my carefully cultivated concentration is being eaten away by the deplorable conditions in this hell hole. But sign the undertaking? Never. It is Dr. Ron Aspinall who comes to my rescue.

Dr. Aspinall is worried about the health of two grannies who are being kept indefinitely under such conditions. He continues to bring up the issue of our treatment in court but Judge Bouck is not moved. And then Dr. Aspinall gets hard-nosed and starts talking about Amnesty International and there is some sort of rally to that affect. Then suddenly, somebody in high places *is* moved and Judith and I are immediately transferred back to Nanaimo Correctional Centre.

What sweet relief! Judith and I are housed in a non-smoking five-bed dorm in the main building. The buildings are old but clean and there is a shower in our dorm and two sinks! What luxury! And the food! It is general prison fare but there are vegetables and milk and bean soups. Judith and I can have our hairbrushes and dental floss. We are the only two women prisoners in the whole place but I don't care. I am breathing fresh air and my bed, while utilitarian, is clean and warm. Now I can concentrate on the trial.

FIFTEEN

In the courtroom, things don't look good. I no longer have any hopes of anything as basic as justice to come out of this trial, because Judge Bouck has gathered up the strings of the law in his fist and is circling us protesters like a chicken-eating snake eyeing a setting hen. We hardly need the Crown Council lawyers to tell us what bad kids we are because there is Judge Bouck doing it for them. Still, some of my fellow arrestees do not seem disheartened. Some, dressed in suits and speaking legalese as smartly as you please, are difficult to distinguish from the real lawyers.

Robert Moore-Stewart, who *is* a real lawyer, representing some of our bunch, hammers day after day on the conflict of interest issue that seems apparent to me, asking for the right to call expert witnesses in the case, people who could testify to the crisis in the Clayoquot, who could catalogue the immediate dangers there to both human and animal life from the landslides, poisoned water, and threatened extinction of entire species. But no.

Aside from Merve Wilkenson, a logger who does only selective logging on his own place, we are allowed no other witnesses. But Merve is wonderful. A man in his late seventies or early eighties, and an arrestee himself, he speaks with calm authority about the devastation left by clear-cutting.

Even without any more witnesses being heard, the trial moves like a Sunday sermon simply because there are so many people involved. But finally it is time for us arrestees to start giving evidence, to talk about why we did what we did on Kennedy River bridge.

As we protesters begin to speak to the judge, trying to romance the stone as it were, I can tell that Judge Bouck is not impressed with any of us.

But I am impressed. I think the testimonies are wonderful. Such different people, with such varied motives. Klaus Hauschild here from Germany on a vacation, regrets the disappearance of Germany's forests and decides to protest the disappearance of ours. Teresa Shanks, a young Canadian college student has lost her semester of school and her apartment in Vancouver because of this trial. Leesa Heyward, a young expectant mother, testifies that she feels her coming child will be threatened by deforestation. The words of another camp song run through my mind while she is testifying, "Earth my body, water my blood, air my breath, and fire my spirit ..."

Darrin Mortson, a young college graduate, gets up and reads *The Lorax* by Dr. Seuss, a wonderful book about trying to save the forest. Judge Bouck is not amused. But later he listens attentively as Crown Counsel Brian Rendell uses a play by Robert Bolt, *A Man for all Seasons*, as an argument why the law must be obeyed at all times. In this play Sir Thomas Moore argues that the law must be obeyed even when the law is wrong, and even if the law benefits the devil himself. When it is my turn to speak I try to answer this line of argument:

"... Sir, there might be some satisfaction for me right now if I could equate MacMillan-Bloedel with the devil, but I can't. MacMillan-Bloedel, and other multi-nationals like MacMillan-Bloedel, have no parallel in human history. They are something new on the face of the earth and their power is awesome.

"MacMillan-Bloedel is not a single entity like the devil. The devil comes down to us over the centuries through Christian mythology as a fallen angel, as a good guy gone bad, if you will. The devil knows of good and evil. The devil has qualities one can speak to, wrestle with, cut deals with. MacMillan-Bloedel as a corporate structure has no human qualities of good or evil because it is a giant, mindless, soulless machine programmed to do one thing and one thing only — maximize profits from the forests. And because it is an entity with no human qualities the MacMillan-Bloedel machine can mercilessly butcher the forests with an immediacy and thoroughness that makes Atilla the Hun look like a pea picker."

But Judge Bouck is not impressed with *my* argument, either. Our arguments do not mean a tinker's damn to him. And later on in the trial Judge Bouck has me ejected from the courtroom for yelling at him. But I am allowed back the next day after making a pitiful excuse for an apology, I apologize only for the way I said what I said, not for what I said, but I think the judge wants me back in the courtroom because it doesn't look good to have a granny languish down in the dungeon cells while her own trial is going on.

I hear of the continuing arrests with utter delight. Every working day there are more, one hundred, two hundred, three hundred, four hundred, five hundred, there are The Midnight Oil arrests, the women and children arrests, the senior citizens arrests, the mass arrests. It is unexpected and spell-binding that so many ordinary citizens have gone to so much trouble to try to save the Clayoquot Sound. They all risk, except the children, getting a criminal record for their pains, plus jail time and a hefty fine. Judge Bouck brings down his Reasons for Judgment on October the sixth. All forty-four of us are found guilty of criminal contempt and on October 13, Judge Bouck hits us with His Reasons for Sentencing.

By peacefully but publicly protesting the destruction of our own rainforests we are inviting the downfall of our entire social and legal fabric, the judge rules after six and a half weeks of trial. Dr. Aspinall is given the heaviest sentence, sixty days in jail and a fine of three thousand dollars. Robert Maher is given forty-five days in jail with a twenty-five hundred dollar fine. I am next in order of severity with forty-five days and a two thousand dollar fine for sassing the judge. Tom Bellaire also gets forty-five days and a two thousand dollar fine, primarily, I think, for commenting that the judge's bench is much higher than anyone else's. But there will be appeals. We have the choice of serving our time and getting it over with, or waiting for our appeals. Roughly half of us opt for getting it over with. Those of us who just want to get it over with are all taken back to Nanaimo.

Inessa is with us again and Judith goes home on a medical leave. There are seven of us women now and about fifteen or so men. We women are put into the same segregated no-smoking dorm that Judith and I had been occupying, but the men have to bunk in with the general population. The issue of cigarette smoking again raises its ugly head.

Our group is largely non-smoking while most of the general prison population smokes rather enthusiastically. While welcoming the young women in our group, a significant number of the general population seems to resent our young men. Mostly young themselves, the regular inmates are for the most part ill-educated and ill-mannered, but not necessarily mean. Except for a few.

These few are called "heavies" and are supposed to be the tough guys. Although Judith and I had eaten in the dining room before when there was just the two of us women, we were grannies and nobody cared where we sat, at least nobody made a fuss about it, we just found an empty chair and sat down. So when we women come back as a group of seven, I hurriedly steer the tray-ladened group toward the back of the hall where there are usually some empty tables. I just want to get the young women seated as most of the general population of men are already eating. Or were until the young women came in. Then jaws stopped working and you could almost hear pulse acceleration in the hall. So I rush the girls to the back to get their bums out of the line of fire and this just happens to be the end of the hall where the "heavies" sit. When the men of our group come in behind us they gravitate to the back of the hall, too, where the rest of us tree-huggers are parked. But then an innocent spill-over occurs. A couple of our men sit down with their trays at one of the "heavy" tables. And the main "honcho heavy" gets up and starts berating us all.

"What do you people think this is, a country club? You act like this is a social club of some kind. You tree-huggers are just going to be here a little while to make your cute little protest, and *you* ..."

Here he pauses with flaming eyes to point his finger at me. "You know they're not supposed to sit here," he goes on accusingly. "You've been here before, you know better ..."

I stare at his pointed finger which is tattooed down to the second knuckle and I can feel the gorge rising in my gullet. I get up to properly address this barnyard bully as our two young men are staring open mouthed, as though they can hardly believe the unspeakable rudeness of this man. They don't seem likely to find their voices anytime soon.

"How the hell do you know what I know?" I yell, using my best God-given hog-calling voice. "Do you think anybody really wants to sit at a table with you? You're a bully! And furthermore I don't know who the hell you think you are, but we have just as much right to be here as you do!"

Am I really arguing over who has the most right to be here, I wonder, for a moment, in spite of my disgust with this man, I almost burst out laughing. But one of the guards, alerted to the loud voices, hurries over and breaks up the rising ruckus. Later, one of the commanding officers comes to see me in the dorm. He advises me that it's better not to argue with the heavies as they can later take out their ire on the men in our group, and the heavies really are heavier, older and meaner. I concur with his suggestion that I avoid exchanging insults with the heavies, but it rankles, just the same. When I pass this very same heavy in the hallway the following morning he speaks politely.

"Good morning," he says distinctly, in a pleasant tone. Is this dreadful man addressing me? I turn around and look. I'm the only one in the hallway. And the heavy is smiling at me.

"I think it's going to be a nice day," he says, still smiling.

I stop in my tracks and glare at him.

"And just why are you trying to be nice when you were so horrible yesterday?" I demand bluntly.

His grin broadens. "Yesterday I didn't realize you were a heavy. Us heavies have to stick together."

And then he lets out a loud guffaw, as though the thought of a granny heavy was just about the funniest thing that had ever occurred to him and then doubled over from laughter, he makes his way down the hall. After that, there is no more trouble in the dining hall, but our men, with the exception of John Vedova and Guy Wera, are all sent to another building, the protective custody building. However, we are allowed to get together with them from time to time along with the lawyers to discuss our appeals.

During the first week two of our women, including Inessa, leave us to go home on house arrest. This is made possible by a monitor placed on the prisoner's leg that signals the police should the prisoner attempt to leave home before full time is served. The rest of us are taken out of the main building and transferred down the hill to a cottage by the lake. Had it not been fenced and locked the place would have been downright homey. The following week I take up the computer course I had started in Burnaby and am designated housekeeper of the cottage. The others are assigned to various outside jobs. Another of our women decides that she has much more interesting things to do on the outside and leaves on the monitor. Now we are just four ... Teresa Shanks, Jane Saville, a young woman who has been rebirthed and renamed Ocean, and I.

The young women go out in the evenings, under guard, of course, to the shop for woodworking, or to the gym. This is my quiet time. I write letters and try to think. I think about the trial and Judge Bouck's decisions and the voluminous mail we jailbirds are receiving in support of our actions and the roasting that Judge Bouck is taking in the letters to the editor columns of the newspapers. Some cabinet members of the NDP try to distance themselves personally from the arrests and trials, and the chief justice of British Columbia calls a press conference and lambastes everybody, including the lawyers in the case. He is, in essence, telling everyone to shut up and accept Judge Bouck's decisions. As I study on these events, I feel almost sorry for the heat that Judge Bouck is taking over his decisions.

I say this, even though I totally disagree with Judge Bouck's ideas and opinions about the law and the citizen's responsibility to the law and to society as he expressed them in our particular case. But I have to admit the man showed a certain amount of fortitude. Judge Bouck came into that courtroom every working day for six and a half weeks and faced forty-odd outraged and sometimes enraged defendants, not people who thought of themselves as criminals and thus felt guilty and morally inferior, but people who were, for the most part, highly concerned with the concepts of right and wrong, who had strong self-esteem and the verbal skills to articulate their sense of outrage and personal injury at the destruction of the Clayoquot Sound.

Some days Judge Bouck was surrounded on all sides by explosions of anger and resentment, never knowing from which side the next snarling attack would come. He was a highly visible target for an enormous amount of pent up frustration. He was a man under siege. Some days he just hung his head in apparent total exasperation and despair, obviously fighting for control. But then I would remind myself that it was he who defended the idea of holding mass trials in the first place as democratic, and that the ensuing confusion would not in any way be injurious to the defendants' rights, so now let the chips fall where they may, yes, go ahead and rain down on Judge Bouck's silver head. Besides, he knew all along who held the real power. And it certainly wasn't us.

Still, in a metaphysical way I came to think that during the trial we were all actors in some sort of creative undertaking that would eventually erupt into something beneficial to society at large. I thought of a process I had studied long ago called "dialectical materialism." In this theoretical process model there is the original thing, or entity that is called the thesis, but it bears within it the seeds of its opposition, which is called the antithesis. Over a course of time the antithesis gains strength and grows larger until suddenly it reaches a stage of crisis and becomes more powerful than the thesis and then a new thing bursts forth, which is called the synthesis. And while the synthesis is indeed a new thing, it has retained within it the qualities of both the opposing original parts. The synthesis can be the birth of a child, the birth of a nation, the birth of an idea, or simply the birth of a new way of looking at things, but the thesis and antithesis are both necessary for this process to take place.

Using this model, Judge Bouck and his opinions represent the original thesis, that the law should be obeyed at all times, even if wrong, and we forty-odd Clayoquot Protectors and the other hundreds of protestors who are being arrested daily on Kennedy Bridge take the part of the antithesis in saying no, that in these instances where the law is clearly and demonstrably wrong, it shouldn't be obeyed. I don't know what the synthesis of the protests and trials will be, but hopefully a new way of looking at nature will emerge, a new regard for the natural world that will incorporate within itself the awareness of the laws of nature, a recognition of the fact that we cannot, as a species, simply destroy the lifelines that sustain us, and that natural law and judicial law will somehow meld and become a new thing.

But I learn that more women are coming to join us from the trial that has followed ours, four new women altogether. We hold circles outside and sing and dance and beat makeshift drums. On Sundays the men from our group across the way respond with singing and drumming of their own. But then it is time for the new women to go home as they received lighter sentences than ours, and finally, it is time for our own release.

People from the CBC TV program "50 Up" are there as I walk through the gates of The Nanaimo Correctional Centre and want to accompany me to Clayoquot Sound. They want to interview me at the A-frame and film the mountains around the cove. I agree to this, as the more exposure of the clear-cutting that has already been done in the Clayoquot Sound, the better. One picture, after all, is worth a thousand words. By the time I walk out of the gates of Nanaimo Correctional Centre I have been incarcerated in British Columbia's jails and correctional centers for a little over four and a half months.

After the filming is over at Cypress Bay I return with the crew to Vancouver for a visit with Barbara Ellen and grandson Julian who is now three years old. After that, a brief visit with Margaret Elizabeth and Andre in Ucluelet, and Marian in Tofino, and then I hail Johnny Tom's water taxi and head back out to Cypress Bay.

My body aches from being tossed hither and yon these last months and my spirit craves respite from the confusion. The cove holds out her leafy arms and enfolds me as the tide gently washes me ashore. I am sorry, I whisper as I embark and start up the winding stairs to the house. I'm sorry. I tried. I tried as hard as I could.

The cove answers, and the mountains. I hear the whispering, the gentle murmurings as the night settles down about. What is being said? I don't know. In the days that follow I listen intently to the language of the cove in the silence of the evenings, but I am not being spoken to, perhaps spoken about, but not spoken to. The perfect unity I had felt at times with this place, that perfect peace, escapes me now. I busy myself with the physicality of my days, trying not to think too much. There is firewood and water to be hauled, clams to be dug, fish to be coaxed onto the line. There are books to be read, a spring garden to be planned. The family gathers in Vancouver at Barbara Ellen's place for Christmas. Immediately after, I head back to Cypress Bay. As the winter flirts with spring and then succumbs completely, I know I am still not right with my cove. Even after the bears stumble out of their winter lairs and amble about looking for food, and the bird population returns in full force, and the giant slugs are lurking underneath the planter boxes waiting for the first sign of garden activity to begin, and the salmon berry bushes are just starting to bloom, I still have the peculiar sensation that the full face of the cove has turned from me.

I think the cove is turning her face because I am no longer very optimistic about saving the Sound from clear-cutting. The cove senses my despair. She does not share the innermost secrets of her soul with summertime soldiers. But how can I be other than pessimistic when I see that the logging of the ancient ones is continuing non-stop? What can one do, I demand of the mountains behind the cove, after one has done the very best that one can? Occasionally I yell at the cedars down by the creek and ask what *they* would have me do? I'm only one person, for Pete's sake, and an old lady at that. I'm tired and I just want to retire and be quiet. Can't you understand that? But the trees are dumb and so are the rocks and the streams and the mountains, and even the stellar jays, who are the biggest beggars and chatterboxes nature has ever designed, seem to be avoiding me. But it is time to go back to civilization for news and supplies. Besides, I want to see my children. I will combine all three of these needs with a couple of weeks in Ucluelet.

But there is a shock awaiting me in Ucluelet, the kind of shock that lurks at the bottom of every mother's worse nightmare — that of learning one's child has a life threatening disease.

SIXTEEN

 Barbara Ellen and Julian are waiting for me.

"Mom, I have cancer," Barbara Ellen announces softly when Julian has been sent to rediscover his old trunk of toys. "I have breast cancer."

I have no life experience to deal with this. Susan's brush with death was over in a couple of days, an aneurism gives its decision forthwith, but cancer ...

"And I'm not having any operations, Mom. I've found a holistic doctor in Vancouver who will treat me herbally. It will be all right, but my doctor says I must rest. I need help with Julian for a couple of months. Michel will take him as soon as he's finished his job in Victoria. Three months at the most. Can you take Julian for that long?"

Of course. Whatever must be done. In the days that follow I am wasted with worry but still I feel I must listen and give over to Barbara Ellen's calm acceptance of the thing, and her resolve to deal with this cancer in her own way. Both Margaret Elizabeth and I can see her thinking on the matter. But Susan and Rose Mary are very upset with this holistic herbal business. My sons, too, as they are informed, are made nervous by this type of treatment. But the one thing we all agree on is that Barbara Ellen must rest. Julian, heart-stoppingly beautiful, and extremely annoyed that his mother, after staying a week, has left without him, looks askance at my old-fashioned notions of childrearing. Julian is more obstinate than any southern mule and has been petted, by Barbara Ellen and her entourage, beyond endurance.

But backed as I am, by forty-odd years of mucking about with kids, at least half of whom were almost, but not quite, as cantankerous as this one, I cannot be got around with piteous cries for help when I have banished Julian to his bedroom, nor charmed with advanced reasoning concerning why he should be allowed to come out of his room immediately and resume his play after indulging in a guerilla attack on our neighbour's flowers.

Especially since the neighbour in question no longer speaks to me because of my criminal record. Actually, I wasn't exactly warmly welcomed back into the Ucluelet community when I got out of jail, with a couple of exceptions, most of the sympathies of this village being with MacMillan Bloedel and as they see it, their loggers. And it is easier to wrestle a hungry alligator to the swamp floor than to convince these people that I am not against the loggers, just against clear-cutting one of the last low-lying old growth rainforests in the world. Anyway, the village is also my village and I don't, at least at the moment, intend to move away. So I will admit, under duress, that Julian may have inherited a trifle of his stubbornness from me. Naturally, we butt heads frequently. He usually winds up, after a confrontation, asking to "speak to the kitties."

The "kitties" are long socks with kitty cat faces that I brought back from one of my trips south to visit my mother. Mama is in her nineties now but still healthy. She lives with my aunt and spends her days gardening, sewing for her grandchildren, cooking, and reading and trying to figure out what really happened to Jimmy Swaggart. She still likes to dress up and go out, too. She bought the "kitty" socks for Julian. When I put the socks on my hands and pull them up over my arms they become puppets, or in Julian's eyes, temporary live kitty playmates.

Gradually, however, because the kitties listen so well, they have also become therapists. Julian tells the kitties of the trauma of his first day in the community playschool, of having his hair cut and washed, of his mother leaving without him after she visits. Only now the kitties are missing. I can't find them. If they don't show soon I will have to find something similar as they have become an important line of communication for Julian.

I have packed a picnic lunch and when Julian wakes we will walk the two blocks to Little Beach. Little Beach, as the name implies, is a minuscule beach that rings a small cove. It's located on the edge of the village, as we are, and while there are expensive homes perching majestically along the cliffs, Julian and I are usually the only ones actually down on the beach. We will take his pail and shovel, but the best part of the beach for Julian is the activity involving the big rocks on the water's edge on the far side of the cove. He likes to turn the rocks over and find the wee crabbies and other diminutive creatures that hide there waiting for the tide to come back.

When Julian flips over a rock and inspects his find underneath he reminds me of the bear cubs at Cypress Bay. I wish I could take Julian there. But I'm afraid. He's just the right size to tumble down the rock face of the steep cliffs to the sea below or to tempt a hungry cougar. After we get back from Little Beach that evening, I call Barbara Ellen in Vancouver. Julian has been with me now almost two months.

"Mom, I'm sure this tumor is shrinking," Barbara Ellen announces in a strong, confident voice. I clue into her optimism. I want so much to believe that she is right. "Yes, I can hardly feel it unless I raise my arm and it gets right over the breast bone," she continues. "Really, Mom. Don't worry, now. I have another doctor's appointment on Tuesday, but I'm coming to Ucluelet for the weekend. Is Julian being a good boy?"

I laugh. Julian is such an intense little fellow, everything, almost literally everything, matters to him too much. He is all nerve endings and if he weren't so smart, he would be impossible.

"Yes," I answer. "But we've lost the kitty socks. Do you have the other pair?"

"Yes, they're here."

"Bring them. Julian needs his therapy. And so do I."

She promises not to forget the socks and I hang up and start trying to bring order out of the chaos of the living room. But my mind lingers on Barbara Ellen. She still refuses to see an oncologist.

Her reason is that she knows what an oncologist will tell her and she doesn't want to hear it. She has already embarked on her own course of action, one that she is convinced is already working. She will not even consider a mastectomy which is what the first surgeon recommended, and will approach a lumpectomy with extreme caution, if ever. She is not convinced that either of these two operations will help her, and, if she has no confidence in them, she does not see why she should have to undergo them. She has given me a book to read, *Peace, Love and Healing* by Dr. Bernie Segal who stresses that a life threatening illness can be an opportunity for restructuring one's life to facilitate growth in relationships and spirituality. Barbara Ellen and Dr. Segal make perfect sense to me. And yet ... and yet....

The following afternoon Julian and I are in the Co-op store in Ucluelet buying groceries. Lately he has been quite cooperative about the shopping, either riding in the basket or pushing it around, eager to help pick out the items for purchase. But today he is full of the devil, hopping around from aisle to aisle, molesting perishables and demanding a popsicle. Finally, I am driven to employ an old method of riot control. I grab a thick strand of dark hair at the nape of his neck and give it a sharp tug. Usually this is all that is needed to return Julian to the real world. But today he is too far off the wall. Instead of whimpering, he gives a sharp loud yelp of indignation and then glares at me while he rubs his hand over the tender spot at the back of his head.

"Damnit, Gramma, that hurt!" he yells out in his clear, childish treble.

Three or four disapproving faces turn our way. Well, and what can one expect from a tree-hugging criminal? I try to hide my face in the grocery basket, not from shame, but because I am about to explode with suppressed laughter. Too late. The laughter bubbles up anyway and this is a terrible mistake because Julian is most decidedly taking note of the effect on me of his outburst and is busy storing this away for future reference. Now I will have to devise some other method of curtailing his high spirits along the grocery store aisles. We declare a truce and finish the shopping. Back home, Julian helps me put away the groceries and then goes to his room to play. After a bit I hear him in the hallway addressing the hated smoke detector.

Julian is positive the smoke detector is out to get him and in spite of all the little stories I have invented to demonstrate that the smoke detector is his friend, he is not impressed. For him, the smoke detector is a dangerous menace. Julian's animosity toward it stems from being scared out of his wits by its scream announcing that the toast I was fixing for his breakfast was burning. It took a few moments of fanning the alerted detector to silence its screams. This made a fantastic impression on Julian and has forever, I fear, put him off toast. When I offer toast now he says, no, thank you, Gramma, I don't like toast, just plain bread, please. And if any visitor who may be offered a sandwich on toast accepts Julian will intercede and try to argue the visitor into appreciating the merits of untoasted bread. Periodically, just to keep the smoke detector at bay and within the confines of the door jamb above the door to his room, Julian must give it a piece of his mind. Curious, I step into the hallway. Julian's back is to me and he is shaking his square, plump little fist up at the smoke detector.

"I will spit at you," he says to the smoke detector, throwing down the gauntlet.

The smoke detector is silent.

"And I will hit you if you bother me," Julian adds, shaking his fist again for emphasis.

There is still no answer from the smoke detector.

"I'm not scared of you! And I will hit you if you bother me and Gramma ..."

I interrupt this macho challenge to take my little grandson by the arm and lead him gently outside. What am I going to do about the damned smoke detector? And it is too rainy and dreary to go to the beach, but the boy obviously needs some fresh air. He settles for riding his tricycle up and down in the covered porchway, pretending he is a bus driver taking his stuffed animal passengers to Mississippi. He has no idea where Mississippi is, but he knows I go there periodically to visit his great-grandma and the name has a pleasing, exotic ring to him. That evening when Julian is in bed for the night, I turn on TV for the CBC "Witness" program.

I usually find this an interesting program, more or less, but tonight it is absolutely hair-raising. It is about the alligators in Florida who are not reproducing because many of them have both male and female characteristics, about fish in the Great Lakes who are suffering from the same malady, and how human reproduction is also being affected by a fifty per cent reduction in the sperm count in men in the last fifty years along with a tripling in testicle and prostrate cancers. Reproductive birth defects are also on the rise in boy babies, and there is an epidemic in breast cancer in women. Younger and younger women are getting breast cancer. The doctors and scientists on the program say that these reproductive ills are being brought about by chemical compounds in the environment that act as estrogens and that these estrogen-like substances are everywhere, primarily in herbicides and pesticides, industrial effluent, and plastics. If sperm count continues to fall in humans there may be extremely serious reproductive problems in just another generation or two because nobody, but nobody, knows how to stop the decline.

After the program is over I turn off the television, stupefied by this information. I think of the tons of herbicides and pesticides that have been sprayed over the clear-cuts on Vancouver Island, including the Clayoquot Sound, the tons of industrial and military effluents that are spewed out into the lakes and rivers and streams and oceans and atmosphere of the earth every day all over the world. And it occurs to me that the earth is beginning to fight back, that she is not going to simply sit and let herself be destroyed, that she will develop mechanisms to get rid of this human virus who is attacking her with such fury. She will see about interfering with the human's reproduction process, so this virus can no longer reproduce. And I don't blame her, she has been patient long enough. A species so stupid as to destroy its own life-support systems doesn't deserve to live. I retire with a heart so heavy I can hardly climb into my bed. The following morning when Julian departs for playschool I decide to go to Tofino to see Marian.

Marian is twenty-four now, a funny, cheery, girl and my Cypress Bay partner. I need some cheering. I can't find my centre anymore. My dreams are chaotic. Other than caring for Julian at the moment I'm not sure what it is I should be doing. At the core of my being where strength and joy used to bubble up there are only dribblings of fear and despair. Marian is working in a restaurant in Tofino for the summer. Housing is at a premium in Tofino, so Marian's boss, desiring my daughter's employ, allows Marian to park her trailer in her yard. I knock on the trailer door and a muffled voice bids me enter. Marian isn't up yet and there is a pack of cigarettes on the counter.

"You're smoking again!" I yell. "And after all the misery you went through to quit. What is the matter with you?"

Marian works the night shift. She struggles up from the fifth wheel bunk and glares in my general direction, still groggy with sleep.

"Stop yelling at me," she responds after a moment. She rises and wraps the scruffy old bathrobe that has been dead for at least three years around her long, slender, mostly nude body and steps down to the narrow landing. I feel explosively angry at her about the smoking.

"I've been having a hard time, Mom," she offers as she pushes her thick mane of red hair from her face.

I am not moved.

"Well, join the club. We're all having a hard time. And what is this about?" I ask, waving some medical bills at her that I have brought with me. I know they are medical bills because they bear the return address of the local clinic. "Don't you have your health insurance straightened out yet?"

"Yes, I do, Mom."

"Then what are these?"

"Probably from my psychiatrist."

"Your psychiatrist?"

"Yes. I've been depressed. I can't sleep and I'm binge-eating and I've been having panic attacks."

"Because of your sister's cancer?"

"Yes. But there's other things, too. It feels like everything is falling apart."

A cold lash of fear wipes at my gut. Are we all going down the depression drain? The thought makes me feel angrier.

"Let me get this straight," I say after this news sinks in. "Barbara Ellen has breast cancer, I have the responsibility of Julian, and you get to see the psychiatrist. If anybody deserves a psychiatrist it's me!"

"Then go get your own."

She is tall and fair-skinned and blue-eyed and only recently, red haired. And at the moment, stoney faced. I look at her and see the distress in her eyes and around her young, tender mouth, and suddenly, the craven fear twisting my gut dissolves and I reach for her, and we are in each other's arms. After a bit of sobbing we can talk calmly enough. It seems that Barbara Ellen's cancer on top of the recent four and a half months I was in prison have taken its toll. Add to that the fact that back in Ontario, for the first time that Marian can remember, her father has entered into a serious new love relationship and is considering remarriage. Marian fears the family as she knows it is going under. I find the strength to assure her that it

is not. She tells me that she has found a reliable couple to stay out at
Cypress Bay until one or the other of us can return to it. She is
sensitive to what I think about the psychiatrist and I tell her about
Julian's "kitties." She smiles.

"You need some "kitties" too, Mom."

"Yes. Julian is going to Port Alberni next weekend to visit his
other grandparents. I'll go out to Cypress Bay then and talk to the
trees. Don't worry about me. And I'm proud of you for seeking out
the help you need to get through this."

"Thanks, Mom. And I really am going to stop smoking."

We have coffee together and then I start home. It really doesn't
matter if I'm late because Margaret Elizabeth is there to receive
Julian from his ride from play school, but I like to be there when he
comes in. When he leaves the house in the morning, he always tells
me to wait for him, that he's coming back. Perhaps I should call
Susan and Rose Mary when I get home, but lately the calls have
been so emotional my spirit quells. Susan and Rose Mary both think
a cancer is a cancer is a cancer. It isn't loneliness and unhappiness
and stress; it is not a symptom of something deeper, as Barbara
Ellen thinks it is; it is simply a wad of cells gone amuck, and the
only way to survive is to cut it out with a knife. Take off the breast,
never mind if it comes back in the other one, cut that one off, too,
wherever it appears, cut, cut, cut, until the breasts are gone and the
lymph nodes, too, and the immune system shot from chemo and
radiation and most of the first line defenses are down. What then?
Where will Barbara Ellen's tender flesh hide from the cruel, pitiless
invasions?

Twenty-seven. So young. So active. Barbara Ellen studied ballet almost from the time she could walk. From the summer session
of The Canadian National Ballet school to sessions in California
and Arizona. When she had the little ballet studio here in Ucluelet,
she also taught aerobics and had begun training to run. *Run, run,
jump, bounce, plie, jete, one, two, three, and four and up and down
and pique, glissade, pas de bouree, pas de basque, run, run, run ...*
How in God's name can anybody this young and physically active
develop cancer?

On the last lap from Tofino, the Ucluelet mountains come into
view. Mostly clear-cut. Some portions of the mountains are greening
up, other portions won't grow much of anything for a thousand
years. Cut the forest down and then give the bleeding earth massive

doses of the equivalent of chemo and radiation, oh, that wonderful reliance on chemicals, the chemical god, the chemical king, if one chemical is killing us, here we can fix it with another chemical, so say the multi-nationals, whose technology-driven mandate is raping our lands and seas and bodies and minds. And then there is the book *The Hot Zone* where author Richard Preston catalogues all of the viruses, both present and potential, coming out of the damaged rainforests of Africa — blood viruses, including AIDS but some far more immediately deadly than AIDS, viruses that have lived in the jungles since their inception and now, faced with the necessity of finding new hosts, are eyeing the human population. And so Mother Nature's corporation is driven by her own mandate and it looks like she is planning to downsize the human population, a little phasing out, as it were, a sort of restructuring of the company by attrition.

I'm in a seriously blue funk again by the time I get home, so I go upstairs to talk to Margaret Elizabeth while I wait for Julian.

Margaret Elizabeth has been my mainstay these past couple of years, she and Andre. Without their confidence and help I probably would not have found the courage to face down the events of the recent past. Margaret Elizabeth listens to my thoughts on Marian's fears. This has a quiet, calming affect on me. By the time Julian comes careening home from playschool I at least have a game plan ready for the rest of the day.

Julian is looking forward to his weekend away. The grandparents arrive to fetch him at the appointed time. I like the other grandparents. Good, steady people, at least fifteen years younger than me. They have a hobby farm and Julian loves to visit them. They stay only for coffee as they must get back to the farm. After coffee I walk out to their truck to see them off. There is a car seat for Julian, stationed in the middle of the truck's cab. Julian is very excited to be going. I am graced with only a scanty kiss. He is strapped into the car seat and then the grandparents get in, ready to pull away. It is only then that Julian realizes he won't see me for a few days instead of a few hours and there have been too many people lately coming and going in his young life. He leans around his other grandmother in the cab and fixes me with his deep, dark eyes, and I see a flicker of uncertainty there.

"I'm coming back, Gramma!" he yells down at me from his high perch in the cab. "Wait for me! Wait for me, Gramma! I'm coming back, you know!"

An overwhelming rush of such pure love surges through my veins that my knees feel weak and foreign to me as I rush up to the truck window. I am lightning struck by the instantaneous adrenalin-soaked recognition that this boy, this sweet faced, passionately alive, keenly intelligent little boy must have his chance to grow up and have children and grow old and see his own grandchildren come into being. I will fight to the death for that and for his mother's life and for the lives and health of my other children and grandchildren, and for other women's children and grandchildren, for Cypress Bay, for the Clayoquot Sound, for the earth itself, for life. How stupid and selfish of me to despair, even for a moment, for I am a product of nature, too, and my voice is also nature's voice. Forgive me mother of the universe for slacking off and losing faith, I will use nature's voice within me with all my heart and soul, oh, yes, I will, for as long as I shall live.

"Yes, my darling," I call up to my grandson's small, anxious figure. My old, strong voice has returned and faith and joy are seeping through the straightjacket of my heart again, winding their way through my blood and bones, leaving me breathless and trembling.

"You mustn't worry, sugar baby. I'll be here. I'll be here waiting for you when you come back. I'll be right here. I promise you."

photo: Marian T. Krawczyk